Overcoming Relationship Impasses

Ways to Initiate Change When Your Partner Won't Help

Overcoming Relationship Impasses

Ways to Initiate Change When Your Partner Won't Help

Barry L. Duncan, Psy.D.

Dayton Institute for Family Therapy
Centerville, Ohio

and

Joseph W. Rock, Psy.D.

Clinical Counseling Associates
Cleveland, Ohio

INSIGHT BOOKS

Plenum Press ● *New York and London*

Library of Congress Cataloging-in-Publication Data

Duncan, Barry L.
    Overcoming relationship impasses : ways to initiate change when
your partner won't help / Barry L. Duncan and Joseph W. Rock.
        p.   cm.
    "An Insight book"--T.p. verso.
    Includes bibliographical references and index.
    ISBN 0-306-43963-8
    1. Family--Psychological aspects. 2. Marriage--Psychological
aspects. 3. Interpersonal relations. 4. Family psychotherapy--Case
studies.   I. Rock, Joseph W.   II. Title.
    [DNLM: 1. Interpersonal Relations. 2. Marital Therapy.
3. Marriage--psychology.   WM 55 D911o]
HQ518.D85   1991
158'.24--dc20
DNLM/DLC
for Library of Congress   91-20802
                                                                                CIP

ISBN 0-306-43963-8

© 1991 Plenum Press, New York
A Division of Plenum Publishing Corporation
233 Spring Street, New York, N.Y. 10013

An Insight Book

Printed in the United States of America

For Natalie and Karen

Preface

In our psychology practices, we frequently found ourselves working on relationship issues with only one member of the relationship present. We used a number of strategies based on ideas
developed in marital and family therapy. Our clients often asked
us, "Where can I read more about these ideas?" In spite of the
proliferation of self-help books in the past few years, we discovered that none of them addressed the approach we were using.

All the strategies we have chosen for this book can be implemented by *one* person trying to deal with a relationship problem.
Many therapists believe that both members of a troubled relationship need to be present in therapy in order to mend that relationship. In the real world, however, both partners are seldom equally
troubled or motivated to change. We have found that by using the
proper approach, one motivated partner *can* have a positive impact. This book was written primarily for those motivated individuals who want to better their relationships, but feel stymied
by recalcitrant or reluctant partners.

Even though our original motivation was to give our clients,
and others in the same boat, fresh ideas on how to handle relationship problems, we also decided to write the book in a way that
would make it useful for counselors as well. Most counselors work
in general practices, as opposed to specializing, and see people

with a variety of problems. Although skilled in dealing with people and their problems, these counselors can't possibly be experts in every type of problem they encounter. By sharing our experiences, we hope this book will give them ideas on how to effectively approach clients whose concerns deal with relationships, but whose partners will not commit to therapy.

In writing this book, we have tried to avoid the two greatest pitfalls of self-help books. The first is describing in great detail and with tremendous insight a particular type of problem or "syndrome" (people with relationship problems and reluctant partners in this case), but failing to give enough specific, helpful ideas on how to cope with it. Many of our clients have come to us after reading self-help books and said, "I felt the book was describing *me*. I could really relate, but I'm still not sure what to *do* about it."

In order to avoid this pitfall, we have devoted most of this book to the description of strategies, suggestions, or techniques one person can use to intervene in a troubled relationship. To flesh out our ideas, we have used many case examples. In doing so, we have altered all identifying information, combined elements of different cases into one example, and changed the specifics of how strategies were implemented, all in the interest of protecting the confidentiality of our clients. However, the dramatic changes produced by these strategies have not been exaggerated.

The second trap into which self-help books can fall is creating a how-to manual in which people are told to do X to handle Y, but are given no clues as to why X should work or how to adapt it to different situations. We have tried to avoid this trap by explaining, as clearly as we can, the theoretical bases and rationales for all the strategies we have presented.

Our challenge was to find ways to present the theories upon which our ideas are based, since they involve a very different way of thinking about relationships and how people influence one another within them. We approached this challenge in three different ways. First, we briefly described the theories and ways in which they differ from conventional thinking about relationships. Then, we picked some common problems couples encounter and presented strategies based on these theories that one person could use. Finally, we outlined categories of strategies, discussed their theoretical underpinnings, and demonstrated their applicability to all types of relationship problems.

The message underlying all we have written is that one person can be effective in making changes in a relationship, even if the other member(s) does not want (or is unable) to directly cooperate. We will present specific ways in which this can be done, as well as general ways of understanding relationships and their problems that will allow the reader to develop his or her own strategies for handling unique relationship difficulties in creative, effective ways.

Barry L. Duncan
Joseph W. Rock

Centerville and Cleveland, Ohio

Acknowledgments

To Alice Penney, Jacki Aldrich, Cathleen Bohn, Steve Drewry, Dorothy Rock, and Connie Scurec for their invaluable help in getting the manuscript into a readable condition.

To the researchers and clinicians at the Mental Research Institute and the Brief Family Therapy Center of Milwaukee for their groundbreaking work and tremendous inspiration.

To Paul Bruening, Mark Hubble, Greg Rusk, and Andy Solovey of The Dayton Institute for Family Therapy for their role in helping to shape and expand Barry's thinking.

To Mort Slobin for being Joe's mentor and friend.

To Norma Fox, executive editor of Insight Books, who was willing to give us a chance.

To our clients for all they have taught us.

And to Pat and Joe Rock, and Doris and Lee Duncan for years of love and support.

Contents

Chapter 1

Playing by the Rules

People visit our offices for relationship counseling when they are stuck. They don't come in at the first hint of difficulty; they seek our professional help after they have tried every possible alternative they can think of to improve their relationships. They have already consulted friends and family. They have read self-help books, and they have watched Phil and Oprah. Nothing has worked. They are stuck.

How do people get stuck as they try to solve relationship problems? One way is by thinking they are trying a variety of creative solutions, when they are really just working with slight variations on the same theme. Consider the following example.

Sharon and Jeff have been married for nine years. She is twenty-eight and he is thirty-three. Since the recent birth of their first child, Sharon has become increasingly aware of Jeff's propensity for giving instructions and pointing out imperfections in her methods of doing things. She understands that, more times than not, he means well and is usually just trying to help when he offers his opinions and advice.

The first thing that Sharon does to address the problem is mention it to Jeff. She explains that when they were first married she needed and appreciated the benefit of his knowledge and experience, but now sometimes feels that he is treating her like a child, and that she doesn't like it. She asks him to please hold his comments and advice in abeyance until she asks for them. Jeff agrees with Sharon that she is a different person from the one he knew when they were first married, and he says that he will make every effort to treat her like the mature, independent woman she, in fact, is.

Initially, Jeff is as good as his word, but fairly soon he resumes sharing his observations of the way Sharon does things and making suggestions about better ways of doing them. When Sharon points this out to him, he becomes defensive and accuses her of overreacting and not being able to accept constructive criticism.

Sharon continues to make Jeff aware of his now "critical, paternalistic, and sexist nature." She hastens to take every opportunity to raise his consciousness about his male need to dominate and keep her in her place. Jeff responds by defensively backing off and withdrawing from conversation in general. When conversation does occur, he seems more apt to criticize Sharon about her "crazy, feminist" ideas, as well as her way of doing almost everything. Sharon and Jeff's latest interactions seem to be best characterized by an unspoken tension.

Sharon decides to try a different approach. She goes "on strike" by discontinuing to do anything that Jeff criticizes. When he comments that the spaghetti sauce needs more garlic, she announces that she is no longer cooking. When he criticizes the pattern in which the grass is cut, she responds by absolving herself of the responsibility to cut the grass. Jeff responds by blowing up in anger, and both Sharon and he say many things that they later regret. Jeff decides to not only stop making comments and suggestions, but also stop talking altogether. Now "an unspoken hostility" seems to best describe their relationship.

This example illustrates three ways in which people get stuck in their relationships. First, Sharon believes she is trying different strategies to improve her relationship with Jeff. In reality, she is trying only slight variations on a single theme: "I will make my dissatisfaction apparent to him, and he will respond with less criticism." People get stuck by trying the same basic approach over and over, even though it might not be obvious to them that they are doing so.

Sharon also demonstrates a second way in which people sabotage their own attempts to improve their relationships. When her first method made things worse, she tried more of the same. The more Jeff shared his comments, suggestions, and criticisms, the more she attempted to make him aware of doing so in hopes that this would reduce his criticism. This trap often happens. A well-intentioned attempt to resolve a small difficulty ends up turning it into a big problem. Of course, Sharon was perplexed since all she was trying to do was reduce Jeff's criticism and improve the relationship. She wound up with increased criticism and an overly sensitive, defensive, withdrawn husband. A relatively benign situation, therefore, can grow into a serious conflict despite an otherwise healthy relationship and the good intentions of the people involved.

A third way this example shows how people get stuck comes from the fact that Sharon recognized the problem but did not succeed in getting Jeff to help solve it. Almost always, one partner notices the problem first. That person mentions it to the other partner and then proceeds to try to solve the problem, assuming the other person to be motivated and cooperative. This can be a faulty assumption. Even if both people agree that there is a problem, they seldom agree on how serious it is or how to solve it.

This book was written for people who are trying to change a relationship for the better without full cooperation from a partner and for people who think they have tried everything and don't know what else they can do. A widely shared belief is that in order for a relationship to change, both partners have to actively participate in changing it. We disagree. We subscribe to a "systems" approach in working with couples. In a relationship system, a noticeable change in one person can set in motion a change in the whole system (that is, the couple). In the chapters that follow, we will give very explicit suggestions to *individuals* who want to work on improving relationships.

★   ★   ★

★   ★   ★

★   ★   ★

We also intend to provide fresh ideas for those who think they have tried everything. You may be wondering how we can give people creative suggestions that are truly different from the methods already used to help relationship dilemmas. To illustrate how suggesting fresh solutions to old problems may not be as difficult as you may think, consider the puzzle above.

The nine dots in the puzzle can be connected using only four straight lines, drawn without taking your pencil off the paper.[1] For those of you who have not seen this puzzle before, take a few minutes to try to solve it.

Now turn to page six and look at the solution. In trying to solve the puzzle, few people think of extending the straight lines beyond the dots, even though nothing in the instructions prohibits doing so. Most people, in effect, superimpose an imaginary square on the dots, which precludes resolution. By acting on the erroneous assumption that the lines cannot extend beyond the dots, you guarantee two things: frustration and failure. These are the identical outcomes people face when they are stuck in an attempt to solve a relationship problem.

It is interesting to note that although you may have recognized after just one trial that a solution to the puzzle was impossible, you probably continued to apply the same solution theme over and over again. You may have varied the speed with which you attempted your solution, the frequency of your attempts, and the intensity of your effort, but your solutions based on the restrictions inherent in the superimposed imaginary square were doomed to failure. Being freed from the constraints of the imaginary square shifts our view of the nine-dot puzzle and makes its solution immediately obvious. New solution options occur as we discard the blinders of certain assumptions.

We all enter ambiguous situations with beliefs and assumptions about how things "should" be and about what rules apply. Until we get our bearings in an unfamiliar situation, we feel confused and uncomfortable. The way in which we begin to make sense out of a new situation is by drawing on past learning and experience that we believe to be relevant. This information can come from our own similar experiences or what we have learned from friends, family, books, television, and so forth. Unfortunately, when we choose ideas and concepts that don't fit the new situation, or make assumptions that aren't accurate, we tend to stick with those ideas and assumptions in spite of evidence that they aren't helping. Too quickly we get locked into one way of looking at a situation, and (1) lose sight of the fact that there are other ways of looking at it (some of which may be more helpful) and (2) become blind to the fact that our assumptions are just that: assumptions, or guesses, about how things are, not facts.

In relationships, we make a lot of assumptions about what the other person thinks, feels, and likes. The assumptions we are most interested in, however, are about what rules apply in various situations. Rules begin to form early in relationships and grow out of patterns that emerge as people begin to relate to each other. Rules can be very simple and straightforward—one partner initiates sex, one partner does the dishes—or they can be more subtle—when both partners are angry, they don't yell. Sometimes the rules are talked about openly, but most times they are not (rules that are assumed, but not discussed). The people involved may not even be consciously aware of these assumed rules. This unawareness causes the most difficulty when problems arise.

Rules, even those based on assumptions, are helpful and useful. One function they serve is to simplify life. When we encounter recurring situations, we don't have to figure out what to do from scratch; we follow the rule that applies to the particular situation.

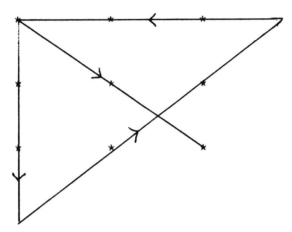

If we had no rules, our lives would be an endless succession of brand-new decisions. How exhausting and confusing!

Since rules are based on previous experience, they also tend to maintain the status quo. We do things basically the same way in which we have done them before. This gives our lives security, continuity, and predictability.

However, the very qualities that make rules useful in day-to-day living can render them harmful when a relationship problem needs to be resolved. The way rules help to simplify life is by limiting options to an acceptable few. When we get stuck in solving a problem, we need *more* options, not fewer. The assumed rules we carry into a situation prevent us from exploring potentially helpful options (again, the nine-dot example), and limit our flexibility.

Also, maintenance of the status quo may provide security during good times; however, in times of trouble, change is not only desirable, but it is also crucial. Rules, and the regularity they foster, discourage change, even helpful change.

So, rules and assumptions can clearly get in the way when we attempt to resolve relationship problems. By limiting options and discouraging change, they get us into ruts in which we try small variations on the same few options over and over. We know that what we're doing is not working, but we don't want to give up and don't know what else to try. Forging ahead with ineffective strategies certainly doesn't help. It makes us feel frustrated and helpless, and, as you saw in the example of Sharon and Jeff, it frequently makes the problem worse.

A fresh perspective is needed to break out of those ruts. Attaining that perspective is what this book is all about. Here is what the old pattern looks like:

Problem → Assumptions (rules) → Limited,
restricted solutions → Worse problem

The first step toward breaking that pattern involves recognizing and challenging unhelpful assumptions. As we mentioned earlier, when you get involved in a situation, it is very difficult to become aware of the assumptions under which you are operating. You are so used to those assumptions, and they are so familiar, that you pay no attention to them and press on not knowing how much you are limiting yourself.

In this book, we will point out both general assumptions about relationships and specific assumptions about certain relationship problems that typically get in the way of finding truly effective solutions. We will also spend some time challenging those assumptions, because many of you have held onto them for so long that you will be reluctant to let them go, even though they are getting in your way.

Once you have successfully gotten past some of the mental rules that have held you back, you will still need ideas on ways to tackle relationship problems that are both different and helpful. We will use systems theory and the experience we have had helping people sort out relationship difficulties to provide you with fresh, helpful strategies. We hope the new pattern that you develop will look like this:

Problem → Flexibility of options → New,
effective solutions → Problem resolved

Before we can describe some new, creative solutions, we will introduce you to some ideas that will place those solutions in a context that makes some sense to you. We will explore, and explode, myths, or assumptions, about relationships that stifle effective problem solving.

A brief foray into communication theory will be necessary to demonstrate how direct communication is not always best and to acquaint you with the levels of communication that exist in every interaction. Most books about relationships stress the importance of good communication. We agree, but we'll take a different slant on what good communication is.

We mentioned systems theory earlier in this chapter, and later we will give you a crash course in what systems theory means. This theory will help us explain a new way to view what causes problems in relationships (a way that does away with the idea of blame) and how one motivated person can make real changes in a relationship, even without active cooperation from a partner.

We will also briefly discuss rules in relationships and how they can sometimes limit solution alternatives. We will take this notion a step further by introducing you to ideas that spring from *constructivism*. Don't let the heavy name scare you. Constructivism offers a very useful framework for understanding how people create meaning for themselves and how they make sense of the world, as well as their relationships. This theory will help us explain how individuals can even make changes in the way their partners think and feel about their relationships.

After we lay the groundwork by presenting these ideas, we'll move on to address specific problems in the areas of communication, power, and sex. We know we can't cover every conceivable relationship problem, so we've chosen ones we commonly see in our practices. Actual case examples will be used to illustrate our points. Before we finish, we will also show how the strategies presented can be used in nonromantic relationships and for individuals with problems not directly related to interactions with others.

We hope you will find our ideas both helpful and interesting. Keep an open mind, because we will try to challenge your old ways of thinking about and acting on problems that threaten the relationships that mean the most to you.

Chapter 2

Interaction, Communication, and the Creation of Meaning in Relationships

The strategies that allow one individual to stimulate positive change in a relationship arise from three related theories: (1) *systems theory*, (2) *communication theory*, and (3) *constructivism*. *Systems theory* has a lot to say about how people interact and how change takes place in relationships. *Communication theory* is a vast subject area which covers the many facets of how people exchange information and understand each other. *Constructivism* provides a challenging description of the relative and idiosyncratic way in which we make sense of our lives and our relationships.

The ideas that spring from the three theories represent a radical departure from many of the prevailing ways of describing people, problems, and change. In the field of mental health, most theories have traditionally thought of human behavior in linear cause–effect terms with either historical (e.g., unhappy childhood) or physical (e.g., bad nerves) explanations for the behavior. Efforts to explain problem behaviors or emotional distress have usually been based on either a medical or Freudian perspective. Both perspectives consider only the individual, apart from his or her relationships, as the unit of study and treatment.

The medical model views problems or emotional distress as symptoms of an underlying mental illness or disorder, usually resulting from biological or genetic malfunction or abnormality of some kind. This disease perspective of human behavior leads to the search for the cause of the so-called illness (its etiology), which purportedly will prescribe treatment in the form of drugs or other means of changing the physical process deemed responsible for the symptoms. From this view, health is essentially the absence of pathology. The medical model has had a lot to say about the treatment of individuals and the diseases or disorders from which they suffer, but it says little about treating relationship problems. After all, how can a *couple* have a disease? How can a medical model explain the problem between Sharon and Jeff? What underlying physical condition accounts for the process that occurs between them?

The influential Freudian model is also a linear cause–effect perspective that links current mental or emotional difficulties with historical events from childhood. Symptoms are seen as arising from trauma or conflict that has been repressed and relegated to the unconscious mind. According to a Freudian view, the symptom (e.g., anxiety, depression) acts as a defense mechanism to keep the traumatic event or conflict from entering the conscious mind. The symptom essentially permits the individual to remain unaware of the event that is pressing for recognition.

Treatment consists of helping the person with the emotional or mental distress to recover the memory of the repressed event, which could be a fantasy or an unacceptable desire (e.g., wishing sexual contact with a parent), and reexperience the emotions associated with the trauma or fantasy. The secret material becomes known and the buried emotions are worked through within the protective confines of a long-term, therapeutic relationship. Then the person can have a "corrective emotional experience," which makes the person more comfortable with the secret and reduces emotional symptoms. Similar to the medical model, the Freudian view has difficulty explaining or treating couples with problems. Describing problems of interaction between people as symptoms related to repressed historical events is not satisfying or helpful. From this perspective, couple problems are usually seen as the fault of individual mental disorders, and one or both individuals must undergo the treatment process discussed above. Which person, Jeff or Sharon, needs to examine his or her childhood relationship with his or her parents to address their concern?

Another important model in mental health is behaviorism. Behaviorists pay little attention to childhood traumas and unconscious conflicts and much more attention to behaviors and their consequences (such as reward and punishment). Linear cause–effect thinking (rewarding a behavior makes it happen more, punishing makes it happen less) is a cornerstone of behavioral thought. Behaviorism has contributed greatly to education, child rearing, and the treatment of many emotional problems. However, the cause–effect thinking upon which it is based does not hold up well with a couple or family. Person A does not affect Person B without being affected in turn. Both affect each other in unpredictable, complicated ways.

After many years of rigid adherence to the above individually oriented models, a growing disenchantment led to the consideration of a very different way of thinking about people, relationships, and psychotherapy. Recently, more and more attention has been devoted to the study of the couple and the family and how individuals relate to one another in social contexts. New ways of thinking are evolving to explain the complexities of relationships and to help resolve the problems and distress inherent in relationships. These different ways of thinking offer a refreshing, illness-free lens through which to observe human behavior and have far-reaching implications and applications. If one studies human behavior through an interactive lens, the focus of study shifts from what goes on inside of a person to what takes place between people, the study of relationships. The shift of focus to relationships between people represents the essence of systems theory. We will consider the mental health implications of a systems view in a later chapter. For now, let us turn to what systems theory is and how it is useful when considering relationship difficulties.

Systems Theory

In recent years we have all been exposed to and probably learned systems theory whether we knew it or not. Attention to Earth Day and saving our planet indicates a growing public awareness of the environment and threats to its ecology. Ecology is itself a systems concept, encompassing the interrelatedness of the multiple forms of life, which create and share a common environment. In any given space, people, animals, plant life, air, soil, and so forth all join together as an ecological system, affecting each other so intimately that consideration of them separately makes no sense. Similarly, a couple or family is a unique kind of ecological system that consists of intimately interrelated individuals.

A system can be defined as a group of elements and the relationships among them.[2] When the elements are people in relationships, the most important feature of the relationship is communication. Relationships are established, maintained, and changed by communicative interaction among the members of the couple or family. As the relationship between individuals in a couple endures, communication sequences form patterns over time, and it is the patterning over time that is the essence of a couple system. Sometimes the enduring patterns begin to create difficulties for couples and, therefore, new patterns are needed. Recall the pattern between Jeff and Sharon concerning the giving and receiving of advice and how such a pattern resulted in relationship problems.

A few of the specific concepts that emerge from systems theory are particularly helpful in describing how couples operate and how effective, relationship-enhancing changes can be made by couples experiencing difficulties and distress. They are (1) mutual dependence, (2) circular causality, and (3) wholeness.[3]

Mutual Dependence

Elements in a system are mutually dependent: They rely upon one another. In some ways, this idea is very easy to understand and accept. People like to think they can rely and depend on spouses or partners and that they themselves are reliable and dependable.

Mutual dependence means much more than this. It also means that what one person does depends upon what the other person does. A simple example of this is a pair of dancers. One leads, the other follows. The follower moves according to cues or signals from the leader, and the leader is able to continue his or her steps only if the follower executes certain moves. When this is done effectively, as by Ginger Rogers and Fred Astaire, the couple moves as one. However, no matter how good a dancer is, if his or her partner can't, or won't, move as expected, he or she will look awkward and clumsy.

It is doubtful that any of you are disagreeing with what we have said so far, but think about what the idea of mutual dependence means. It means you are *not*, in the context of a relationship, acting *completely* of your own free will. You are constantly being influenced by your partner, and vice versa. This idea, while obvious to most of you, is a little hard to swallow. We like to think of ourselves as free agents, acting independently. This is an attractive idea, but a ridiculous one. We don't act the same way around our parents that we do around other people their age. We're different with friends than we are with strangers. People don't control us, but they clearly influence us, and we influence them. The more closely involved you are with someone, the greater the degree and scope of that influence.

For the purposes of this book, the most important aspect of this concept is the idea that everything you do in a relationship is influenced by what your partner has done and is doing and will influence what your partner does subsequently. A good analogy is bidding in bridge. The person who bids first influences how all three of the other players will bid. Their bids influence how that first player bids next. A slight change in the way one person makes a bid can dramatically change the final bid, how the hand is played, and the outcome of the game.

Our example of Sharon and Jeff also illustrates how mutual dependence operates. Sharon tried to do some things to get less criticism. Jeff responded by criticizing more and pulling away. Sharon tried even harder, and Jeff pulled away even more. So each person's actions helped determine what the other did, and each person's actions affected the relationship as a whole.

A marriage, then, is not just a static and fixed relationship between two rigid individuals, although it may seem that way. Marriage is a fluid, ever-changing relationship between two people and their individual ways of behaving. The overall relationship is determined by how the spouses behave in relation to one another. No matter how entrenched one's behavior is or how strong one's personality has developed, each individual is influenced by the other on an ongoing basis. The result is a dynamic flow and exchange of information that is mutually influenced by both persons. Put one person on a deserted island and he or she will have a specific pattern of behavior. Place that person in an office environment, and a different behavior pattern will emerge. Finally, put that same individual in an intimate relationship and he or she will have another pattern of behavior, largely depending on the behavioral pattern of the spouse. *Once you recognize your partner's dependence upon your pattern of behavior, you can consciously plan and change your own behavior, thereby influencing your partner and the relationship in a constructive manner.*

Circular Causality

Mutual dependence is closely related to another characteristic of systems: circular causality. This concept is important because it addresses the question of what causes things to happen in relationships. Virtually every couple we see is interested in what, or who, caused their problems, but they usually express that interest in terms of looking for guilt, blame, or responsibility. In short, they ask, "Whose fault is this?" Circular causality offers an alternative, more helpful way of looking at this issue.

Most people, when asked to comment on why they do things, will respond in terms of cause and effect: "I walked out of the room because she yelled at me." Although the description of cause and effect may be accurate, and probably is from the speaker's point of view, it is limited in its scope. There is another, and very different, way of looking at cause and effect.

Consider the following example. A husband has a nagging problem, and his wife has a drinking problem. If the husband is asked why he nags, he will say, "I nag my wife because she drinks." Not surprisingly, the wife replies, "I drink because my husband is such a nag." Each statement is true depending upon whose point of view you adopt and at what point in the process you step in to observe.

The systems perspective on this example is that the husband nags because the wife drinks because the husband nags. Circular causality does not see people as influencing one another in a straight-line, "A-causes-B" way. Rather, influence among people in relationships is reciprocal and mutually dependent: I react to you and you react to my reaction, and so on. Choosing the point at which the causal chain begins is pointless and arbitrary.

One implication of circular causality is that the circle can be broken or interrupted at any point, regardless of how the problem started or how long it has been around. If one person in a couple changes his or her behavior noticeably and consistently, the other person's reactions will change, which will change the first person's reactions. In this way, one person can positively impact a troubled relationship. The other partner's active cooperation is not necessarily required.

We often hear from our clients, "My husband/wife should be the one talking to you. He/she has the problem." First of all, as we have seen, it is not always obvious who has the problem. Just look at our previous examples. Does the wife have a drinking problem, or does the husband have a nagging problem? Does Sharon have a problem with constructive criticism, or does Jeff have a problem with control and sexism? We hope you are thinking that determining *who* has the problem is entirely arbitrary and depends on *where* in the sequence of events you choose to look.

Based upon circular causality, it doesn't really matter too much who has the problem. One person, either person, in the couple can interrupt the causal circle and move the relationship in a different direction.

We see a lot of people who feel hopeless and powerless. Their relationships are falling apart and their partners don't want to come in for help. The idea that one person, either person, can initiate meaningful change in a relationship, which comes from thinking in systems terms, helps him or her to feel stronger and more hopeful.

Wholeness

The third systems concept is wholeness. As you might expect, based on what you have learned about systems thinking so far, wholeness is intimately related to the ideas of mutual dependence and circular causality.

We are sure that you have heard many times the saying that "the whole is more than the sum of the parts." In its simplest terms, that is what the concept of wholeness states. Specifically, as wholeness relates to the ideas we will be discussing, a couple is more than two individuals who happen to be together. The system of a couple includes the two individuals, their interactions with each other and with other systems (family, work), and more. So when two individuals come together in a relationship, something is created that is different from and larger and more complex than those two individuals when they were apart.

It is also important to keep in mind that a couple is a *dynamic* system. This means that a couple is constantly changing and adapting to pressures from within it and outside of it. A system is said to behave as a whole when a change in one part (person) is responded to with a change in each other part (the other person in a couple), and the system as a whole (the relationship).

This aspect of wholeness suggests that when one person makes a change, the other person will respond with a change and the relationship itself will be different, and not just in ways directly related to the specific problem that was addressed. For example, if Sharon is able to apply one of the creative solutions found in this book to her problem effectively (a change in one part), Jeff will respond with decreased criticism and advice giving (a change in a related part). This could reduce the overall tension level between them and allow them to communicate better and enjoy each other in ways unrelated to the problem under concern (a change in the system as a whole).

What we are saying is that a small change in a specific area can lead to a positive "ripple effect,"[4] in much the same way that the impact of a stone thrown into a calm pond affects the surface well beyond the small point at which it enters. When there are many problems in a relationship, people assume that a major overhaul is required. Many times, a small adjustment, strategically employed, is all that is needed.

The challenge, of course, is to find a way to change that will produce a positive ripple, not a negative one. Also, the change has to be a real change, not just a minor variation on previous solution attempts (as Sharon used).

We hope you will take some time to digest the ideas from systems theory that we have just presented. They represent a considerable departure from the ways we traditionally think about relationships, how they function and how they change.

Cause-and-effect thinking has been portrayed as inaccurate in describing patterns of interaction in relationships and unhelpful in producing change. The ideas that one person can produce meaningful change in a relationship, and that a small change can and will lead to a ripple of other changes, are not part of conventional wisdom. Nor are the implications that change can occur quickly and that it can happen without the knowledge or cooperation of one member of the couple.

As unusual as these ideas sound, they have been found to apply to couples and families and to work in producing changes in those systems. Remember: A lot of your thinking has been shaped by ideas developed to explain how *individuals* function. The world of the couple operates under a different set of principles and assumptions than the individual. The good news is that the strategies that have been developed from systems concepts do work, even when both partners aren't equally motivated to change.

Before we move on to communication theory, there is one important qualification we would like to make about systems theory. Mutual dependence, circular causality, and wholeness address your ability to influence patterns of interaction that you find distressful and that are destructive to your relationships. These concepts should not be interpreted to mean that each individual's behavior has equal significance, equal power, or is equally productive of relationship problems. If you are in a relationship with an alcoholic spouse, you *do* have influence but you *are not* responsible for that individual's drinking. Keep in mind that there is a distinction between influence and responsibility and also between the one actually *enacting* the serious problem behavior (e.g., alcoholism, violence) and the one engaged in the problem behavior pattern. The ultimate responsibility for behavior lies within the individual. We make this qualification because sometimes people infer that they are equally at fault for a spouse's alcoholism, battering, or other seriously dysfunctional behavior.

Communication Theory

A couple is essentially one person communicating with another person. How else can there be a relationship? Everyone reading this book is aware of the importance of communication in relationships. The difficulty comes in figuring out exactly what *communication* means and how to change it if it is not going well. We hope to shed some light on this complicated subject by presenting three assumptions relevant to understanding the ideas presented in this book. They are (1) all behavior, verbal and non-verbal, is communicative; (2) all communication defines, maintains, or changes the nature of a relationship; and (3) listening is an active process.

All Behavior Is Communicative[5]

Nonverbal communication is a topic familiar to most of us. We know that gestures, tone of voice, and facial expressions are important in understanding what someone is saying. Many books have been written about body language, addressing what people "say" by their posture, distance from the other person, position of their arms and legs, and so forth. What gets lost in these considerations of subtle, nonverbal methods of communicating is that *all behavior is communicative.* What a person *does* sends a powerful message to people with whom he or she interacts.

Everything a person does in relation to another is some kind of message being sent. There is no such thing as *not* communicating. Even silence or the apparent lack of verbal behavior is conveying some message. So in the presence of your partner, you cannot not send messages, which is to say that everything you do can be seen as communicative and relevant to your relationship.

A spouse who routinely comes home late for dinner without calling may be saying, "Your inconvenience is unimportant compared to what happens at work" or "Your feelings are not a priority to me." The spouse who prepares dinner may not comment in response to the late spouse. Yet the silence may be a worse indictment than a verbal scolding.

Perhaps the most important aspect of viewing behavior itself as a powerful means of communication is that such a recognition significantly increases our options when verbal communication is not working. In other words, if you have tried to change your relationship problems by talking, ad nauseam, and that has not been helpful, then looking at your behavioral options may provide a more fruitful way to positively impact the problem under concern. In some ways, behavior can be viewed as an even more powerful method of communication that conveys an individual's true intentions in a given situation. We will return to this idea in Chapter 3. For now, please consider that *both verbal and nonverbal behavior convey messages and offer avenues to change distressful patterns of interaction to productive and satisfying ones.*

All Communication Defines, Maintains, or Changes a Relationship[6]

As we have seen, communication occurs both verbally and nonverbally. Communication also occurs at different levels, even though most of us focus our attention on only one, the *content level*.[7] The content level of a message is simply the literal meaning of the words. The phrase "my back itches" means just that at a content level, and "I love you" holds no additional meaning. The content of words is what most people use when trying to understand what a partner is saying. It is also what is often brought up in marital counseling sessions to prove points and win arguments ("But yesterday you said . . . "). Unfortunately, as we will see shortly, content from previous discussions becomes relatively meaningless when separated from the other, more important level of communication that accompanied it when it was originally delivered.

The more important, but less obvious, level of communication is the *relationship level*.[8] This aspect of communication indicates how the sender of the message is attempting to influence the receiver in a given situation. It conveys a command or directive concerning the sender's needs and is an implicit attempt to influence the receiver. For example, "My back itches" may mean "Scratch my back." "I had a rough day" may mean "Leave me alone," "I need your support," or "Fix me a drink." Even "I love you" can be an implicit command, depending upon the circumstances. It may mean, "Tell me that you love me." Kurt Vonnegut captures the implicit command of "I love you" in this passage from his novel *Slapstick*.

> "Eliza . . . " I said, "so many of the books I've read to you said that love was the most important thing of all. Maybe I should tell you that I love you now."
> "Go ahead," she said.
> "I love you, Eliza," I said.
> She thought about it. "No," she said at last, "I don't like it."
> "Why not?" I said.
> "It's as though you were pointing a gun at my head," she said . . . "What else can I say, or anybody say, but 'I love you, too?'"[9]

The implicit command or indirect influence in communication can be difficult to understand and accept. It implies that when we are communicating with other people, we are trying to influence them indirectly to do what we want them to do. This can be hard for some people to accept because it sounds like manipulation—which it is, at least to some degree. But influence is unavoidable in communication; it is inherent in how we interact. Just as one cannot *not* communicate, one cannot *not* influence when communicating. The words that you are now reading are attempts by the authors to influence your thinking regarding communication. Whenever we interact with other people, one item on our agendas is to get our needs met, or to get our points across. We communicate these needs explicitly, by asking directly for what we want, and implicitly, by making indirect attempts to get what we want. Saying that one way of influencing is better than another misses the point. Both direct and indirect ways occur routinely.

The most significant point to be gleaned from this discussion is that we attempt to influence our partners all the time without the benefit of conscious planning; the implicit commands are largely automatic and occur outside of awareness. Consequently, we often address the most important parts of our lives, our relationships, in an extremely haphazard fashion. Awareness of the implicit influence inherent in communication allows for its planned use in improving relationships. Many of the strategies in this book involve a conscious utilization of this implicit aspect of communication.

In addition to conveying an implicit, or indirect, command or directive concerning the sender's desires, the relationship level also functions to define the very nature of the relationship. For example, the statement, "The garbage can is overflowing," not only conveys the obvious, but may also convey the implicit directive, "Take the garbage out." The original statement serves another function as well: It defines a certain relationship between the sender of the message and the receiver, that is, one in which the sender has the right to comment on the state of garbage and expect the receiver to follow the implicit directive. In other words, communication also establishes rules in a relationship. Usually, the rules must be inferred, but couples do sometimes talk about them, for example, "When it comes to the kids, I call the shots," or "We will act as equals in this marriage." But whether or not such explicit definitions occur, the relationship is defined implicitly whenever you communicate with each other.

All communication, therefore, defines, maintains, or changes a relationship. Communication establishes rules in each situation (e.g., who takes out the garbage) and either maintains those rules or changes them. In every sequence of communication between individuals in a relationship, the opportunity exists to either maintain things as they are or redefine them. We are not advocating that you attempt to figure out your partner's motives or implicit commands or definitions. Rather, we are suggesting that you look at how *you* are defining the relationship through *your* communication and make changes accordingly in a helpful way.

The game of bridge, once again, provides an excellent example of how the three levels of communication interact to give meaning to communication. In bridge, there are conventions, ways of communicating something different from the actual meaning of the words. Consider the convention of "one club." On the content level, "one club" as a bid means "I have an opening bid in clubs." However, the convention of "one club" conveys an implicit command which is quite different from the content level. It says to the bidder's partner, "I have major suits in my hand that are equal. Tell me, through your bid, which suit you can support."

That is still not the whole story. Also at the relationship level, "one club" communicates "I am taking charge of this hand, and you are to follow my lead." In other words, the nature of the relationship between the partners is defined for that hand.

To conclude this discussion of the levels of communication, let us emphasize that there is always more than one level to communication, and that what a person says is merely one aspect of the total message. The relationship level is always present, and it often involves indirect, unconscious attempts to influence the other person's behavior and the rules of the relationship itself. Many of the strategies we suggest later in this book are based upon the idea that it can be helpful to use the relationship level in a consciously planned, but still implicit, manner in order to help the relationship.

Listening Is an Active Process

When we think about communication, we think of a speaker and a listener. The speaker is actively conveying a message, and the listener is passively receiving it. But this is a very inaccurate perception. Listening is an active process. When people speak to us we have to make sense out of the words they produce. We compare their ideas to beliefs and attitudes we hold and to perceptions about the speakers we have already formed. We take into account gestures, tone of voice, and facial expressions. We also consider the circumstances. In addition to all of this, our needs influence what we hear. For example, a man who has been left by his wife and is very lonely and sad gets a consoling hug from a female friend. He interprets it as a come-on and starts to kiss her, and she is shocked. She has hugged him before, but his needs help him give this hug a different interpretation.

The idea of listening as an active process is relevant to our purposes in a number of ways. First of all, it means the listener helps create meaning. Much of this process tends to be automatic and done subconsciously. We are seldom aware of how our beliefs and attitudes affect how we hear, or the ways we interpret non-verbal communication, much less how our own needs affect our perceptions. By paying attention to these factors, however, we can make them conscious. Once they are conscious, we can control them.

This means we can choose how to interpret a given communication. Words or behaviors which have hurt us before (due to how we have perceived them) no longer have to have this power. It also means we can choose to interpret a message in a way that is different from what the sender intended. Just because people intend to hurt or manipulate us doesn't mean we have to co-operate by giving their messages the meanings they want us to get. In later chapters, specific ideas on how to do this will be explored.

The flip side of the coin is that often the listener's understanding of a message is already different from the sender's, and that can cause problems. For example, if a woman believes her husband is stressed out and needs time away from her and the kids, she might suggest he go away for a week. If her husband interprets this as "she's trying to get rid of me," the whole point of her message has been twisted, and caring is perceived as rejection. This may be the most common problem seen in couples: The message sent is not the message received.

Another way differences in perception create difficulties occurs when one person gets defensive because the other sees things differently. An example of this is a wife who comes home and complains to her husband about how she is being treated by her boss. The husband, trying to be objective and to calm her down, suggests that what her boss has been doing really isn't so bad. She feels misunderstood and gets defensive—goes into more detail about her boss, accuses her husband of not caring, points out how she always listens and understands when he complains about work.

Even if perceptions are genuinely different because people

see things differently, or have different attitudes or values, it is not always helpful to express or defend those differences. Many of the change strategies we will present involve finding ways to understand and express your partner's view of a situation so as to reduce defensiveness and change old, conflictual patterns.

Constructivism (Meaning Creation)

Systems theory provides one with a way of looking at relationship difficulties that permits one person to effect significant change in relationships. Communication theory allows for the consideration of both direct and indirect methods of influence, as well as verbal and nonverbal means. Communication theory emphasizes the importance of the listener and how the receiver of a message participates in the creation of the meaning of the message. Expanding upon the significance of the listener, constructivism provides one with further understanding of the interactional nature of relationships and the process through which people make sense of their lives. Constructivism is a theory of how people create meaning in relationships. Meaning is our thoughts, feelings, perceptions, and experiences all rolled into an organized whole.

From a constructivist point of view, people do not discover reality; they invent it.[10] Reality consists of "constructed" or created meanings, which, in turn, organize perceptions and experience. The creation of meaning serves the purpose of making our lives more describable and predictable by pulling together the vast amount of information that we process daily.

Saying that we invent reality does not mean that there is no objective reality. The book you are holding in your hands is real. Rather, constructivism suggests that we create reality or meaning about social relationships through the interactive process called communication. Meaning, therefore, arises from our interactions with others and is generated from the dynamic social exchange of verbal and nonverbal communication.[11] Meaning creation is a continual process that flows from a couple's interaction. The implications of this view of meaning generation are powerful. We are suggesting that you not only have the power to change your interaction with your spouse by altering your behavior, but also have the capacity to influence change in how your partner thinks and feels about the issue under concern.

Recall Jeff and Sharon and the problem that developed from Jeff's propensity to point out better ways for Sharon to perform whatever task she was doing. Most likely, Jeff's reality was that he was only trying to help Sharon and save her time, and that she was being needlessly hypersensitive and defensive. Sharon, on the other hand, had a constructed meaning that Jeff was controlling and sexist and persisted in treating her like a child, despite her repeated protests. From Sharon's perspective, no wonder that she responded in a hostile fashion.

If Sharon changes her part in the circular process, she will enable a change in Jeff's behavior as well. She would also be encouraging or setting up the conditions for him to create a new meaning regarding his or her behavior. In other words, changing the interactive process itself generates new meaning; you can set up an experience for your partner and yourself that challenges the usefulness of the current meaning and enables a more helpful meaning to develop. By allowing such an experience to occur, you permit your partner to arrive at a new meaning on his or her own. Because your spouse arrives at the new meaning independent of your attempts to tell him or her the right way, the change is far more likely to endure and become a *meaning*-ful change.

Sharon told Jeff many times about his bothersome behavior, but to no avail. Creating the conditions for him to reach a conclusion on his own may be a far more productive way for her to influence change. People ascribe meaning to social interaction in an ongoing fashion that permits a continual possibility for not only change in behavior, but also change in attitude and feelings. This goes well beyond mere behavior modification. We are asserting that *you can create a context for relationship change that allows an ongoing opportunity for the generation of more positive meanings and, therefore, more satisfying relationships.*

Summary

These ideas are the basis for a number of the creative solutions to relationship problems that will be outlined throughout the rest of this book. So if you are a little confused now, don't worry. We are suggesting a very different way to think about relationship problems, and this is bound to be a little difficult to digest at first. We will get much more specific on how to carry out these suggestions in subsequent chapters.

Before we move on, let us recap some of the implications these theories have for dealing with relationship problems. The systems theory concept of mutual dependence holds that everything you do influences your partner and is influenced by what your partner has done and said. Circular causality suggests that it doesn't matter who has the problem or when it started. Either partner, acting in a truly different way, can create a meaningful change. Finally, according to the concept of wholeness, a small change can, and will, create other changes by rippling through the whole system. Small initial change can lead to large, meaningful change. Overall, perhaps the most important message that systems theory sends is that one motivated person, using effective strategies, can turn a relationship around, even without the active participation of his or her partner.

Communication theory also has a lot to say about where to look to make changes in relationships. Behavior as communication suggests that both verbal and nonverbal behavior convey important messages and that each can provide options for changing distressful patterns in relationships. Consideration of the relationship level of communication leads to the conclusion that attempts to influence the other person and the relationship, often implicitly, are a routine, normal part of communication. Another way to interpret the relationship level is that manipulation, albeit automatic and unplanned, happens to some degree all the time. Implicit communication can remain indirect, but it can be conscious, intentional, and helpful to a relationship in certain limited situations. Communication theory offers the hopeful perspective that we have the continual capability to positively influence how both people see a relationship.

Listening as an active process is another facet of communication theory that opens doors to creative problem-solving. Since we help to create meaning as listeners, we can choose how to interpret messages and, therefore, gain much more control over how we respond.

Finally, constructivism is a theory of how we create meaning in our relationships that suggests one person can effectively influence a change in what a behavior or situation means to the other. Setting a context for the generation of more helpful meanings is much of what this book is about.

While these ideas can help open doors to new possibilities for coping with relationship problems, there are factors existing in all of us that create resistance to these ideas. A potent source of this resistance is based in a number of myths about relationships that are held by most members of our society. Before we proceed with specific strategies to produce change in relationships, we will describe and hopefully discredit those myths.

Chapter 3

Myths about Relationships

In Chapter 1, we discussed rules and assumptions, and how they can keep people stuck in old patterns and stifle their creativity in attempting to solve problems. Some of the most difficult assumptions to recognize and change are those based on societal myths. A myth can be defined as "a notion based more on tradition or convenience than fact," or "one of the fictions or half-truths forming part of the ideology of a society."[12]

Even though myths are nonfactual half-truths, a majority of the members of society continue to believe in them. Those beliefs guide behavior and perpetuate old, ineffective habits and patterns. Since relationships—and particularly, committed, romantic relationships—are key threads in the fabric of society, many myths have been woven around relationships and how they function.

Relationship myths impede attempts to make constructive changes in relationships, much in the same way that perceiving the imaginary square inhibits solution of Chapter 1's nine-dot problem. Myths can have a particularly strong influence for two reasons: (1) they have been around for so long that we are not even aware of what they are and how they affect us, and (2) even if we do recognize them, they fit so well into the cultural belief system that it doesn't occur to us to challenge them.

This chapter will examine myths that we have found to be counterproductive to resolving relationship problems. We will attempt to show how inaccurately they describe relationship reality, and we will offer alternative viewpoints on how relationships, and the people in them, function. These new perspectives, which will often appear at first to challenge common sense, are much more conducive to developing creative solutions to problems.

Myth #1: What People Say Is Very Important and Has a Big Impact on What They Do

As we discussed in Chapter 2, all behavior is communicative and, therefore, sends messages about the nature of the relationship. Of particular interest are situations in which words and behavior give conflicting messages. Consider a husband who says, "I'll leave you if you don't stop drinking," but continues to stay as his wife continues to drink. Or consider a wife who says to her husband, "I love you," but has affairs and lies to him constantly.

Many people stay in destructive relationships because they believe or pay attention to the words, not the behaviors, when the two send opposing messages. This is not surprising in a society that places such emphasis and value on words: "A man is only as good as his word," "Say what you mean and mean what you say." These ideas may be countered with "Actions speak louder than words," but the truth is that most of us don't have much training or experience in "listening" to behavior. In spite of the fact that we are all aware that people can say one thing but do another, many of us still hold the belief that people will do or act in accordance with their words.

Take, as an example, the case of Linda, a young woman who entered therapy confused, frustrated, and depressed. What was even worse for her was the fact that she felt she had "no good reason" to feel as she did. Upon further examination of her circumstances, it became clear that her problems centered around her relationship with her boyfriend, David. Linda had been seeing David for three years. He frequently told her he loved her, and that spending time with her was more important to him than anything. Yet things kept getting in the way: work, softball, his friends.

Linda was upset with herself. How could she be unhappy? After all, she had a wonderful man who loved her and wanted to be with her. When she finally expressed to David her frustration with their lack of time together, he was outraged. Didn't he always tell her he loved her? Hadn't he been faithful? What more did she want?

What he said made Linda all the more confused and guilty as well. How could she have questioned David's love? How selfish she must be to make such unreasonable demands on him. Linda was quite depressed by that time and thoroughly convinced it was all her fault.

Linda was unaware of her belief that "If David says something and means it, he will certainly act in accordance with what he has said." Obviously, to her therapist, this was not what David was all about. Linda was on the receiving end of a *double message*.[13]

A double message occurs when two conflicting messages about a given topic or issue are simultaneously sent by one person to another. Usually, one message is verbal while the other is non-verbal, comprised of tone, gestures, or actions. A simple example is someone who says, "I'm very angry with you," but is smiling while saying it. The recipient of the double message is unsure what to believe or respond to.

In the example of Linda and David, the double message consisted of the contradiction between what David said and how he behaved. On the one hand, he said he loved Linda. On the other, he seldom found time for her. The effect of such a conflicting set of communications can be devastating, especially when there are no additional cues to help decipher the true meaning. Linda was left to figure which message was true. When she tried to get more information by directly asking David about the discrepancy, she got no help. In fact, he may well have been unaware of the mixed messages he was delivering.

An extreme example of a double message is the battering relationship. The battered wife is beaten, but told she is loved. The result, assuming she stays in the relationship, is usually disorientation, depression, and loss of self-esteem. The battered spouse winds up believing it is her fault.

A person who receives, but doesn't recognize, a double message finds himself or herself in a no-win situation. A correct response to one message is the incorrect response to the other. This dilemma has been labeled the *double bind*, and some researchers believe that such double binds can lead to serious difficulties.[14]

Most of the people we see in our practices who are caught in double binds begin to question their own perceptions and wonder if they are "going crazy." One thing that contributes to this phenomenon is that the people who deliver double messages don't realize that they are. Their motives are not conscious ones, so they are not aware of the meaning of their behaviors. Consequently, they can be very convincing in denying any contradictory messages, since they absolutely believe they are telling the truth. The recipient of the double message, already confused, quickly loses confidence in his or her judgment in the face of the other's certainty.

One way to avoid being caught in a double bind is to attend to what people do, not to what they say, when the two messages conflict. Behavior tends to be a far more tangible and meaningful expression of beliefs and values than words. This is, of course, easier said than done. If we hear a politician rail against high taxes, but then see him vote for a tax increase, we know what to believe and we are not confused. However, in relationships in which we participate, not just observe, and which involve our needs and feelings, the picture is not nearly so clear.

Unfortunately for Linda, she listened to David's words when his behavior was much more indicative of his commitment to her. She unwittingly became a victim of her own belief that what people say has a big impact on what they do. We have seen that myth disproved time and time again, and that the people believing it are left confused and helpless. Once we accept that words often fall short of accurately depicting someone's intentions and that we can't really guess many times what someone else really means, it becomes obvious that what we must count on is behavior. In the long term, behavior is what gives evidence of our true intentions.

Myth #2: People Can and Should Understand and Explain Their Own and Others' Motives

This myth holds that understanding the reason why you or someone else does something is crucial to solving a problem. Extending this idea to relationship issues means that no problem can be resolved until we know why it is happening. This means tracing it back to when the problem started and looking at each partner's motivation for acting as he or she did. In order to truly understand these motivations, we have to examine each person's background long before the two partners ever met. From this perspective, any attempt to deal with a problem in terms of how it currently exists is only scratching the surface.[15]

We see two major shortcomings to this view. One is that searching for "why" produces only possible explanations. Behavior is the result of a tremendous number of interacting influences in a wide variety of different areas: biological, psychological, interpersonal, situational. For every explanation we arrive at, another, deeper-seated one, can be speculated. We never get answers to "why" questions, only plausible-sounding guesses. The bottom line is that mental health professionals and behavioral scientists still don't know with any certainty what causes even the simplest behaviors. So if you think you know why you or someone else did something, please realize you are only guessing.

A second reason that leads us to suggest you abandon the myth of needing to know why is that knowing why seldom produces a solution. *Understanding* a behavior or pattern and *changing* it are often two completely different phenomena.

As an illustration, consider the problems of Dan, a man who entered therapy because his wife constantly criticized him. Dan described his wife, Kim, as a hard-driving perfectionist. She worked as a personnel manager for a large corporation and was working evenings on her M.B.A. at a local university. Her first husband was a "bum" who couldn't hold a job and was completely irresponsible.

In addition to the problems Kim had had with her ex-husband, she was an Adult Child of an Alcoholic (her mother had a drinking problem). Her father was very demanding and difficult to please, which led Kim to push herself even harder to live up to his lofty expectations of her. She was, in fact, the family "hero" who tried to solve, or at least distract attention from, the family's problems through her own hard work and achievement.

Given all this, it was easy for Dan to understand why she was concerned about his pulling his weight (even though it wasn't a problem) and why she was so perfectionistic and driven. In fact, Dan probably did a better job of explaining his wife's personality than his therapist could have. However, he still had no idea of how to change things for the better. He understood her past, but couldn't alter it, and even though he knew why she criticized him, he was still hurt. Dan could, however, examine his current response to her criticisms and attempt changes in his behavior so that she would necessarily change hers. Changing the overall experience of the criticism pattern may also result in different meanings assigned by both Dan and his wife.

Historically, mental health professionals have done more than their part to perpetuate the myth of "why." Freudian theory, which dominated psychotherapeutic thinking in the early part of this century (and which is still very influential), held that insight was critical to therapeutic progress. In order to change, a patient needed to allow a therapist to help uncover layers of the subconscious mind, thereby getting to the deepest roots of the problem. Therapy of this type is like an archeological expedition in which the therapist and patient gradually uncover layer after layer of past and deeply hidden explanations for current behavior.

Many competing theories that look to current behaviors and ways to change them as key elements in therapy now exist. Still, the influence of Freudian thought on our culture is significant. Most people still believe looking for "why" is important. We believe that his is often an impossible quest—motives and influences are too varied and complex to be understood—which doesn't lead us to useful solutions anyway.

We are not suggesting, however, that looking for the "why" is never appropriate. Seeking the causes or explanations of problems is not inherently self-defeating to problem-solving *all* the time. Gaining insight into our childhood and adolescent development, as well as our families of origin, can provide us with a very useful understanding that enables us to recognize how we play out our past in current situations. What we are arguing against are the excesses or extremes of such explorations into the "why" of any problem. We are results-oriented therapists, who believe that if finding explanations in the past helps you solve your relationship difficulties, then you should continue to do what is working for you. If searching for the "why" is not providing you with solution alternatives, then we suggest you consider *what* is happening now between you and your partner and *how* that pattern can be changed.[16]

Myth #3: In Close Relationships, Being Completely Open and Honest Is Critical If the Relationship Is to Work

Prior to discussing this myth, it is best that we define our terms, because of all the myths, this one will probably provoke the strongest emotional response. We will take "honesty" to mean telling the truth, that is, not lying or deceiving. "Openness" will refer to not holding back any of the truth. A person who is being open and honest tells the truth, the whole truth, and nothing but the truth. The subjects of those revelations can be events, ideas, opinions, feelings, or motives.

One obvious problem with this idea is that it is probably impossible for anyone to be totally honest. You can only be honest about things of which you are aware. As we have seen in Chapter 2, we are often unaware of the relationship level of our communications and the needs that motivate that level. Situational factors influence what we say much more than we would like to think. In order for someone to be totally and completely honest, he or she would not only need to be aware of all internal needs, desires, and beliefs, but also all external factors influencing him or her. In addition, he or she would have to be motivated, at all times, to share all those experiences with his or her relationship partner. Neither of us has ever met such a mythical creature, nor any close approximations. So when you pat yourself on the back for your unflinching honesty, or castigate someone else for not opening up or knowing him or herself, please think twice. There are undoubtedly many things of which you, too, are unaware.

For the sake of discussion, let's first assume that one can be totally open and honest in a relationship. Given that this is possible, honesty of expression is not always the best policy. What is overlooked is that the impact of a message is entirely dependent upon the message's *interpretation* by the person receiving it; communication is a two-way process. In other words, the open and honest message occurs in the context of a relationship, with all of its inherent complexity. What may seem like an open expression of true feelings by the sender may be cruel nagging to the receiver. Remember the example from Chapter 1: Jeff's open and honest attempts to help Sharon by sharing the benefit of his experience were interpreted by Sharon as condescending and sexist.

Another example may further illustrate. Sheila, a mother of a seventeen-year-old son, would like him to be considerate of her needs and inform her when he stays out past his curfew. At each subsequent infraction of the household rule, Sheila, believing in the myth of honesty, expresses her anger, hurt, and frustration about her son's behavior of not simply letting her know when he was staying out later than curfew. She also expresses her honest expectation that he will notify her in the future if he is going to be out late. To her dismay, her son continues to not honor her request.

Much like the imaginary square limits alternatives and detracts from other perspectives that are more helpful, honesty in certain circumstances can similarly preclude problem resolution. Sheila's attempts at influencing her son's behavior ignore the power struggle that exists between her and her son. The struggle for power between a parent and an adolescent in the process of becoming an adult is a far more important variable to consider than honestly expressing one's feelings. When the context of a power struggle exists in a relationship, open and honest communication is very likely to be interpreted as something entirely different and usually as a demand for compliance. Sheila is likely being interpreted as saying, "I am the parent here and I want you to do what I want."

Communication is not so simple as to be restricted to merely what the words mean. In addition to expressing content, the words also convey meaning through the relationship level. The mother says, "It makes me very angry when I'm not informed when you are out after curfew." At the relationship level, mom is demanding compliance with the rule, and she is saying that she has the right to demand compliance because she is in power by virtue of being a parent.

Openness and honesty, then, aren't entirely open and honest. Expressions of honest communication can be ways of getting what we want and may also be ways of jockeying for power in a relationship. The person who professes to be open and honest can say almost anything and rationalize it without considering the other's interpretation or reaction.

Those who insist on pulling out the honesty trump card, maintaining that any other way of handling problems is merely playing games, are preferring to play the game of not seeing that they are playing games.[17] They are, in effect, denying that their honest expressions are attempts at influencing others to get their needs met. They are also denying that those same honest expressions often represent ways of attaining power in relationships.

If the person with whom you are communicating is unable or unwilling to respond honestly and openly, like Sheila's adolescent son, honesty and openness may well be a bad idea at times. Being open with someone who will use what you tell him or her to manipulate you or gain power over you is like playing poker and showing the other players your cards before you bet. It is a nice gesture, but you will often lose. Another point is that an open and honest expression must be interpreted as such by the receiver of the message for it to be truly open and honest. Honesty of expression involves both sender *and* receiver.

We do advocate openness and honesty. It can enhance closeness and trust and make both people feel better about the relationship and themselves. We also advocate that honesty and openness be tried *first* and continued until it is clear that it is not reciprocated and is, in fact, making things worse. We are only saying that honesty and openness is not the only way, and, in some situations, certainly not the best way.

Myth #4: A Good Relationship Is One in Which Both People Give Unselfishly

In our practices, we notice that most of our clients have a great deal of ambivalence when it comes to this myth. They know that they need to help meet their own needs and take care of themselves, but the idea of giving unselfishly sounds so good and so idealistic. As a result, when people begin taking better care of themselves, they experience a lot of guilt. Let us go on record as saying that unselfish giving is not a prerequisite for a good relationship. In fact, attempts to do so usually create more problems than they solve.

No matter how good our intentions, most of us have an idea in the back of our minds of what makes a relationship "balanced."

I may be able to give seventy-five percent and my partner only twenty-five percent, and that can feel all right to me. However, if it goes to 80–20, I will begin to feel resentful. The numbers are, of course, arbitrary, but the idea of balance is always there, and resentment inevitably follows if things are out of balance for too long. In other words, feeling as though you are on the giving end of things all the time becomes unsatisfactory and usually leads to relationship problems.

When one person in a relationship feels he or she has been giving too much and stops doing certain things, the other partner usually feels angry. After all, something is being taken away, and it's often something he or she never asked the other person to do to begin with.

Jack and Margy provide a good example of how the process occurs. Jack moved into Margy's house after a brief courtship. Margy was very busy with work and school at that time, and Jack, being a nice guy and madly in love, decided to help her out by doing more than his share of the housework and taking care of her two large dogs. After a while, Jack felt he was doing too much and was being taken for granted. He fully realized this one day while he was scooping up a large pile of dog dung. He confronted Margy and accused her of being selfish and lazy and taking advantage of his good nature. Margy was amazed and angry. She didn't know how burdened he had felt, and she had never asked him to do all those things anyway. In addition, she believed he was being insensitive to how busy and stressed she was.

Giving is an important part of any relationship. However, it needs to be kept in perspective. All of us expect something back for what we give. It helps to let the other person know what that is. Balance is also important. Rather than expecting to meet all of each other's needs, be sure to stay in practice at meeting some of your own. It adds stability to a relationship and reduces the risk of resentment.

You might say, "But those problems won't occur if both partners keep giving to each other." This is not necessarily true. We see many couples in which both partners feel they have been doing a lot of giving, and neither feels he or she is getting much in return. How can that be? What is usually happening in those situations is that what one partner gives is not what the other wants, and vice versa. Therefore, neither gets his or her needs met, though both are trying very hard, and both feel resentful.

We have found that *selfish* has become a dirty word for some people. Yet people who are happy in relationships have always found a balance between being selfish and unselfish. It is that balance that allows relationships to work. Complete selfishness certainly does not lend itself to being a participant in a healthy relationship, but it turns out that neither does utter unselfishness.

Myth #5: In Any Situation There Is Only One Reality or One Truth

In closing this chapter on myths about relationships, we would like to look at a myth that affects relationships but is much broader in its scope. That myth is the idea that there is such a thing as truth or reality in a given situation. When couples come into our offices, they often look for a judge, not a therapist. They know that only one person can be right and that the other must be wrong. Not only do they think the therapist will make that determination, but they also believe it is the key issue of their problems. Unfortunately, truth is neither that objective nor that simple.

Reality is entirely dependent upon who is observing and describing it, especially in complex situations such as interactions in relationships. Each person constructs his or her own reality based upon beliefs, values, and needs he or she brings into the situation. There is no objective relationship reality, only subjective evaluations of it. Therefore, there are multiple views of reality—as many views as there are people describing it. Each one of us sees only through the filters created by our unique perspectives and experiences, that is, through our created meanings. (See the discussion of constructivism in Chapter 2.)

When two people have very different stories to tell about the same situation, it does not mean that one is lying, although each partner usually believes that about the other. Rather, each is describing reality from his or her frame of reference, viewed through his or her perceptual lenses. In marital therapy, we find that there are almost always at least three perspectives on any given situation: one for each partner and a third for the therapist. All are valid; none is the truth.

A lot of time can be, and usually is, wasted trying to convince your partner that you are right. This time is spent much more efficiently trying to understand the other's point of view and using that understanding to change your own behavior in a way that will help the relationship.

In this chapter, we have described and, we hope, discredited five relationship myths that tend to rigidify behavior and limit creativity in solving problems. Keeping in mind the concepts described in Chapter 2, we will now move on to outline specific strategies for handling relationship difficulties. In the next three chapters, we will address the general areas we have found to encompass most problems in romantic relationships: communication, power, and sex. Subsequently, we will expand our scope to include strategies relevant to all types of relationships.

Keep your minds open. These ideas will be quite different from what you have traditionally heard about how to handle problems, and we all tend to be a little resistant at first to truly different ideas. Then again, if the old, traditional methods for dealing with problems had worked, you wouldn't be reading this book.

Chapter 4

Communication Problems in Romantic Relationships

Starting with our discussion of communication issues, we will begin to look at problems encountered by adults who are engaged in romantic relationships. We include in that category people who are married, living together, or dating. Within this broad category, the degree of commitment can vary tremendously. What is important is that there are two adults involved in a relationship involving relatively frequent contact, which permits patterns of interaction to develop.

This chapter will address three common communication patterns that often bring individuals to therapy. The first is lack of communication, in which one partner feels distress concerning the other's unwillingness or inability to talk about things. The second communication problem involves a pattern in which one partner is consistently sad or negative and the other person feels frustrated in his or her attempts to help or cheer up who we call the "chronic complainer." Third, we will examine an accuser–denier pattern of communication that frequently evolves when one partner accuses the other of lying. In addition, this chapter will present a discussion and negotiation format intended for those individuals who have not exhausted direct attempts at verbally resolving their relationship difficulties.

Lack of Communication

This pattern manifests itself when one partner complains that the other won't communicate. Unlike most of the other problems we will discuss, the roles in this pattern consistently separate along gender lines. It is most often the male partner who is seen as relatively silent and the female partner who is distressed about this. When people with this problem come into our offices, we typically hear, "He won't talk to me" or "She says I don't communicate with her."

The gender patterning of this problem should not be surprising given what we tend to learn growing up in American culture. Women are encouraged, from an early age, to express their feelings and to be sensitive to others' feelings and to social cues in general. Men, on the other hand, learn it's not "manly" to do so. Sociologists, psychologists, and journalists may tell you that's changing, and we hope it is. However, we still tend to see men who have difficulty discussing feelings, and women who feel uncomfortable with that state of affairs. Women, in this situation, often interpret the relative silence as a lack of caring or commitment or trust, while the men see themselves as strong, silent types, à la John Wayne and Clint Eastwood.

This brings us to an issue that will recur throughout this book. That issue is "Whose problem is it?" The female partner sees it as the man's problem: "He doesn't know how to communicate." The male partner interprets it as "She's not comfortable when I don't talk a lot." From a systems perspective, no one owns the problem. Both people are involved in the relationship patterns, and both contribute to the development and maintenance of problems in that relationship. More important than who "owns" the problem is, we believe, who is feeling the most discomfort in the situation.

This is the person who is the most motivated to change, and this is the person to whom we will direct our suggestions in this book.

In the case of lack of communication, it is most often the female partner who is more uncomfortable. Consequently, most of our attention will focus on her and what she can do in this situation. First, as with all the subsequent problems we discuss, we will look at the most common ineffective solutions people have tried in order to solve the problem.

Let's consider some of the "sensible" and "reasonable" ways women try to cope with the dilemma of an uncommunicative partner. Probably the most common is to encourage him to talk, usually by asking him questions: "How was your day today?" "What's the matter?" "Why don't you ever talk to me anymore?" In some situations asking these questions can help (as can all the solutions we will list), but we are examining the situations in which sensible solutions don't work. If someone believes he has nothing to say, or doesn't want to talk, he probably sees the questions as intrusions or irritations. It may well make him more reluctant to speak.

Other people attempt to schedule time to talk. The partner who is trying to change the pattern will get the kids to a baby-sitter, turn the television off early, or plan a quiet dinner for two. Unfortunately, lack of time isn't always the problem, and sitting there, with no distractions, and still having nothing to say can be doubly frustrating. At this point, many women get frustrated and back off. They give their partners the message, "I've tried all I can. I give up."

Let's examine the difference between backing off *reactively* in anger and backing off *actively* in a planned fashion. Women who try to get their husbands to talk often feel they have no choice but to stop trying. However, they back off reactively in anger, with no hope that any change will occur. Since they communicate that anger and lack of hope, positive change seldom happens. An example of this kind of communication problem is the case of Brenda and Keith. Keith is a middle manager in a large corporation, where he has worked since graduating college. Brenda is a housewife, who has given up a career in business to raise a family. Both are in their early thirties, and they have three school-age children.

Brenda came in for help because she was concerned that Keith was falling out of love with her. Her prime source of evidence for that contention was that he never talked to her anymore. When Keith came home from work, Brenda would be busy with dinner and the children, so conversation was difficult. Later in the evening, when the children were in bed, Brenda made sure she was available to talk. Keith seemed to prefer to read business publications, watch television, or drift off to sleep in his easy chair.

At first, Brenda tried coping with this situation by initiating more conversation. She tried to keep up with Keith's projects at work and ask specific questions about them. He generally didn't want to talk about work. So she would tell him about her day or about the children. Occasionally, he would grunt an acknowledgment, but tended to keep his eyes glued to the magazine or television set.

Since her attempts to get him to open up didn't work, she tried harder. Some evenings, she would get a baby-sitter for a couple of hours so that they could go for a walk or a drive by themselves. She asked him to spend some time with her each night just to talk, without his reading or watching television. He agreed, but had little to say either during those times or on their walks and drives alone.

Now Brenda felt worse. They had time together, but he still had nothing to say. What was even more frustrating was that Keith seemed to have no trouble talking to anyone else. Brenda began to get depressed and believe that there was something wrong with her. At this point she came in for help.

Generally, female partners try strategies that involve encouragement, making themselves more available to the male, and trying hard. We often make the assumption that trying or striving is the thing to do when we are faced with problems. But this is not always good to do. Imagine that you are holding a wet bar of soap. You are afraid you'll drop it, so you try hard not to by squeezing it and putting more pressure on it. Naturally, the bar of soap squirts out of your hand. There are certain things in life (and in relationships, in particular) that happen naturally. If you try to force them to go in another direction, you can disturb the process and the rhythm and make the problem worse.

In the case of getting a partner to talk more, assumptions are made such as "He's holding something back," "He doesn't care," or "He wants to talk, but doesn't feel comfortable talking to me." Remember, those are just assumptions, and unconfirmed, unproven assumptions can exaggerate problems and lead to ineffective solutions. From talking to the silent partners, we have found that their beliefs in these situations were more often "She's putting a lot of pressure on me," "She's trying to change me," or "She's getting too dependent on me." To make it even more frustrating, the men are often not fully aware of their own reactions until they are encouraged by a therapist to explore them. So they don't even tell their partners what's going on (of course).

What are some things couples in this situation can try? One is to do something that is a noticeable change from your previous strategies. As we've said, most people get locked into an idea ("I'll make it easier for him to talk") and try small variations on the same theme over and over. They do this because they don't challenge their own assumptions and their own perceptions of what the rules are. Break out of the rut. Do something that is really different.[18]

The second general message is to focus on a noticeable change in *your* behavior, not the other person's. By just looking at your impact on the other person you are making it too important for that person to change, and you are placing too much emphasis on that person's behavior as a source of your happiness and contentment. We will suggest things to try that may allow the other person to change, but that will make you feel better about yourself if you try them in the spirit in which they are suggested. Of course, according to a systems perspective, you set the stage for the other person in the system to change when you do something noticeably different. That change may not manifest itself in the way you wish it would, and it may not even be visible. For instance, the other person's attitude toward the situation could change. Nevertheless, by doing something different, you create an atmosphere conducive to a change in the overall system, and even a small initial change can set a positive ripple effect into motion.

More specific to this situation, remember that the nontalker may feel pressured, while the more communicative spouse feels out of control ("I can't make him talk"). One strategy the female partner could try is to make herself less available for conversation, stop initiating conversation, and cut it short when it does start. This not only removes, but also reverses, all pressure on the male partner. Also, this gives the female partner more control. She's not trying to make him talk, so she's not failing. If he talks, she decides when the conversation is over. The entire pattern is changing, and the power shifts.

A second specific strategy that can be tried involves reinterpreting the meaning of the silence. She assumes he should be talking more and that his silence connotes lack of caring. He learns, perhaps in a less than conscious way, that his silence gives him power. If the female partner can begin to interpret, out loud, the silence as being a positive thing, it will change its meaning for both of them.

For instance, the silence can mean "He doesn't want to burden me with his problems," "He's comfortable enough with me to not feel he has to talk," or "Things are O.K., and he'll tell me if a time comes when they aren't." What we're suggesting is that the more talkative partner say to the quiet partner things like, "I really respect you for being able to keep your problems to yourself," or "I feel good when you're quiet, because I know that means everything is all right between us." By doing this, the female partner learns, by hearing her own voice saying it, that there are less gloomy ways of looking at the situation. If he disagrees with how she is interpreting it, he has to speak up and tell her, and she succeeds because he's started talking. His continued silence implies agreement, so she still comes out ahead.

A third strategy involves the dissatisfied, more talkative partner making positive changes in her life that are *not* directly related to the relationship. We suggest getting involved in exercise programs, hobbies, clubs, or closer friendships. We know this strategy runs the risk of sounding like tired folk wisdom: "Keep yourself busy and it won't bother you so much." That is not our intention. The idea is to take more responsibility for making yourself happy and place less emphasis and pressure on the relationship doing it for you.

An important change can occur when you do more for yourself. Not only does your partner see you treating yourself as more important by devoting more time and energy to your interests, but you see yourself doing that as well. We all have a part of us that watches and judges what we do, and that part has a lot to say about our self-esteem. When you treat yourself better, you observe that and your self-esteem grows ("I must be O.K. if I'm treating myself as worthwhile"). When you feel better about yourself, you generally need less from others in the way of attention and assurance.

Let's get back to Brenda and Keith. The strategy for Brenda was twofold. The first part directly addressed the communication issue. She was instructed to make herself less available for conversation, to initiate conversation less frequently, and to halt the conversation before it went on for too long. Her second task was to focus more on activities she could do without Keith that she believed she would enjoy and from which she would get a sense of accomplishment.

Brenda implemented the suggestions. She was able to completely stop asking Keith questions to get him to talk. Instead, her conversation consisted of statements about things she wanted to bring up or found interesting, many of which required no response at all from Keith. She did very well at abruptly ending conversations once they had started. She would remember something she had to put on her shopping list and leave the room to do it. She would keep a magazine in her lap and go back to reading it at the first lull in the conversation. And, more subtly, she didn't try too hard to keep the dialogue going.

Not being as available for conversation became easier as she pursued other interests. She went out with friends more and talked to them on the phone after the kids went to bed. She took a course at college and often had homework to do at night. Brenda also realized she had been overlooking one of her favorite pastimes, reading mystery novels. She got back into that.

Keith's changes in response to Brenda were dramatic, if not rapid. For the first few weeks, he seemed to enjoy being left alone and was happy to let her go her own way. After about a month, he began to get more curious about some of the things she was doing and started to ask her questions, to which she responded very briefly, of course. Finally, he appeared to get a little jealous of the time she was spending doing other things and he asked her if they could find a way to spend more time together.

This example and its outcome may sound contrived or too good to be true because the strategies we suggest represent dramatic departures from old patterns. Often, the changes in response to these new actions are also dramatic and often surprisingly rapid.

Remember the systems way of thinking. If one part of the system changes, the other part has to adjust. If the change is not minor and predictable, the other parts of the system need to make more pronounced changes to adjust.

Also, keep in mind that Brenda may well have felt a lot better even if Keith hadn't opened up. By focusing less on him and how little he talked and more on what she wanted to do, she de-emphasized the communication problem and emphasized her own needs and importance.

In summary, the relationship problem addressed in this section is one in which one partner complains that the other does not communicate enough. *What* is said is not the issue. *How much* is said is. After exploring some common strategies people employ to handle this problem, which are often ineffective, we presented three ways to approach the problem differently. These three are (1) become less available for conversation and do not try hard to initiate and maintain it; (2) interpret the silence (of your partner) in a positive way in order to negate any power the partner may be expressing through silence ("I'll show you that you can't make me talk"); and (3) focus less on the relationship and more on satisfying yourself.

The Chronic Complainer

This pattern occurs when one partner seems sad, pessimistic, cynical, negative, or depressed—and verbalizes it—while the other partner is distressed by the complaints and frustrated in his or her attempts to help. As difficult as it may be to imagine, if you are in a relationship with a person who chronically complains about a particular issue or about everything, you have an important part in maintaining and perpetuating those very complaints that you most dislike. Let's examine this situation from the complainer's point of view and look at some common, but ineffective, strategies that are often used to deal with the complainer.

One aspect of the chronic complainer's pattern that is very important but seldom recognized is that ordinarily the complaint has at least some basis in fact. More times than not, chronic complainers have experienced a life circumstance or a set of life circumstances that have given them good cause to feel depressed or pessimistic. It may even be true, at times, that they are doing remarkably well to continue their everyday responsibilities given the situation with which they must cope. So most often a chronic complainer has good reason to complain. A sad or depressed person usually has a life circumstance that would create a sad emotional experience in most people. A pessimistic person can find much in our violent, half-starved, racist, sexist, headed-for-nuclear-disaster world about which to be realistically cynical.

Unfortunately, people tend not to consider the validity of the complainer's position and, therefore, attempt to help in the most commonsensical, but ineffective, way. When most people are confronted with a chronic complainer of either a sad or cynical type, they tend to try to cheer the person up or to counter the pessimism with optimism. Often they will spend much of their interaction describing the positives of life and conveying the general message that things will get better. In other words, people become cheerleaders for the complainer. They come home from their jobs, where they tend to interact on a more normal basis with people, and change immediately into a cheerleading uniform.

The problem with the cheerleading strategy is that it often doesn't work despite the enthusiasm of the cheerleader. The chronic complainers interpret the cheerleading as lack of understanding. Even worse, the chronic complainer may feel that the cheerleader is being condescending about the issues under concern. Cheerleading minimizes and trivializes the complainer's concerns and often puts complainers in the position of having to prove that they really are depressed or deserve to be cynical. If they can't be happy, they'll at least be right. People who are sad or depressed may interpret the attempts to cheer them up as an indicator of how bad off they really are: "I must be really seriously depressed if I have all these reasons to be happy and am still depressed."

Another losing strategy with a chronic complainer is ignoring the complaining and trying to avoid discussion of the sensitive areas altogether. The person using this strategy steers conversation away from problem areas and essentially attempts to walk on eggshells around the complainer so that the gates of negativism are never opened. The general effect of the gatekeeper strategy is that the gatekeeper stays continuously tense and on guard, and the chronic complainer feels more compelled to express his or her concerns. The gatekeeper strategy may also be interpreted as a lack of interest and caring.

Let's consider the case of Bob and Nancy, who moved to a midwestern city from the beautiful southeast because Bob was promoted. Nancy was understandably somewhat distressed after the move because she had moved away from her family and friends, had quit a job that she had for years, and had given up a house with many good memories. Virtually everything in her life had changed overnight. Bob, on the other hand, was overwhelmingly enthusiastic about his position and was very pleased about the move because it was the right thing for him to do in his career.

Bob noticed his wife's sadness and cynicism and tried to get her to see the bright side. No matter how hard he tried to emphasize the positives, she would usually respond with more negatives. Nancy began complaining about everything: "The people up here are not as friendly," "There's nothing to do up here," "I miss our family and friends," and "I wish we could go back home." Bob retorted with, "Everything will be fine, just give it a chance," "You need to get out more and meet people," "It's not as bad here as you think," "I'm making friends at work, why aren't you?" Bob pointed out great things to do and positive things about the new city at every opportunity. He invited new acquaintances from work over for dinner and cocktails. He seemed to have a perpetual smile on his face while he was around Nancy. Nancy seemed to get worse instead of better.

Bob began quickly to change the subject whenever Nancy began to complain. He felt tense around Nancy and avoided conversation altogether. Then Nancy complained about Bob's distancing. Bob, becoming more and more frustrated, and angry with Nancy for her inability to accept the move and make the best of it, withdrew even more and occasionally blasted Nancy for her negative attitude. Bob decided to consult a therapist because, as is often the case, the cheerleading and gatekeeping strategies are very demanding and frustrating and will eventually wear down the most energetic among us.

The harder a cheerleader tries, the worse things will ultimately get. In many ways, the strategy to help the problem has itself become the main perpetuator of the problem. A cheerleader makes the assumption that information of a positive nature and encouragement will help the complainer, even though it repeatedly doesn't work (remember the nine-dot puzzle). And because nothing is helping, the cheerleader also begins to make the assumption that complaining is a static or unchangeable position. Of course, we know that if the cheerleader makes some changes in behavior, it will enable the complaining spouse to make corresponding changes.

A far more useful assumption to make with persons who are expressing sadness or pessimism is that the person has ambivalent feelings about the issue under concern. For example, when a complainer says, "I hate living here," he or she is probably telling the truth. However, it is also probably true that a whole range of feelings also exist in regard to "living here." The complaining individual is most likely ambivalent and expressing only one extreme pole on the continuum of feelings about the subject. By choosing to respond with optimism and counter such a remark, the cheerleading spouse further entrenches the complainer in a negative position and essentially invalidates the feelings the complainer is trying to convey. By not allowing the sad or negative feelings to be expressed and accepted, the cheerleader pushes the complainer into expressing the extreme pole on the continuum of feelings over and over again.

If one allows and even encourages expression of the negatives and accepts the complainer position, one also allows the complainer to express other more positive feelings along the continuum. In other words, if you allow chronic complainers the freedom to express themselves, you also allow them the freedom to see another side.

The strategies for enabling a change in a chronic complainer involve taking the complainer's position, about whatever topic is under concern, and validating it. You validate the position by agreeing with the complainer and recognizing the inherent truth in the complaints. Rather than cheerleading and further entrenching the negative belief, convey a message of understanding and support. Let the complainer know that the complaints are valid and that the complainer has every right to feel distressed: "Yes, you're right. Your job is really stressful. I don't see how you can take all that pressure," "Really, I'd be crazy too if I had to deal with kids all day," "I sometimes wonder why we even keep going on, given the way we are constantly burdened by all the hassles of plain, ordinary, everyday existence." The best message to convey back to a complainer honestly accepts, validates, and slightly exaggerates the issue under discussion.

Rather than avoiding the forbidden topics that will result in the complaints, *encourage* the complainer to express the complaints by *initiating* conversation about the topics yourself. Again, if you can, it is better to initiate conversation on a more negative, cynical, or pessimistic tone than the complainer usually adopts. These strategies free up the complainer to make different choices about what feelings he or she will express. Rather than opening the gates of negativism, these strategies have the capability to bump the complainer to a more positive position.

Let's return to Bob and Nancy. Bob took our suggestions, went home the first night, and began honestly accepting and validating Nancy's negative expressions about the move. Moreover, Bob initiated discussion about the negative aspects of the situation by regularly expressing his own honest feelings of regret about the move. He also complained about his job, sometimes noting that there was certainly a down side to his promotion as well. Although the change did not occur overnight, Nancy began finding other topics for conversation and sometimes interrupted Bob's expressions of regret about the move and frustrations with the job with suggestions for weekend activities. Sometimes, Nancy even assumed a cheerleading role, reassuring Bob about the move and sharing her belief that in the long run the promotion and relocation would prove to have been a good decision for the family.

By accepting Nancy's position and validating it, Bob allowed Nancy the freedom to express other opinions and feelings. She no longer had to continually prove how bad things really were. By being honestly sad and skeptical, Bob enabled Nancy to be more open to optimism.

In this section of the chapter, we have looked at a problem we called chronic complaining. Like all problems in relationships, this problem is influenced by two people. One is the chronic complainer, who may be sad, pessimistic, or cynical for good reason. The other person is the well-intentioned spouse or lover who attempts to help the complainer by cheering him or her up, or by avoiding the topic of the complaints altogether. Both strategies, cheerleading and gatekeeping, are ineffective and ultimately wind up intensifying the problem and frustrating the problem solver. We recommend the following strategies for an individual who is tired of cheerleading and gatekeeping: (1) accept, validate, and exaggerate the complainer's position; (2) encourage the complainer to express the issues under concern; and (3) honestly express your own negative feelings and initiate conversations about the topics of complaint at every opportunity, thereby giving the complainer the freedom of choice to discuss other issues and positive feelings.

Lying

This exceptionally common problem involves two roles: accuser and denier.[19] We find these roles to be about equally divided between men and women in our clinical practice. The roles are fairly self-descriptive: The accuser continually confronts his or her partner with suggestions that the partner is either lying or avoiding discussion of issues of which he or she wishes the accuser to remain ignorant. The denier spends his or her time defending against those accusations.

Lying is usually suspected in three basic situations. The most obvious situation involves what is happening during the time the couple spends apart. Infidelity is, of course, most often the overt or underlying accusation. Frequently, the communication about this issue is quite indirect, and it comes up in questions such as, "You were supposed to be home three hours ago, where were you?" and "Why are you spending so much time at the office all of a sudden?" The issue of suspected infidelity overlaps quite a bit with jealousy, which will be dealt with in more detail in a subsequent chapter. Nevertheless, the topic of what is occurring when the couple is apart is a key one in the classic accuser–denier pattern.

A second common situation involves concern over the degree of caring or commitment one partner has. The accuser claims he or she is much more emotionally invested in the relationship and produces evidence to support that claim: "I'm always the one who says 'I love you' first," "I never stay out late with my friends," or "We always do what you want." Again, the pattern in which one person attacks and the other defends becomes apparent. The implication here is, naturally, that the denier is lying about how much he or she cares about the accuser.

Most everyone agrees that ninety-nine percent of all marital arguments revolve around three basic subjects: money, sex, and children. How money is spent is the third common situation in the accuser–denier pattern. Money always disappears faster than we expect it to, and the tendency to blame that on your partner is tremendous, since you know that *you* have been financially responsible.

What is often overlooked is that when planning budgets it is very easy to forget certain items. Also, if a partner's life style differs considerably from your own, it is very difficult to understand the kind of necessary expenses that style entails. For example, a salesperson incurs quite different daily expenses than his or her teacher spouse does. Nevertheless, the partner who feels he or she is getting the short end of the stick turns into the accuser and wonders if money is being secretly spent on someone else, on gambling, and so on.

In this section, we will look at the problem from the perspective of the denier, for a number of reasons. First of all, the denier may be lying. We have no way of knowing. Yet in treatment, the accuser routinely wants to enlist our aid in playing detective to help uncover ironclad evidence of deceit. Doing so usually just plays into the accuser–denier pattern and doesn't allow for change in the interaction. Part of that pattern is playing detective to find evidence of lying. When that happens, no one can win. A lack of evidence never proves innocence, since maybe the detective hasn't looked hard enough yet. But a hint of ambiguous evidence that a person is lying can help one to presume guilt.

Basically, guilt or innocence isn't the issue here. The interactional pattern of one person accusing the other of lying and the other denying it is. Together, we will look at ways for the denier to try to break the pattern, since he or she is usually most willing to give up on the guilt–innocence and detective traps.

We don't want to ignore the accuser, though, so if you think you fit into this category and wish to break the pattern, we can suggest, briefly, some things for you to consider. What kind of traps do you set for your partner? Do you withhold information to see if he or she will contradict what you know to be true (ask where he or she was when a friend already told you)? Remember those traps often depend on information from unreliable sources, and to set up the traps, you, the accuser, have to lie about what you know.

Another key strategy for accusers is to ask a lot of questions and look for inconsistencies in the answers. We tend to forget a number of things when we do this. One is that people are inconsistent. Consistency is a myth, and inconsistency does not imply willful deceit. Another thing we forget is that we can get confused, and that the inconsistency may be a product of faulty memory or communication and not of lying. Generally, if you are an accuser, keep in mind that you tend to presume guilt and play detective poorly, but nevertheless have faith in your findings.

Now, let's get back to the denier and how he or she attempts to cope with the accusations of lying. The first thing most deniers try are defending and explaining. They vigorously deny any wrongdoing and put a lot of energy into explaining why things might appear the way they do. Occasionally, the denying partner will even go so far as to produce witnesses or evidence of his or her own. Naturally, in an accuser–denier pattern that has gone on for some time, this doesn't work. First of all, guilt is presumed, so the evidence isn't believed. Second, by protesting too much, the denier looks guilty ("If he or she isn't guilty, why is he or she getting so upset?"). Finally, remember that this is an interactive pattern. The content, the specific thing the denier is accused of, changes from episode to episode, but the underlying process ("He or she is a liar, and I'll catch him or her this time") remains constant. So, even if the denier gets off the hook one time, there will probably be other times.

The next thing the denier usually tries, after explaining and defending, is getting angry and indignant. After all, he or she is being falsely accused. However, this reaction just makes both people more defensive and can make the denier look even guiltier since the strong reaction can be seen as protecting a guilty conscience. Sometimes, when this pattern goes on for quite some time, the denier decides to do what he or she is being accused of. The idea is, "I'm getting the blame anyway, so I might as well have the fun I'm supposedly having." At this point, the relationship gets into even more serious trouble.

An example of the accuser–denier pattern is David and Alice. They are both in their early forties and have been married for twenty years. They work for the same company; David is in engineering, Alice in marketing. They have no children. Alice has always been more outgoing than David and has more friends.

Problems began when a man was hired to work with Alice's marketing team. She became friendly with him, and they talked a lot, often eating lunch together. Alice contended that they never socialized outside of work, but David had difficulty believing that. He assumed that they were having an affair and accused Alice of it. He would say things to her such as, "Listen to the way you talk about him. I can tell how you feel" and "You spend more time talking to him than you do to me." The fact that the man was younger than David, and attractive, did not help matters.

Alice, of course, denied David's accusations, which made him more suspicious; he thought she was getting too defensive. So he enlisted a friend of his in Alice's department as a spy, to watch her and the man. He found out what he already knew: They talked and sometimes went to lunch together.

David's questioning became relentless, and Alice grew tired of explaining herself. She began to get angry and started to fume the minute David brought up the subject. Finally, she threatened divorce and even moved in with a friend for a couple of weeks. David improved for a little while after that, but then got back to his old routine. As you can see, Alice followed a fairly predictable and reasonable pattern of responses to David's accusations. Predictably, Alice's responses didn't work because her denying strategies did not convince David of her innocence or alleviate his fears.

Before we explore more effective ways that Alice and David could have handled the situation, let's look at the assumptions the denier makes. One is, "I owe my partner an explanation, and if I don't give one, I'll look guilty." How ridiculous. First of all, why do you owe someone an explanation when you're being accused of something you didn't do? Moreover, as we've seen, you will probably look guiltier if you explain too much, rather than not at all.

A second assumption is, "If I'm innocent, it's not fair for me to be accused." That belief makes self-righteous anger and indignation imperative. However, the anger usually makes the problem worse. We all think life should be fair, but it seldom is. People who continue to expect it to be fair walk around very angry and frustrated. Of course, being unjustly accused isn't fair. Would you rather yell and make it worse, or do something effective to make it better?

The first alternative solution to the denier's dilemma is simple: Don't explain or defend. If you did not do what you have been accused of, say "I didn't do that." When confronted with, "Well then how do you explain . . . " or "What about . . . ?" *respond with silence* or say "I don't know." This extremely simple solution is effective for a number of reasons. It's hard to argue with someone who does not argue back, so the situation doesn't escalate. Also, by denying, but not explaining or defending, you don't appear guilty by reason of protesting too much. Finally, accusations are often made primarily to get an argument or fight started. If one partner won't go for the bait and fight, the strategy of accusation stops working and is eventually dropped.

When the accuser continues to question and confront, take the "don't explain and defend" solution one step further. Respond to further accusations with a statement that reflects the accuser's insecurity about the situation under concern. For example, "You're afraid that I'm having an affair," "You're concerned that you are not attractive to me anymore," or "You're feeling insecure about my love for you," and so forth. This strategy of reflecting the insecurity of the accuser breaks the cycle and permits a more meaningful exploration of the issues involved. It also allows the denier the opportunity to reassure the accuser or problem-solve ways in which the denier may help the accuser with his or her insecurities. In any event, helping, exploring, and understanding are noticeably different from arguing and defending and are likely to result in a different response from the accuser.

The second alternative strategy is, strange as it might sound, to not only agree with the accusation, but to also carry it a few steps further: "You're right. I gambled away all our money today. Not only that, I bet it all on long shots that had no chance of winning. I'm hopeless." This strategy accomplishes a couple of things. One is to break the accuser–denier pattern right at the start. There is no denier now, so the game will have to change. Don't just agree sarcastically, because that will often be seen as an evasion and provoke stronger accusations. Say it so it is ridiculous enough to make the accuser wonder, but seriously enough to make it possible. People change when they are confused. This often succeeds in confusing the most dedicated accuser.

Another goal accomplished by this strategy is to change the *feeling tone* of the interaction, or the emotional context usually associated with the problem. In the accuser–denier pattern, the underlying feeling is serious and grave and implies "This is a truly big deal." By agreeing and getting ridiculous, the accused partner is saying, "This is kind of silly, and I'm not going to let it become a life-and-death issue." Once the situation becomes less grave, it becomes more workable. In fact, in most of the patterns described in this book, the problem has been a persistent one, and a number of attempts have usually been made to cope with it. As this happens, the problem becomes a "big deal," since a lot of time, thought, and emotional energy are devoted to it. It can get to the point where it feels like every time the pattern recurs and is handled badly, it poses a serious and imminent threat to the relationship. That creates a lot of pressure, and it is difficult to try new, creative things under a lot of pressure. This strategy, as well as most of the others in this book, has a goal of lowering the emotional intensity surrounding the problem and putting it in a different, less crucial perspective.

The danger in using this technique is that regardless of how wild and crazy you make the exaggeration, some accusers will believe it and get very angry. If you fear that to be the case, we suggest you warn the chronic accuser: "Sometimes when you accuse me of things, I'm going to lie and agree with you. But, I won't tell you when that is. See if you can guess." That will, hopefully, both confuse the accuser and temper his or her anger. If you're still scared that this will provoke your partner, stick to the first two strategies (don't explain or defend, and reflect the insecurity), which are less risky.

Meanwhile, let's return to David and Alice. Alice came in for help when she felt she had tried everything. It was suggested that she use the agree-and-exaggerate strategy. The next time David asked what she had done after lunch with her friend, Alice replied, "Yes, I was with him. We went to a motel and screwed all afternoon. Want to hear some details?" This was very effective since it was out of character for Alice and since David knew from his spy that she was really at work. He didn't know what to say, but evidently believed she wouldn't tell him if she really had been at the motel. His accusations immediately decreased dramatically. When he did break down and start accusing her, Alice exaggerated his accusation. The feeling then actually changed to the point where they were able to joke about the same topic, when only weeks before, their twenty-year marriage had been threatened.

To summarize this section, the problem we have called "lying" has a pattern with two roles: accuser and denier. Lying may or may not actually be involved. Our suggestions are primarily geared toward helping the denier, the one who is accused of lying, since that is the person we most often see in therapy. We suggested two different ways for the denier to deal with this pattern: (1) don't explain or defend, and reflect the insecurity which involves not actively denying or even responding directly to the accusations, but rather commenting on and thereby validating the underlying insecurity that may exist in the accuser, and (2) agreeing with and exaggerating.

Changing the Rules

Sometimes in our practices, we encounter clients who present the relationship difficulty as an inability to talk constructively to their partners about the relationship and its problems. Their partners may be willing to talk about the relationship, but are unwilling to consult a therapist. Consequently, the clients who sought therapy are looking for some "communication" format to organize a discussion of the problems and a negotiation of solutions. These individuals often believe that they have not exhausted verbal negotiation options and would like a coherent framework for a productive exchange of ideas. If both individuals of a couple do want to openly negotiate the rules of the relationship, the discussion itself can be both relationship enhancing and problem-solving.

In such an instance in which both individuals are motivated for the discussion and a structured format has not yet been tried, we recommend a negotiation exercise based on Don Jackson's "marital *quid pro quo*" formulation.[20] The quid pro quo, which is Latin for "something for something," is designed to allow for both a nondefensive discussion of problems and a negotiation of how resolution of the problems may occur. As you read what follows, please keep in mind the concepts we presented in Chapter 2.

The quid pro quo assumes that the relationship needs to be redefined to accommodate all the changes that have occurred in each individual, as well as in the relationship itself. The relationship rules that formed when the relationship started no longer apply in a constructive way. The couple has outgrown the original rules and the patterns of communication that arose from them. Continued application of the rules through repeated patterns of communication can exacerbate problems, making problem resolution more difficult with each passing day.

If one considers the developmental transitions inherent in the individual and marital life cycle, it makes common sense that couples may need to reestablish rules that adjust to life transitions. Relationships, like people, are not fixed entities that merely gather years of life experience without adjusting to that experience. Individuals and their relationships change in response to the changing demands of life; people mature as they struggle with these ever-changing demands and continually evaluate their values and priorities.

Recall Sharon and Jeff. One way to conceptualize their difficulties would be to say that Sharon simply outgrew the original rules of the relationship that defined her role as subordinate to Jeff's role. The passing years, combined with her life experiences of advancing in her career and becoming a parent, led to an end result of dissatisfaction with the relationship. The communication patterns that maintained the rules that she perceived kept her in a subordinate position became a source of continual irritation.

The quid pro quo offers a method of taking the implicit relationship level of communication and making it explicit so that it may be discussed and negotiated. The purpose of the quid pro quo is to redefine the relationship rules in a more satisfying way for both partners. Please be advised that this exercise is very difficult and is likely to evoke a variety of emotions because you will be discussing sensitive topics. Please discuss this with your partner and gain his or her explicit approval before proceeding.

Start the quid pro quo by finding a comfortable place to sit where you may face each other and hold hands. Do not begin unless you both are committed to spending one hour of uninterrupted time. Flip a coin to see who begins. Start by telling your partner all the traits, characteristics, attitudes, and behaviors that you would like to see more of or less of that would make the relationship more workable for you from your *entirely* selfish point of view. Say, "I would like to see more patience with the kids," "I would like to see less working on Saturdays," and so forth. Do not editorialize, justify, rationalize, or explain yourself; just say what you want more of or less of.

Take ten minutes to complete this segment. There will be pauses and that's okay. Take your time and think about what you want to say. Fill the ten minutes however you like. You may start with general things and go to specifics or vice versa. It doesn't matter. What is important is that you share with your partner what will make the relationship better for you without diluting your message with excess verbiage or explanation.

Your partner needs to pay close attention and listen carefully because he or she will be required to summarize your list of "more of's" and "less of's." Your partner should maintain comfortable eye contact and say nothing in response. At the end of ten minutes, your partner should repeat your list back to you *without* adding any of his or her opinions. Let your partner know if any items were forgotten and ask him or her to repeat these forgotten items.

After your partner has summarized your list of more of's and less of's, it is his or her turn to share what will make the relationship more workable. It is tempting to rebuff or counter the first person's presentation, but please control your urge to do so. When your partner has finished, repeat his or her list and allow him or her the opportunity to remind you of any items you missed.

Again, remember that this is a difficult task and periods of silence are common. This is a challenging task because we are generally unaccustomed to making the implicit level of communication (the relationship level) explicit. Two thoughts to keep in mind throughout this exercise: (1) when repeating the list of more of's and less of's, do not comment, refute, or elaborate upon the list; and (2) when it's your turn to talk, do not respond or react to things that your partner brought up.

After you both have listened to each other's ideas of a more workable relationship and repeated back those ideas, you may proceed with the second phase of the quid pro quo exercise. Since you went first before, it is your partner's turn now. Your partner should tell you all the ways he or she has contributed negatively or destructively to the relationship. This phase takes five minutes. Please say it like this: "I have contributed in a negative way when . . . " Do not editorialize, justify, or defend *why* you contributed negatively; just say *how* you did it or *what* you did. When you "own" something negative and then rationalize it, you dilute your ownership message and it has no impact. For example, "I contributed in a negative way to the relationship when I flirted at parties, but it usually happened when I had too much to drink and after we had a fight."

While it's reasonable to assume that many influences led up to the flirting and that it did not occur in a vacuum, it is helpful to share only things for which you feel you can own responsibility. From a systems viewpoint, the flirting is part of an ongoing sequence of events and the individual is ultimately responsible for his or her behavior. This phase of the exercise requires you to take the perspective of the relationship itself and how you have negatively impacted it.

After your partner finishes, reverse roles and take your turn sharing your own negative contributions. In this phase, you do not need to recall what is said.

Upon completion of the quid pro quo exercise, take a few minutes to reflect upon what was said. Do not discuss specific issues that were raised, but rather discuss your impressions and experience of the exercise itself. Was it difficult for you? Which part was the most difficult? Was expressing your selfish point of view easier or harder than taking the perspective of the relationship? Is there a connection between what you want from your partner and how you have contributed negatively? Did anything new come up? Remember to discuss how the exercise felt and what it meant to you, not the specifics that came up.

Sometimes the experience of the quid pro quo permits the realization that the very ways we have contributed negatively have prevented us from getting what we want from our partners.

The things we want most are those things that we have probably sabotaged with our own behavior. For the couple who has not attempted a straightforward discussion of their relationship, the quid pro quo can allow each person to actually listen to the other's point of view. Understanding your partner's frame of reference and accepting it as valid in its own right is a very powerful relationship tool, as well as the most necessary ingredient to any negotiation process. After discussing your experience of the exercise and brainstorming its meaning, set aside another time to repeat the exercise, but in a slightly different format.

This time, repeat only the first part—the more of and less of part. Instead of listening and repeating your partner's list, record what your partner tells you. After you have shared your lists with one another and recorded your partner's list, exchange the recorded lists. Now prioritize your wants, numbering them in order of importance. Do not discuss your list or your relationship issues or problems until the next meeting.

Now the real negotiation begins. Once again, flip a coin to determine who goes first. That person begins with the number one priority on his or her list, the most important and meaningful issue in the relationship. For example, "I would like you to be more supportive." Two steps follow the expression of the first item. First, the speaker must define the item in such a way that it is very clear what he or she wants. Specifically, and in concrete terms that your partner will understand, what exactly are you wanting more of or less of? What would you *see* that would allow you to know that things were beginning to turn toward the desired change? What would be the first step your partner would take to address the issue under concern? What would "more supportive" look like? How would you know that your partner was being more supportive? Try and think of what the *first* indicator would be of your partner beginning to be more supportive, and negotiate for it at that level. Think small, though, because small noticeable changes lead to big changes much like a snowball rolling down a hill (remember the concept of wholeness). A first noticeable step toward being more supportive may be your partner asking you how the day has gone and listening to your response. The first aspect of negotiation entails defining specifically what the desired change is and clarifying what an initial step toward positive change would look like.

The second step in the negotiation process involves the speaker who began the exercise asking the other person the following question: "What can I do that will permit you or make it easier for you to ask me about my day and listen to my response?" (The systems thinking is hopefully apparent.) "How can I set the stage, through my own behavior, for you to give me what I want? How can I stack the deck of circular causality so that I may be dealt the cards I want to receive?" Think for a minute of the change of operations this exercise requires. Instead of telling your spouse about how your needs are not being met, you are asking your partner how you may help him or her meet your needs.

After the listening partner has indicated how he or she can be helped or enabled to perform the desired change, an agreement is reached and a new, tentative relationship rule is established. The couple essentially agrees to try out the rule and observe what happens in their interactions around the rule. In our example, the person being requested to be more supportive suggests that it would help him or her be more supportive if he or she were greeted with a kiss and a "hello." It is also suggested that if the person requesting more support indeed has a bad day, then he or she will share that information.

The roles are then reversed and each item on the lists of priorities is addressed one by one. Usually, one priority for each person is enough for one session. Once an agreement has been made, put the agreement in writing so that each of you knows exactly what the agreement is. Try the new way of addressing what you want from the relationship and observe the interaction that is the result. Pay particular attention to how your partner responds to your new way of getting what you want. Also note any differences in how you feel during the enactment of agreements.

The quid pro quo is not a cure-all for relationship difficulties, but it can be useful for couples who feel they have not exhausted attempts at discussing their differences. The quid pro quo was described in three stages. The first stage has four parts: (1) saying what you would like to see more of or less of that would make the relationship more workable, (2) repeating each person's list back to him or her, (3) saying how you have contributed in a negative way to the relationship, and (4) discussing your experience of the exercise, not the problems or issues. The second phase has three parts: (1) repeating the more of and less of aspect, (2) recording your partner's list and returning it to him or her, and (3) prioritizing your own list of more of's and less of's. Finally, the third phase involves four parts: (1) expressing a particular more of or less of item on your priority list, (2) specifying in concrete terms what would be an indication that your partner was taking the first step toward making the desired change, (3) asking your partner what *you* can do to permit or make easier for him or her to make the desired change you are requesting, and (4) agreeing to try out what you have negotiated (the new rule) and observing your partner's response and your own thoughts and feelings when the situation occurs.

Chapter 5

Power Disparities in Romantic Relationships

By far the most common source of problems in relationships involves the distribution of power. Many specific issues—what car to buy, where to go for dinner, who gets the "last word" in an argument—have at their root an attempt to get control or power. The reason we see so many couples making a big deal out of insignificant issues is that the smallest issue can symbolize who is in control and who is being controlled. So, if one partner "gives in" on a minor point, it can mean to him or her that the other partner has achieved the upper hand in the relationship.

Why is power, or control, so important? Many of the reasons are obvious. A relationship between two people has to involve give-and-take. If one spouse has power, he or she presumably gives less and takes more. In other words, the more powerful partner gets his or her needs met more often and has to sacrifice less. Also, we all like to be in control. If I am in control, I direct what happens; I call the shots. I am seldom surprised or caught off guard. If I give up that control, I am told what to do, and my life becomes unpredictable; I don't know what will happen next. I am vulnerable; I get nervous.

In a good relationship there is ideally a balance of power. Unfortunately, this ideal is not always realized and neither party is happy with the unequal power. The powerless, disenfranchised partner feels cheated and resentful and, consciously or unconsciously, finds ways to even the score (as we will see in our section on dependent, but critical partners). The powerful partner, on the other hand, gets resentful because he or she has too much responsibility and carries a disproportionate share of the load.

In a relationship with a power disparity, no one wins. Yet the struggle for power underlies virtually every relationship quarrel. Regardless of the subject, people try to impose their wills, viewpoints, ideas, values, or preferences on others. These power struggles are intimate parts of all the problems we discuss in this book.

In this chapter, we discuss two relationship patterns in which power is the key issue. One involves the dependent but critical partner who needs his or her partner to do things, but tries to regain the power lost to dependency by criticizing the ways those things are done. The second pattern is a common one in troubled relationships. It involves one partner having control in a variety of areas, such that the relationship begins to resemble that of a parent and child, with the powerful partner treating the other like a child.

Dependent but Critical Partner

In any relationship, there is a division of labor and responsibility. Decisions as to how those are divided are based on a number of different criteria including skills, interests, societal sex roles, and availability of time. However, in many relationships one partner depends on the other excessively, to the point where there is a tremendous disparity in responsibilities. This dependence can cover everything from food preparation, money management, and transportation, to emotional support and decision making.

Dependency on the part of one member of a couple can occur for a variety of reasons. In some instances, one spouse has a physical disability (heart condition, amputation or paralysis of legs, stroke, chronic back problem) that renders him or her physically incapable of doing some things independently. More often, social deficits or lack of skill in tasks of everyday living create the dependency. Examples include people who can't do simple household chores, balance a checkbook, or do shopping; people who are painfully shy and rely on a spouse to make friends and initiate social plans; and people who are locked into rigid, stereotypical sex roles which dictate that a woman is not allowed to do certain things and that a man can't do others.

Regardless of the cause, there results an imbalance in responsibility. However, in this pattern, unlike the domineering partner relationship, the dependent partner seizes a great deal of power by letting the other do things, but continually and relentlessly criticizes how these things are done. If the more responsible partner cooks, his or her meals are tasteless. If he or she provides transportation, he or she takes the wrong routes, drives badly, and is never on time. If he or she handles finances, there is never enough money because it is being mismanaged and squandered. (This pattern is also seen, frequently, when an elderly, but previously independent parent becomes disabled and an adult child or child-in-law has to do things the parent used to do him or herself.)

By being tirelessly critical, the dependent partner keeps the other defensive and off balance. Thus, the dependent partner is in control ("Do things for me and do them my way"), and the responsible partner feels obligated, trapped ("I have to do these things"), and angry and resentful since his or her efforts are not appreciated. Not surprisingly, it is the responsible partner who most often shows up in a therapist's office feeling frustrated, angry, and, often, guilty. This is predictable, since it is the responsible partner who is stripped of power by the constant criticism from his or her dependent counterpart. Thus, we will direct our discussion and suggestions to the partner upon whom the other depends and of whom the other is critical.

Let's take a look at how the partner who is being criticized tends to react. The first attempt that is usually made in the face of criticism is to try to do better or to try harder. Along with this strategy, the nondependent partner defends himself or herself, explains his or her reasons for doing something a certain way, and/or makes excuses. Naturally, none of this works because the real issue is power, not the particular activities (housework, money management, etc.) being debated. So, no explanation or excuse will be adequate, and no performance will be acceptable.

When the first lines of defense don't work, the responsible partner usually turns to anger, arguing, and confrontation: "I do everything for you, and all you do is complain. If you don't like the way I do it, do it yourself." Not only does this not work, it leads to guilt and depression, particularly if the dependent partner is physically disabled or appears totally helpless to do things for himself or herself. So, the responsible partner goes ahead and completes his or her duties and feels guilty for having picked on someone who is helpless. Guess who still has all the power?

The case of Eric and Barbara serves as an excellent example of the dependent, but critical pattern. They had been married 30 years when Eric suffered a stroke. At first, he was confined to a wheelchair, being partially paralyzed on his right side. Gradually, he was able to get around fairly well using a walker. Still, he couldn't drive, do many household chores, or prepare his own meals. It was only with assistance that he could bathe and dress himself.

Barbara, being a good and dutiful spouse, did these things for him or helped him as he did them. However, in his eyes, she couldn't do anything the right way. She drove too slowly, picked out the wrong clothes for him to wear, and was never there when he really needed her. He was constantly angry and would yell at her and criticize her in ways he had never done before. He had always been a little cranky and stubborn, but he had also been fiercely independent and able to do things his own way.

Barbara tried to do things better, but could never quite get the hang of doing things Eric's way. She wanted to leave him when he yelled at her, but felt she couldn't because he needed her. When she yelled back at him, she felt guilty. After all, he couldn't help what had happened to him. She began feeling trapped, not wanting to be at home, and became depressed and lethargic. It was at this time when Barbara came in for help. Eric didn't come in with her because his only problem, from his perspective, was that Barbara didn't know how to do things right.

This may seem like an extreme example since Eric had an obvious, legitimate disability. However, even in less "legitimate" cases, the helplessness of the dependent partner is every bit as compelling, and the issues of depending upon someone and then criticizing his or her attempts to help are quite the same.

In this pattern, the responsible partner makes some assumptions. One is, "I owe it to him or her to be helpful." Another is, "I shouldn't be critical of or angry at someone who can't help him- or herself." These two assumptions conflict with a third one: "I'm going out of my way to be helpful and I should be appreciated." Remember, when people make assumptions, they pick a narrow and arbitrary way of looking at a situation and use it (as if it were the only way to see reality) to limit their options and create negative feelings.

What are some other, more helpful, ways of looking at this pattern? One is that helping in obvious ways is not always helpful. Picking up the pieces for an alcoholic often just allows that person to remain an alcoholic, because he or she is shielded from the consequences of his or her behavior. Parents always want to protect their children, but effective parents know that learning from mistakes is a critical part of development. In this case, doing things for someone who wants the help, but can't graciously accept it, may be counterproductive. You may be giving your partner what you think he or she needs, but what he or she doesn't really want.

So, while your perspective might be that you are helping, the other person's might well be, subconsciously, that you are robbing him or her of independence and self-respect. If that belief exists, or even if it co-exists with a belief that you are being helpful, resentment will occur and fuel criticism. In addition, the give-and-take that defines a relationship needs to continue—or, in some cases, needs to begin. If creative ways to restore some balance to the power in the relationship are not found, destructive and competitive ones will continue.

In all power-related conflicts, it is important to find ways to get away from the specific conflict or argument and to address the underlying power struggle. Even in seemingly rational discussions, the hidden agenda is "I'll prove I'm right and make you give in." No one wins these arguments, because even if one person concedes defeat, he or she is resentful and looks for ways to get revenge, or to get some power or control back. A key strategy in the power-related patterns described in this chapter is to get power by giving it up. This is called "onedownsmanship."[21] In a power struggle, people are trying to go "one-up," or show who has control. This is a verbal struggle. The dependent partner criticizes and, by defending him- or herself, the other partner inadvertently goes one-down by buying into the assumption that "I owe an explanation."

Keep in mind that only words are involved here. We suggest that the partner being criticized agree with the criticism and, perhaps, even expand on it: "Yes, I'm a terrible driver, and I can't believe you're brave enough to ride with me," or "Not only am I a lousy cook, but generally I'm a rotten husband. I'm amazed you continue to put up with me." You are only agreeing with words; you are not in any way changing your behavior. (It is critical that you not sound sarcastic, which just creates hostility.) By doing this, you go from a no-win to a no-lose situation. Before, if you argued and lost, you lost. If you argued and won, you got defensive and played the other person's game, which gave him or her the power; so you still lost. (When we way "win," we mean the relationship is enhanced. "Lose" means it is damaged.)

Using this new strategy, you can't lose. If you agree and the other person accepts it, you still do whatever you want; the argument's over, and you didn't get angry and defensive. Therefore you win. If the other person disagrees with you (remember, you are now accepting criticism), he or she is absolving you of blame. So you still win.

Reread this strategy again and again. We know it's somewhat confusing because it represents a very different way of thinking. People think they have to win an argument, or prove innocence, to win. We believe you win when you break the old pattern and when you decide what the new pattern will be.

People who try this strategy are often amazed at the results. Their partners usually have no idea what to say. They also feel a lot better. It feels good not to be defensive and not to argue. This strategy allows the other person to change without compelling him or her to do so. Rather than defensively responding to the power issues and trying to stay one-up, the person does not feel threatened and can respond based on the issue involved, his or her own needs, and/or the relationship context.

A second, less dramatic strategy is one we've mentioned before. It involves, simply, not defending yourself or explaining yourself. Criticism only works if the person being criticized takes it seriously and defends against it. By responding to criticism, you give it credibility and get yourself more worked up. Instead, you can be silent or walk away. Again, when you respond to criticism, you play the other person's game by the other person's rules. Remarkably, most people go for the bait over and over, even though they get hooked into a no-win contest every time.

A final strategy we suggest you consider when dealing with a critical partner is to interpret the person's message the way *you* want to—the way that allows you to guiltlessly do what you want. When a person criticizes you every time you cook for him or her, you could interpret such criticism as saying, "Don't cook for me." You respond: "Since you always dislike how I cook, I guess you're trying to tell me you don't want me to do it anymore, but you're too polite to tell me directly. I get the message. I won't cook for you, in spite of how much I would like to." If the other person argues, you can always fall back on, "You're just trying to spare my feelings. I know you don't want me to cook." In place of "cook," fill in any activity for which you are criticized. By doing this you are saying, indirectly, "From now on, when you criticize me, it means you want to do it yourself." And you are saying it in a way that does not cause confrontation, since the only argument the other person can make is to say you are really doing it well enough already.

Basically, the core of this strategy is for you to think of what the other person does, decide what meaning you want to give that behavior, and feed that perception back to the other person in a way that makes it sound like what you are doing is just what that person wants you to do. If this is too complicated for you, keep in mind the simplest way to view it: "When you criticize me, it means you don't like what I'm doing, so I'll listen to you and stop." When utilizing this strategy, it is very important to clearly maintain a one-down position, which does not convey confrontation or an "I'll-show-you" attitude. You do not want to come across as meaning, "O.K., you've been treating me badly, and now you'll get yours." Rather, you want to sound, not feel, defeated. The message should be "I tried my best and failed, so I won't inflict myself on you in that way anymore." But remember, if you are going to sound sarcastic, don't say anything. You want to sound resigned and less knowledgeable, skilled, and powerful than the other person. Essentially, you are giving up power to get more control.

Meanwhile, let's return to Eric and Barbara. As you will recall, Barbara couldn't do anything right when she helped Eric, and he constantly yelled at and criticized her. The strategy Barbara used was twofold. First, she began agreeing with and extending his criticisms: "Yes, I'm really pretty stupid, and I can't think of anything I know how to do right." She also tried less hard to please since trying to please him never worked anyway.

Her second assignment was to interpret Eric's criticism in a way that allowed her to do what she wanted. The message she and her therapist came up with was, "Eric, you say you need me and want me around, but every time I am around, you yell at me and criticize me. So I guess I really get on your nerves, but you're too polite to tell me directly. From now on, when you yell at me, I'll know I'm getting on your nerves, and I'll leave if I can." Eric protested that that wasn't what he meant, but Barbara just replied

"You're just sparing my feelings. I know I get on your nerves." And she stuck to her guns. When he got abusive she left to see her friends or to take herself out to dinner.

As we expected, Eric's criticism decreased markedly. Not only could he not upset her by criticizing, since she just agreed with him, but if he criticized her too long or too loudly, she would leave. As he stopped being critical, Barbara found she wanted to be home more. Evidently, there were some things Eric really didn't want Barbara to do, because he began doing them instead of criticizing her.

In this first section of our chapter on power-related issues, we examined the pattern in which the dependent partner relies on the other in a variety of ways, but is relentlessly critical of how the other partner performs those duties. We made three suggestions to the criticized partner: (1) agree in words, but not in action, with the criticism; (2) don't explain or defend; and (3) interpret the other person's message in a way that allows you to stop doing things for him or her, for his or her own good, which basically involves saying that the criticism means that the person does not want your help, so you'll stop.

In the pattern just described, the dependent partner held more power through the use of criticism. The next pattern we'll discuss involves a dependent and dominated partner who is virtually bereft of power to the point where the relationship resembles that of a parent and child.

The Domineering Partner

The pattern described in this section is certainly the most common power-related problem that comes into our offices. In this situation, the domineering or "parental" partner is in control of virtually every aspect of the relationship: money, decision making, social life, conversation topics, and so forth. Unlike the relationship with the dependent but critical partner, the power disparity is not due to a lack of skills or abilities on the part of the less powerful partner (who we'll call the dominated or powerless partner). From early on in the relationship, one member of the couple took charge. Why this happens differs from situation to situation and is not always clear. Some people are just naturally take-charge people. Others don't like taking responsibility and are happy to hand it over to someone else.

Some people like to theorize that, in a power-disparate situation, a woman has found a substitute father, or a man a substitute mother. The idea that the dominated partner is looking for a parent is a little hard to swallow in most instances. However, to an observer, the relationship ends up looking more like parent–child than adult–adult. Grown men and women actually come into our offices and tell us they aren't allowed to go out with their friends or to write checks. If you hear yourself saying "I'm not allowed to ... " to your friends or family, please pay close attention to the rest of the chapter.

Some people are perfectly comfortable in the child role. They like being taken care of, dislike responsibility, and don't mind leaving their fates in someone else's hands. For many other people who find themselves in a dominated position in a relationship, it is not nearly so pleasant. When you are treated as less capable and responsible than you genuinely are, and when someone else calls all the shots, it can have dramatic effects on you—commonly, decreased self-esteem, lack of confidence, and depression. But don't get the wrong idea. The person in the powerful, parental role can be very kind and nurturing. He or she can be very unselfish and sensitive to the other partner's needs, like any good parent.

Still, it is a good idea to keep the parent–child analogy in mind. A parent can be kind and caring, but the child is never his or her equal in power. That's all right, and even important, in a true parent–child relationship. However, in an adult–adult relationship, the powerless partner can easily feel inferior, helpless, and trapped. As the dominated partner feels less able and confident, he or she becomes less willing to try new things or to rebel, and the disparity in power grows. And as the powerless partner is called upon to do less, he or she becomes less able to do things from lack of practice.

To summarize, one partner is domineering and powerful, but not necessarily selfish or unkind. It is clear that that partner calls the shots, while the other partner is dominated and relatively powerless. The dominated role may be attractive for a while. We all have fantasies of being taken care of and having no responsibilities. However, over time, the reality becomes much less pleasant for most people. It can be fun to be treated like a child, but it is not ordinarily fun for an adult to consistently feel powerless, dependent, unequal, or less competent. Unlike the previous pattern, in which the dependent partner aggressively captured power through incessant criticism, the dominated partner in this situation is virtually powerless, and any attempts to speak out against the arrangement sound like the helpless protestations of a child.

Let's now look at the strategies dominated partners use to try to reduce their discomfort. First, the dominated party usually tries to do a better job of following the rules the other partner sets up. These rules are guidelines for behavior—how to keep the house clean, what time to be home from work, and so on—set up by the powerful partner. If those rules are broken, the less powerful partner is criticized, obviously ("Can't you do anything right?") or subtly (silence). This criticism, of course, is much like a parent scolding a disobedient child. Trying to do a better job of following the rules rarely works. Even if the dominated person succeeds in obeying the rules, he or she is just buying further into the submissive, childlike role. Plus, the domineering partner can always change the rules, or set standards that are too strict to be followed.

The next solution tried by a dominated partner is to assert himself or herself and not give in. Occasionally this will work, but not too often. For one thing, the less powerful partner has little practice in standing up for himself or herself, and seldom does it well. Secondly, it is a bold action to take, since that person has relied on the other so long that he or she questions his or her own judgment. Finally, and most importantly, the domineering partner has a lot of power, and wants to keep it that way. So he or she will pull out all the stops to put down a rebellion. The more dominant person usually argues better, uses examples of how the other partner's decisions have been bad in the past, or threatens to stop doing anything for the other person. Basically, making an out-of-character attempt to be assertive seldom works because it comes in the context of a parent–child relationship and is treated like a child's attempt to overrule a parent—amusing, but futile.

A less conscious attempt to deal with this problem involves the powerless spouse actually becoming more childlike as he or she is consistently treated like a child. The person might spend money irresponsibly, drink more, not take care of the house, miss appointments, and forget things. In short, the person being treated like a child begins to become more of a child. And, since it happens without the person's awareness, the childlike partner becomes critical of him- or herself when irresponsibilities are pointed out, and his or her self-esteem drops even lower than it had been. Moreover, as that person becomes more childlike, it allows the partner to extend parental authority, and eventually the power disparity becomes more exaggerated.

You might ask why this happens. An obvious, but simplistic answer is that when a person is cast in a role long enough and consistently enough, he or she gets better at playing the part.

A more complex and satisfying answer involves the idea of passive-aggressive behavior. The term "passive-aggressive" may sound strange since the two words seem to be opposites. When they are combined, they refer to the behavior of a person who indirectly shows anger at another by doing something, by doing something poorly, or by doing something aggravating while acting or being unaware of how aggravating it is. Such behaviors often appear very childish and usually only serve to reinforce feelings of powerlessness. Examples of passive-aggressive behavior are forgetfulness, lateness, inefficiency, illness ("Not tonight, I have a headache"), and irresponsibility. People who don't feel powerful enough to stand up to someone at whom they are angry often resort to this type of behavior to irritate and get back at the person. The person is often unaware of the purpose of his or her behavior and is therefore surprised to be accused of doing something on purpose.

At any rate, passive-aggressive behavior doesn't shift the balance of power, but it does annoy the domineering spouse. Therefore, it is a strategy dominated partners use in order to get some slight satisfaction. But passive-aggressive behavior also creates more tension in the relationship and doesn't create any lasting changes (although we will show later how it can be channeled into an effective strategy if used on purpose, not subconsciously).

A couple that exemplifies the parent–child, power-disparate pattern is Donald and Roxanne. Donald is a forty-year-old professional who is well respected and successful in his field. He was the oldest of eight children in a single-parent family. He helped his mother raise his siblings, and many of them look up to him as a father figure.

Roxanne was working as a model when she met Donald, but began working part time after they had a child. Roxanne was from a smaller family, and there were no strong parental figures in her household. Her mother was more interested in her own social life than in her children. The men with whom her mother got involved were never around very long, and when they were, Roxanne spent a lot of time fighting off their advances.

At first, Roxanne like Donald's take-charge, dominant style. He made a very good living and gave her a comfortable life style. He made decisions for her and took care of details. He also had a lot of expectations of her and had strong opinions on how everything should be done. As she found herself unable to meet all of his expectations—dinner at a certain time every day, her taking self-improvement classes, ways their son should and shouldn't behave—she felt criticized more and more. He wouldn't discuss things because his way was the right way. Every once in a while she would "rebel" and not cook dinner, or go out with a friend. He would get quiet when angry or disappointed, and she would end up feeling so guilty that rebelling was never worth it. She felt helpless, stupid, and incompetent. She began to drink heavily, and she found herself becoming less and less responsible—housework didn't get done, she missed appointments, she wouldn't go shopping.

One important reason why people get stuck in this pattern is because they look at content instead of process (as we described in Chapter 4, in our section on lying). The content is the specific issue under discussion—what time to be home from work, how well the house should be cleaned. The process is the underlying pattern, or game, that takes place over and over, regardless of the subject matter. In this instance, the game is "Who's in control?"

The powerful partner is in a no-lose situation. If the less powerful partner acquiesces to his or her rules, the domineering partner wins. If the partner puts up a struggle, it is in reaction to the powerful partner, and the struggle is a defensive one. As we discussed earlier, even when you win a defensive struggle you lose, because you have bought the assumption that you owe an explanation or that you have to defend your behavior instead of questioning the other person's right to tell you what to do in the first place. So, even if you stand your ground, you haven't challenged the other person's power or control. The rules guiding the relationship stay the same.

Generally, there are three phases in breaking a pattern. They are (1) recognizing the old pattern; (2) somehow disrupting that pattern; and (3) establishing a new pattern. In this case, the pattern is that one partner is in control and that arguing over specific issues is pointless, since they are only important in that they allow one person to demonstrate control over the other.

An important aspect of any attempt to break this pattern involves the dominated partner's getting some control or power. As we have seen, direct attempts to do this often fail if the game has been going on for quite some time. We will look at two more subtle but effective ways to break the old pattern.

The first strategy is an extension of onedownsmanship. In this instance, taking a one-down position involves doing what you want to do and then agreeing if you are criticized or blamed that you were wrong to do it.

In order for the domineering–dominated game to work, the dominated partner has to (1) do what the other person wants, or (2) feel guilty for not doing so. Obviously, by doing what you want to do, you break the first part of the pattern. But, since you're used to doing what the other person wants, how do you not feel guilty when you "disobey"?

The dominated partners usually have mixed feelings about doing what they want to do. On the one hand, they feel they have the right to make their own decisions. On the other hand, they think they should comply with the other person's demands (since it has always been that way and because they feel insecure and unsure of themselves). When defending yourself, you are verbalizing one side of the mixed feeling ("I'm allowed to do what I want"); but the other side ("Maybe I shouldn't have") stays in your mind and makes you feel guilty. If you can say out loud to your partner, "You're right, I should have done it your way," what stays in your mind is, "That's not true, I can do what I want." You feel more sure of yourself and less guilty, and arguments and defensiveness are avoided since you're agreeing with your partner's criticism. We call this agreement partly insincere, since you know you did what you did on purpose and would do it again. But part of you ("I shouldn't have") does agree, and that's the part you're verbalizing.

To summarize this simple, but complex sounding strategy, you do what you want to do—act independently of the other person's expectations. Then, if you are criticized or blamed for doing it, you verbally agree that you were misguided, but behaviorally continue to do what you believe is best.

In the old pattern, the powerless partner probably felt manipulated constantly by the other person's calling the shots. The other person probably wasn't mean or deliberate, but it was manipulation all the same. By changing the pattern in the way we described, you gain control in two important ways. First, you are doing what you want. Secondly, you are not getting defensive or guilty, both of which weaken your resolve and make you backslide and atone for your independence. Finally, by changing your behavior, you disrupt the power distribution in the situation. This could motivate your partner to reverse his or her perceptions of the interaction and change his or her behavior in a way that takes into account a more equal distribution of power.

Some people have a hard time not arguing or defending themselves. They are proceeding on the ridiculous notion that in every situation someone is right, and that you have to show that the person is you. In an argument, the person who is right doesn't necessarily win. Either the best arguer wins, or both people lose, since they wind up more angry at each other and less able to see the other's point of view. We think you win when you do what you want and feel all right about doing it.

A second strategy involves, to put it indelicately, *constructive payback*.[22] This strategy can be especially useful, in combination with the one just described, when the domineering partner is coercive, verbally abusive, or relentlessly critical. In situations like these, the less powerful partner can feel unable or afraid to directly express anger or resentment. And, in power-discrepant relationships, the dominated partner normally gets resentful.

Constructive payback is an indirect way to both express that anger, and to let the other person know he or she can't get away with being abusive, by purposefully using passive-aggressive behavior. Being passive-aggressive involves doing something that bothers the other person (being late, stupid, inefficient), but looks unintentional. As we said earlier, passive-aggressiveness is generally ineffective if it is done subconsciously, because, then, you don't have control over when you do it and can feel guilty about it since you didn't choose to do it.

Here are some examples of constructive payback. A man complains daily about how his wife cooks dinner. She deliberately overcooks or undercooks the food for the next week and apologizes profusely for her ineptitude. Another woman tells her husband that he can never match a shirt and tie that look good together. So he wears the same shirt and tie for two weeks straight, driving her crazy, and tells her every day how many compliments he gets.

The payback need not have anything to do with the actual circumstances surrounding the criticism, as in the examples above. A man can criticize his wife for spending too much time with her friends, and she can pay back by "accidentally" blocking his car in with hers when she knows he's in a hurry, or "forget" to pick up his dry cleaning just before he leaves on a trip.

Yes, this does sound childish. But it also serves some important functions. It helps blow off anger without confrontation, since you never admit you're doing it on purpose. It shows the other person that unacceptable behavior on his or her part will meet with unpleasant consequences. Also, it's fun and can loosen up an otherwise "heavy" situation. By doing silly and immature things like this, you give yourself the message that the situation is not life or death. If this strategy is implemented cleverly, it can lower the emotional intensity of the whole situation (see section on lying in Chapter 4). It is important *not* to choose critical, emotion-laden situations as the subjects for payback. Instead, look for mildly irritating, but noticeable ways to put across your message. The sillier and less consequential, the better.

Finally, payback confuses the domineering spouse and allows him or her to start viewing his or her behavior in a different light. Confusion is often a necessary precursor to behavior change: "Why is my spouse acting so weird? I need to attend more to him or her and find out."

It is probably obvious that the constructive payback strategy can be very frustrating to the person who is on the receiving end of it. With most people, that frustration is uncomfortable, but not dangerous. In fact, it can motivate positive changes. However, there are some people who have a very low tolerance for frustration and who are easily provoked to violence. If you have any reason to believe your partner is such a person, do not try this strategy. The risks will outweigh the benefits.

One way to test whether you are being too confrontational is to see if your behavior fits into the one-down mold. You should not be making mistakes, forgetting things, or performing poorly in a nasty, vengeful, or powerful way, but rather in a forgetful, clumsy, or powerless way. Your behavior should not present itself as a challenge to the other person.

It is also important to remember another point we stressed earlier. These strategies ought only be used when direct attempts at communication have been tried and have failed. An honest and direct approach should always be considered first; but continuing this when it doesn't work is self-defeating and destructive to the relationship.

If you use one or both of the strategies just outlined, things will change. At first that change may not be pleasant. People who have power and see themselves losing it will fight to hang onto that power. Your partner may get louder and more critical, or try to be even more controlling. This is normal. When change occurs and one person doesn't really want it to, the first thing he or she does is try to do more of what he or she was doing before.

Nevertheless, stick to your guns. A person who escalates his controlling behavior is confused and threatened. The confusion can act as a catalyst for change, since people who are confused are uncomfortable and look for new ways to behave to lessen that discomfort. If his or her escalation doesn't work, the pattern will be broken, and a new, more equitable one can be established. Let's see how the situation turned out for Roxanne and Donald.

As you will recall, Roxanne felt she was being treated like a child, controlled and criticized by Donald and made to feel guilty whenever she didn't comply with his wishes. Her first assignment was "Do what you want and agree with him if he says you are wrong, but keep doing what you want." She did so, and very well. She and their son spent more time out of the house, she spent more time with her friends, and she didn't cook dinner every night, and certainly not at the same time every night. When Donald told her how irresponsible and selfish she was being, she replied, honestly, that she felt bad about neglecting him. Nevertheless, she didn't alter her new behavioral course. His first reaction, predictably, was to get more critical and to set up more rules. If he got particularly unpleasant or verbally abusive, Roxanne kicked in Strategy 2, the payback. She would do laundry, but misplace his socks. She would cook his favorite meals, but leave out key ingredients. She was careful to accompany these lapses with apologies for her ineptitude.

Within a few weeks, Donald seemed to get the message that dominating Roxanne through a power play would not work. He became less demanding, discussed things with her more, and actually asked her opinion occasionally. Evidently, Roxanne's changes allowed him to see her and their relationship differently. Roxanne, for her part, was happier even before Donald changed, since she was doing what she wanted and not feeling guilty about it.

In this section, we looked at a pattern in which one partner is in control of the most important aspects of the relationship. The domineering partner plays a parental role in many ways, and the dominated partner feels relegated to a child's role. We suggested two alternatives for the dominated partner, when more direct, open strategies have failed: (1) Do what you want to do and, if criticized, agree you were "wrong" to do it, but continue to do it; and (2) use a constructive payback approach in which criticism and overcontrol are responded to with "inadvertent" mistakes and "forgetfulness" that make the other person's life slightly more difficult.

Problems that revolve around sexuality will be the subject of our next chapter. Power and communication are also involved, but the sexual nature of the issues are central. Specifically, we will explore the issues of jealousy/trust and disagreements about how often to have sex.

Chapter 6

Sexually Related Problems in Romantic Relationships

Sexual intimacy is obviously an important component of any romantic relationship. Naturally, any facet of a relationship that has assumed such a place of importance is bound to be the focus of problems. And it is. The plethora of books and articles written about sexuality speaks to both the increasing emphasis placed on it in relationships, and the fact that people have a great deal of concern about their sex lives.

In this chapter, we will examine the two most common sexually related difficulties we see in our practices. The first problem to be addressed does not have its basis in the bedroom. It is an issue we call *jealousy/trust*. Many books about sex have been criticized as how-to manuals due to their focus on the mechanics of sex. However, key aspects of couples' sex lives have little to do with what happens in bed. Quality and quantity of communication, mutual respect, and feelings of emotional safety and trust have much more of an impact on most people's levels of sexual intimacy than do the partners' technical proficiency or choices of cologne.

Of the issues that are related to what does, or doesn't, happen in the bedroom, sexual frequency is the one about which we hear the most complaints. Impotence, "frigidity," premature ejaculation, and other performance-related problems are certainly the cause of a great deal of concern for couples. How-to sex manuals often address these issues very effectively. Differences in preferences regarding sexual frequency, on the other hand, lend themselves more readily to solutions generated by an interpersonal, systems-oriented approach.

Regardless of the specific issues addressed, all sexual matters have a tendency to take on an exaggerated importance for a number of reasons. Many people have learned to equate sex with love and feel unloved if they are not treated as sexually desirable by the partner. In addition, men and women alike place sexual matters high on the list of factors that go into determining self-esteem. Finally, in spite of the increasing openness about sexuality in our society, frank and open discussions about sex are difficult for most couples. This silence inhibits problem-solving and allows difficulties or misunderstandings to grow and fester. The overall effect of these factors is to give sexual issues a lot of power and excess meaning. Hopefully, the ideas we will present will help to return sexual problems to a more realistic perspective by demystifying them and rendering them capable of being solved.

Jealousy/Trust

Jealousy and trust issues in relationships have a great deal in common in that both involve one partner's suspecting that the other isn't being completely loyal or truthful. They are also similar in that the person who is the object of the jealous feelings or mistrust cannot remove the problem. Suspiciousness remains that the person who is believed unfaithful or untrustworthy is "just acting" loyal or faithful and acts differently when not being observed.

In order to demonstrate a pattern that represents both trust and jealousy issues, we have chosen the extreme example of a relationship in which an affair has occurred. Some aspects of this pattern are unique to this example and do not apply to all jealousy or trust problems. Many different real or imagined actions can destroy trust, and jealousy certainly isn't always the result of a real indiscretion. Nevertheless, many of the strategies which are effective in dealing with this specific pattern are also helpful for general trust and jealousy issues.

An affair is a very difficult occurrence for a relationship to survive. The hurt and anger that result probably never leave the couple completely. Surviving an affair is much like surviving the death of a loved one, because the relationship as it was prior to the discovery of the affair is forever lost. When a loved one dies, we gradually come to grips with the loss by actively grieving. No one ever completely gets over the hurt, pain, and anguish of the loss of a loved one. What does occur is acceptance of the loss and realization that it will always hurt to some degree. The pain remains, but its intensity can be greatly lessened. Accepting an affair is much the same as coming to grips with a death. The partner who must accept the "loss" needs to experience and express the entire range of emotions associated with the affair.

Unfortunately, the partner who had the affair rarely helps facilitate this "grieving" process. Rather, he or she tries to deal with the situation through minimization, avoidance, and indignation. Believing that the subject will die if it is ignored, he or she never brings the topic up and quickly steers conversation away from it when it is mentioned. When discussion can't be avoided, the importance of the affair is minimized in many ways: "It was only sex, not love;" "It's over, let's get on with our lives;" or "It meant nothing to me."

These strategies usually backfire. The other partner already felt hurt, angry, and betrayed. Now he or she feels dismissed and misunderstood. So he or she brings up the affair even more and more strongly emphasizes how hurtful it was and how detrimental it was to the foundation of trust in the relationship. Any jealousy that was previously present intensifies and feels justified ("I knew you were fooling around, and I was right.")

As the perceived attacks by the hurt partner increase (talking more and more about the affair, emphasizing its significance), the partner who had the affair gets more defensive and indignant

("How long do I have to go on like this?" "When do I stop paying for my crime?"). This person is already defensive since he or she feels guilty. The mistaken belief that the issue of the affair should be resolved more quickly than it has been allows this partner to begin to feel wronged. This leads to more negative emotion and greater distance between the partners. Let's see how this pattern played out in the following example.

Rob and Sarah had been married for about ten years. Rob worked as a chemist, and Sarah as a systems analyst. Their jobs kept them both very busy. Over time, a lack of intimacy and general malaise developed in their relationship. Sarah entered into a sexual relationship with a man with whom she worked. The affair became public knowledge after this man confessed his indiscretion to his wife and told her he wanted a divorce. His wife went to Sarah and her husband's workplace and confronted her. The wife loudly announced her knowledge of the details of the affair. She went to Sarah's boss and almost got Sarah fired. Finally, she called Rob and filled him in, in exquisite detail, on the specifics of Sarah's relationship with her husband.

When Rob's initial rage diminished, he and Sarah decided to see a therapist. They were able to work through a lot of the hurt, anger, and guilt. Their marriage appeared to be back on solid ground.

A few months later, Sarah's job required that she and a number of her colleagues (male and female) attend an out-of-state business meeting. She returned from this outing to a barrage of questions from Rob. He wanted to know with whom she went to meals and how she spent her evenings. In spite of feeling somewhat put upon, Sarah honestly and completely answered his questions.

It didn't end there. More questions and suspicions ensued. Rob seemed to withdraw more and more, and usually involved himself in other activities when Sarah was at home. Sexual contact was nonexistent. On the rare occasions they did talk, the conversation concerned Sarah's activities and whereabouts.

Finally, Sarah became very angry and blasted Rob for his attacks and accusations. She defended her integrity and told Rob she had been giving him no reason to mistrust her. Rob, of course, pulled out his trump card and said, "I can never trust you after what you did." Sarah replied, "What am I supposed to do? That was almost a year ago. Why can't you get over that so we can go on with our lives?"

Rob said that he could never forgive or trust her. He didn't, however, want a divorce. He preferred to live with Sarah as a roommate for reasons of financial convenience. He refused to go back into therapy since he saw no purpose in it.

There are two strategies that are very effective in turning this type of situation around. The first involves frequently encouraging the partner who feels betrayed to express his or her feelings about the affair and for the other partner to listen *nondefensively*. This strategy accomplishes a number of things. First of all, it allows the partner who is trying to deal with the affair the chance to grieve. All emotions surrounding the issue can be explored, experienced, and understood. This "working through" is key to eventual acceptance.

Minimization and avoidance are also handled by this strategy. The partner who had the affair actively initiates discussion of the affair and its ramifications. The affair is treated as being significant, as are the feelings it has created. The partner dealing with the affair has no need to emphasize to his or her partner how important and painful an issue the affair is since it is already being treated that way.

This strategy also addresses power issues. The person who has to adjust to the idea that his or her partner has had an affair suffers an incredible reduction of power in the relationship ("I have no power if I can't even control whether my partner remains faithful"). By encouraging discussion of the affair, the agenda of the person who feels betrayed is given priority. This restores some of the lost power and control without necessitating a prolonged power struggle.

Another strategy that can be helpful in handling the trust and jealousy issues in this type of situation is having the partner who had the affair provide a detailed account of his or her daily activities before it is requested. A diary should be kept and information presented in mind-numbing detail. Frequent phone calls reporting whereabouts, activities, and companions should also be made.

Although some people feel that such a strategy is demeaning and unreasonable, it serves important functions in breaking destructive patterns and rebuilding trust. Information is presented before it is requested, breaking the questioning-defensiveness cycle. The information overload makes it less likely that accusations of giving partial or incomplete data will be made. Finally, this allows a number of "positives" to accrue to the account of the mistrusted partner, since most, if not all, the activities described will be routine and harmless. In order for this overabundance of information to have the desired effects, it must be presented in a matter-of-fact fashion, with no hint of resentment or sarcasm.

A footnote to both of these strategies is that it should be expected that the issue of the affair will resurface from time to time. This is perfectly normal and should be handled the same way it was initially. The issue does not go away. It gradually recedes into the background.

When Sarah sought therapy, she was at her wits' end and virtually resigned to the fact that her marriage couldn't work. The therapist discussed with Sarah the strategies outlined above and the rationale for them. She made an immediate turnaround and began initiating discussion of the affair. She tried hard to get Rob to express his feelings and she made it clear that she really wanted to understand how he felt. Sarah not only gave Rob a detailed written account of her activities daily, but she also called him once or twice a day to let him know what she was doing.

At first Rob reacted with skepticism. Sarah explained that she realized she had been making things worse and was determined to try to help him work through the residual feelings he had about the affair. Although he was guarded at first, Rob eventually was able to open up and let her know what was bothering him. As expected, Rob began to tire of the discussions and stopped reading Sarah's daily activity logs. Sarah persevered, however, until it was abundantly clear he had had enough. Meanwhile, Rob got used to talking to Sarah again and approached her on subjects other than the affair. Slowly, their relationship improved to the point where it was closer and more intimate, in many ways, than before Sarah's affair. At the time Sarah ended her therapy, the issue had not resurfaced, but her therapist prepared her for that possibility, and she felt capable of handling it.

In this section, we presented a pattern which often follows one partner having an affair and used it as an example of how to deal with trust and jealousy issues. The strategies presented were (1) encouraging expression of feelings about the affair; (2) initiating discussion of the affair at every opportunity; (3) keeping an exceptionally detailed diary of daily activities and reporting them to one's partner; and (4) expecting the feelings about the affair to resurface and repeating the three previous strategies when it does.

Sexual Frequency

It should come as no surprise that differences regarding sexual frequency are common among couples. Yet, for some reason, most people seem to have the expectation that their partners will have very similar, if not identical, preferences regarding sexual frequency. However, since desired sexual frequency is an individual preference, it varies tremendously from person to person. Even couples who start out compatible in this area often find their preferences drift apart over time, or that specific situations (work stress, birth of a child) change them temporarily.

Ideally, when these differences appear, they can be openly discussed and a mutually agreeable solution negotiated. In other cases, there is a physical basis for diminished desire on the part of one partner, and medical treatment can provide a solution.

Therapists become involved with couples unable to utilize one of these two solutions. Often, the cause is emotional or interpersonal, not physical, and many people are just not able to openly talk about sexual issues. However, a large number of people believe sexual frequency is not something that can be negotiated ("Either you want to do it, or you don't").

When a difference in desired sexual frequency turns into a full-scale relationship problem, it is usually the result of a series of events that starts with one partner's decision that there is a problem. It is almost always the partner who desires more sex who comes to this conclusion. He or she begins by stating the problem and directly requesting more frequent sex. The *verbal* response from the other partner is usually encouraging ("O.K. Let's try to get together more often"), but the *behavior* frequently remains the same or changes only briefly.

At this point, the partner who feels deprived pulls out all the stops. He or she brings up the topic of sex more and more. Adult movies, sexy clothing, suggestive remarks, and manufactured romantic situations (candlelight dinners, nights before a roaring fire) are all tried in the hopes of rekindling romance.

The other partner, who is being aggressively pursued, begins to feel pressured and often responds by backing away further. The person who has been doing the pursuing takes this badly, of course. He or she feels unloved and rejected and may even begin accusing his or her partner of being involved with someone else.

The case of Dennis and Nadine is illustrative of this pattern. Sex had never been an issue in their relationship. Nadine realized that sex was a little more important to her than it was to Dennis, but she was satisfied. Recently, however, some things had changed. As the couple had planned since they first got together, Dennis had returned to school full time about a year ago to complete his bachelor's degree. Nadine was very supportive of this because she knew it allowed Dennis to leave a dead-end job he hated. The couple had planned for the change in every way. Nadine had already completed her marketing degree and secured a challenging job with a computer firm. Her job was working out well, and she was making enough money to support Dennis while he finished his college course work.

Dennis's new schedule meant that he got home around 8 P.M. (He also had a part-time job.) After dinner, he would immediately begin to study and often worked until past midnight. Nadine, having recently finished college herself, understood that Dennis needed to study, but she thought he might be overdoing it just a bit. As a result of Dennis's study habits, the couple seldom went to sleep at the same time, since Nadine had to get up quite early to go to work. This significantly decreased their opportunities for sexual contact. When opportunities did arise, Dennis seldom took advantage of them. Nadine tried to be patient and waited a few months before mentioning her dissatisfaction to Dennis.

NADINE: "Dennis, I've been meaning to talk to you about, uh, our sex life, or, really, our lack of one. I know you're very busy with school and everything, but I would really like to figure out a way for us to have sex more often. I really miss having sex on a semiregular basis."

DENNIS: "Yes, I've really been busy. Probably taking three hard science courses at the same time was not such a good idea; just the time I spend in lab alone is driving me crazy. Maybe we could set aside a time for us to have sex."

NADINE: "Well, I'd rather it just sort of happens. Maybe if we just try a little harder to fit it in, we can work it out that way."

DENNIS: "O.K."

Time passed and nothing really changed. Dennis always seemed to have deadlines, tests, or lab reports that prevented him from going to bed when Nadine did. When they did got to bed together, Dennis was too tired or didn't feel like having sex. Nadine started thinking that the zest had left their sex life and that she needed to liven things up a little. She went out and bought sexy lingerie. She began initiating more, even though Dennis didn't seem to be interested.

From his perspective, Dennis thought Nadine was overreacting. He knew that he had a very demanding schedule and that it was important for him to do well in school. Dennis became somewhat annoyed and frustrated with the whole issue of sex. He began staying up even later.

Tension continued to grow between them. Nadine tried to cut through it with humor, but her humor often had sexual connotations. Dennis failed to see the humor and got more defensive instead. He avoided interaction at all levels with Nadine and began studying at the campus library. Things came to a head one evening when Dennis came home late from the library to find candles lit throughout the house, iced champagne in a bucket, and a negligee-clad Nadine awaiting him.

NADINE: "Hi, honey."

DENNIS: "Nadine, what's going on?"

NADINE: "What do you mean?"

DENNIS: "You know what I mean. The candles, you nearly naked in that sleazy nightgown. I'm really sick of all this pressure about sex. You're obsessed with it. I wish you would just understand that I'm temporarily too busy and too tired to indulge all your sexual whims."

NADINE: "Temporary? It's been six months! How long is it going to last? You've lost all interest in sex. It's like we're roommates, or brother and sister, and I'm tired of it. I've tried to be patient and understanding. You said you would try to do something about it, and you haven't. If you really cared about me, you would make a little bit more effort. How am I supposed to feel? You reject me constantly. It's like you don't even love me anymore."

DENNIS: "How can I love someone who's so insensitive to my situation? I avoid coming home because I know I'll have to face your pressuring me for sex and pouting and whimpering when I refuse. I'm just too preoccupied right now. Can't you see that?"

NADINE: "You're preoccupied with another woman, that's it. All those nights at the library—how could I have been so stupid. You've been seeing someone else, haven't you?"

It went downhill from there. Dennis got furious and left. They didn't speak for days. When Nadine tried to make up, Dennis suspected her motives, and she felt rejected again. Finally, she consulted a therapist.

Nadine made a number of mistakes. She focused on the content level ("I want you to make love to me"), and lost track of

Dennis's response to the relationship level ("You're making demands on me, and I have enough pressure already"). She believed his words ("I'll try") and not his behavior (he didn't try). She assumed a direct approach would work and that if he cared, he'd respond. Finally, when her approach didn't work, she tried more of it.

The basic strategy in this situation is to completely remove all pressure for sex, direct and indirect. The pressure comes not only from direct conversations about sex and the problems with it, but also from all the behaviors the other person *perceives* as pressure. What is intended is not what's important. How the actions are interpreted by the sexually disinterested partner is important. No pressure for sex means no initiation of sex or conversations about it, no sexy clothes, no romantic rendezvous.

This approach is made even more powerful when accompanied by clearly nonsexual affection—affection for affection's sake, not foreplay. Kissing hello and good-bye, holding hands, and other nonthreatening signs of affection are what is needed. Nonsexual affection allows the sexually frustrated partner to establish a track record of affectionate interactions that do not lead to intercourse. This allows the other partner, over time, to begin to reinterpret such affection as indicators of love and caring, not as overtures for sex.

A second component of the overall strategy involves putting sexuality back in a healthy perspective by focusing on other, enjoyable aspects of the relationship. As the couple becomes preoccupied with, and sensitive to, sexual issues, other things are deemphasized. Anything that has historically been mutually enjoyable should be rekindled: time together with friends, playing tennis, going to movies, cooking a meal together. As we have pointed out before, sometimes the best way to solve a problem is to stop trying to solve it.

The final part of the strategy involves the sexually frustrated partner making himself or herself less available to the other partner. Yes, we have just suggested that the couple needs to do more enjoyable, nonsexual activities in their time together, but the partner who feels neglected needs to create fewer opportunities for sex. Following a pattern of initiating, pressuring, and practically begging for sex, that partner appears desperate and at the other's beck and call. This seldom enhances one's desirability.

In addition, if someone runs away when pursued, the message he or she is sending is "I need more distance." However, when the distance gets too great, that same person will look to close the gap. Moving away from the partner who has been looking for distance allows that person the opportunity to achieve a comfortable amount of space and to begin pursuit when that space becomes uncomfortable. The partner who has felt neglected needs to pursue individual interests and friendships and to be sure to be engaged in activities around the house when his or her spouse has free time that could be used for amorous pursuits. Not only should he or she not initiate sex, but he or she could also pleasantly decline invitations and overlook subtle overtures. The basic idea is that the person who has been chasing needs to do a little running away. This reduces perceived pressure and frees the other partner to accept the role of pursuer.

Nadine did her best to take the pressure off, but it was a struggle at first. She had spent so much time and energy convincing Dennis (and herself) that she was desperate for sexual contact, that it was hard for her to reverse her tactics. She tripped up a few times early on and made overtures, but gradually was able to back off. She also had difficulty dealing with her impatience. She wanted change, and she wanted it quickly.

As she got caught up in her new approach, an interesting thing happened. She became a lot less preoccupied with sex. When she spent time with Dennis, it was spent doing things they had always liked: watching old movies, playing cards with friends, talking about ideas, not about sex. In her increased time alone, she got involved in a local political organization. Initially, she had joined to be less available to Dennis, but she found she really enjoyed it. She had the opportunity to act on her political convictions and made a lot of new friends who shared many of her values.

As a result, Nadine exuded a vitality she had not felt for a long time. Her sexual struggle with Dennis had left her depressed and bereft of self-esteem. Dennis commented that she had returned to being the woman he married. He found himself excited by and attracted to her.

But what about their sexual frequency? Dennis became interested again, but this time Nadine genuinely found it difficult to fit him into her schedule as often as he would have liked. A couple of months after her therapy had ended, Nadine called her therapist to report on an interesting variation on turnabout being fair play. She came home late one night from a political fund-raiser to find Dennis, clad only in bikini briefs, sipping champagne by candlelight, waiting for her.

The problem of differences in desired sexual frequency involves an escalating pattern in which one person tries harder and harder to excite interest in sex in his or her partner, with paradoxical results. The three-pronged strategy we outlined involved (1) removal of all pressure accompanied by nonsexual affection, (2) time together spent in mutually enjoyable, nonsexual activities, and (3) reduced sexual availability on the part of the partner who previously sought more.

Chapter 7

Beyond the Couple

Further Implications and Applications

Thus far we have looked at the problem areas of communication, power, and sex and have offered strategies to deal with specific situations that often arise in our clinical practices. However, the viewpoints expressed in this book and the suggestions that follow have much broader applicability than only to those specific problems. The approach espoused in this book can also be applied to any relationship difficulty—with spouses, children, colleagues, bosses, or family members. In addition, many of the strategies can be used to address problems of individuals that are not directly related to interactions with others.

Now that you have gained experience with the ideas we presented in Chapter 2, we would like to further your understanding of our approach so that you may apply these ideas in a variety of situations. In service of that goal, and to set up the strategies in the ensuing chapters, this chapter will present three therapy models that use systems theory and constructivism directly to develop solutions to problems that people bring to therapy: (1) the brief strategic approach of the Mental Research Institute (MRI),[23] (2) the solution-focused approach of the Brief Family Therapy Center (BFTC),[24] and (3) the eclectic strategic approach of the Dayton Institute for Family Therapy (DIFT).[25]

These systemic models of psychotherapy challenge traditional thinking about mental health by focusing on people's resources rather than their deficits and on the social and developmental context of the client's problem rather than its underlying pathology. This chapter will discuss the mental health implications of such a view and will present a normal life cycle perspective of human behavior. The strategies that flow from the three approaches will be presented in a broader framework that organizes them into six categories, which will enable you to more easily apply them to other problem areas.

Problems, Not Pathology

The brief strategic approach of the MRI is an outgrowth of the family systems movement and evolved concurrently with many approaches to family therapy. One group of researchers studying families containing a schizophrenic member was the Bateson Project, which investigated the communication patterns in such families. One of the early discoveries was quite radical; what was thought to be solely a mental illness belonging to an individual may not be an illness in a medical sense. It may not, in fact, be a disorder at all; rather, it could be seen as an orderly pattern that had meaning in the families or other social settings in which it occurred. The behavior labeled schizophrenic was viewed for the first time as part of an ongoing system of social interaction.

The research of the Bateson Project culminated in the double bind theory of schizophrenia[26] (remember the double message that we described in Chapter 3). Until the double bind hypothesis, most other family-oriented descriptions of human problems were awkward translations of Freudian or medical views; problems were often described as symptoms of underlying family pathology, as well as intrapsychic conflict. The double bind theory, based in communication and relationships between people, had the powerful capacity to describe human dilemmas as interactional in nature and freed the emerging field of systems from the limitations of Freudian and medical perspectives.

Two members of the original Bateson Project, John Weakland and Jay Haley, became interested in the work of Milton Erickson, a psychiatrist known for somewhat unorthodox, but effective treatment methods. To give you a flavor of what we mean when we say unorthodox but effective, consider the following story often told in therapy circles about Erickson.[27]

Erickson consulted in a hospital in which a man who professed to be Jesus Christ lived for many years. The man had initiated virtually no contact with another human being beyond his occasional mumblings about being Jesus. No productive behavior or communication had occurred for years. As is often the case with problems of long duration, most mental health professionals give up, declare the person to be unchangeable, and justify their positions with the references to the "severity" of the pathology.

Erickson held a very different view about treatment and his view allowed him the freedom to try innovative ways to attempt change. Carrying a carpenter's tool box, Erickson approached the man professing to be Christ and said, "I understand you have some carpentry skills and I need some shelves built in my office." The man was put in the position of denying his divine nature or of doing something productive for the first time in many years. He chose to build Erickson's shelves, during which time Erickson developed a close relationship with him. The man was ultimately discharged from the hospital. Erickson practiced with a creativity that was not burdened by the conventional wisdom of his day; it was this creativity that interested Weakland and Haley.

After several years of studying Erickson's innovative methods, both Haley and Weakland went on to integrate Erickson's ideas with communication theory and systems theory, forming the basis for what is now known as strategic therapy. Haley went East and later cofounded the Family Therapy Institute of Washington,

D.C. with Cloe Madanes.[28] Weakland joined Don Jackson at the MRI in Palo Alto, California.

From those influences, an approach evolved that to this day is still considered maverick and unorthodox by many mental health professionals. Be your own judge.

Recall from Chapter 1 our discussion about people who get stuck in trying the same old solution over and over again. This simple but elegant idea comes from the MRI, which suggests that people's attempted solutions, the very ways they are hoping will improve problems, contribute most to the problems' persistence and escalation. The MRI sees problems beginning from some ordinary life difficulty, of which there are usually many in most of our lives. This difficulty may come from an unusual or chance event like the loss of a job or a car wreck. Most often, though, the difficulty is associated with one of the transitions regularly experienced in the course of living one's life and raising a family. (See later section on "Normal Life Cycle.")

Most people will handle these difficulties *with* discomfort, but *without* the distress that usually leads to seeking therapy. During these difficult times, we fall back to coping styles that have previously worked for us. Most times they continue to work, but sometimes they don't. For example, Christine and Robert are having a difficulty with their fifteen-year-old daughter, Megan, who is achieving below her potential by receiving C's and D's. For the past five years, under similar circumstances, Christine and Robert grounded Megan and intensely watched over her studying habits in response to poor school performance. It had always worked before, and Megan would improve her grades by the end of the following grade term—until now. Christine and Robert are at their wits' end. They first tried grounding Megan from the phone, then the TV, then total house arrest. Nothing has had an influence on the grades; in fact, things are getting worse to the point that Megan recently ran away for two days.

The MRI would view this circumstance as a problem that grew from a difficulty arising from a normal developmental transition, namely Megan's transition from childhood to adolescence.

Christine and Robert applied solution strategies that they have previously employed with success. They continued to apply what worked when Megan was a child even though they knew it wasn't working with Megan the adolescent. For such a difficulty to turn into a problem, only two conditions need be fulfilled: (1) the difficulty is mishandled (the solution attempts don't work), and (2) when the difficulty is not resolved, more of the same solution is applied.[29] Then the original difficulty will be worsened, by a vicious cycle process, into a problem whose size and nature bear little resemblance to the original difficulty. Megan's running away has little apparent similarity to the original problem with grades.

Problems, then, develop from chance or transitional circumstances encountered by individuals and families evolving through the life cycle. The problem, once *perceived* as a problem, becomes not only the original difficulty, but also all the meanings it has accumulated through attempts to solve it. Based on these accumulated meanings about the problem or how to solve it, people will try variations of the same solution pattern over and over again. This occurs despite the best intentions of those involved, and the fact that the solution attempts are recognized as not helping. The solution, in essence, *is* the problem.

This simple view of how problems develop may be understandable, yet hard to really accept. It may not be difficult to believe that people handle life changes inappropriately, but what makes people persist with ineffective solution attempts despite their own experience that their attempts are not working? Some explanatory scheme is needed to address this amazing propensity of individuals to act in such irrational and unproductive ways. Enter the Freudian and medical models. These models and the concept of mental illness are little more than explanatory schemes that describe behavior that appears irrational or self-defeating. These models explain that people behave in unhelpful ways because they have mental deficits or personality disorders.

The MRI does not believe that persistence in mishandling problems must require mental, personality, or emotional defects in the family or in the individual. The human experience of emotional and interpersonal difficulties are therefore seen as *normal* responses to trying times. The MRI interactional view enables a contextual view of human behavior that depathologizes problems in living.

The significance of not looking for illness or pathology in persons seeking help for personal or relationship problems can hardly be overstated. All therapeutic strategies employed by the therapist rely on the assumptions the therapist makes. These assumptions structure the therapeutic strategy at every level. How the therapist interprets and conceptualizes the problem situation of the client influences not only the nature of the helping relationship, but also what information will be relevant, who will be seen in treatment, what will be said, and how results will be evaluated.

Unfortunately, many psychotherapists continue to consider the individual as the sole unit of understanding and do not attend to the individual as part of a unique relational and developmental context. What happens in therapy is that a person will present a complaint or set of complaints to the therapist and the therapist will reinterpret or translate the complaint to the model to which he or she subscribes. The therapist's reformulation of the complaint into a theoretical model will enable treatment to proceed down a particular path flowing from the theory.

Consider the example of Deborah, a woman who felt considerable distress on a periodic basis, but was not quite sure why she felt so bad. The therapist she saw was a psychiatrist who asked her a series of questions about her eating, sleeping, and sexual habits. Given that Deborah reported difficulties sleeping recently and admitted to feeling somewhat hopeless at times, a diagnosis of depression was reached. The therapist conceptualized the problem as an illness resulting from a biochemical imbalance involving the neurotransmitter serotonin or norepinephrine. Treatment would consist of antidepressant medication and perhaps hospitalization.

Now on antidepressant medication, Deborah was referred to a therapist who worked with the psychiatrist so that she could learn to manage her illness. The therapist, practicing a derivative of the Freudian model, investigated Deborah's childhood relationship with her parents and discovered that Deborah's father had died when she was six. The therapist believed that Deborah's depression (she was now formally diagnosed) was related to repressed and unresolved feelings about her father. The therapist, a psychologist, administered several psychological tests. Although costly and time-consuming, according to the therapist's model, the test results would be helpful in understanding Deborah's intrapsychic make-up. Treatment would consist of a long-term therapeutic relationship that would enable an intensive pursuit of the unconscious causes of Deborah's depression.

Not completely understanding the relevance of the treatment in addressing the original reason she entered therapy, Deborah stopped therapy for a while and reentered with another therapist. This therapist, operating from a nonillness, systems perspective, investigated Deborah's current situation and what she was doing to try and make herself feel better, as well as what others were attempting. Deborah's opinions and ideas regarding her distress led to a frank discussion of what she thought was contributing to her unhappiness. Deborah shared her sadness about her youngest daughter going to college and her concern about her relationship with her husband. Rather than a doctor–patient exchange, the discussion was more conversational and Deborah felt as if she were the expert regarding her problem. Treatment consisted of a mutual exploration of what the problem meant to Deborah, as well as the therapist suggesting options that she might try to help herself feel better.

Obviously, such differences in conceptualization and treatment of the proposed case also make for some radical differences in prognosis, as well as ramifications for Deborah and her family. The theory of the therapist not only dictates what sort of therapy is selected, but also how drastic and lengthy it is expected to be. If a therapist looks through a pathology or illness lens, he or she is quite likely to find an illness. Once found, a path is set and then must be followed. If a therapist looks through a lens that views people as having the resources and skills to solve their problems, then a different path for problem resolution is discovered. This health-based perspective on psychotherapy can be largely attributed to the approach of the Mental Research Institute. Removing the pathology blinders has enabled a shift from what is wrong with the individual experiencing a problem to what can be done to improve the individual's situation. Two derivatives have evolved from the MRI that expand the MRI's problem formation model and nonpathological way of viewing human dilemmas. We will now turn to those models.

Solution Focus and Meaning Revision

The approach of the BFTC is called Solution-Focused Brief Therapy,[30] which highlights its major difference from the MRI model. Rather than focus exclusively on the problem itself, proponents of this approach—Steve deShazer and Insoo Kim Berg—pay close attention to what is happening in the client's life when the problem is *not* occurring. This model pays particular attention to exceptions to the problem and pursues an amplification of those exceptions. As a systems-oriented approach, the BFTC attempts to empower clients to initiate small changes that will ripple into larger changes (remember wholeness).

Focusing treatment on exceptions to the problem and how the client lives when the problem is not expressed opens many new options for problem resolution. The task becomes one of encouraging what is already occurring, amplifying that process, and understanding how clients are *already* solving the problems on their own. Helping people understand their existing skills and appreciating their inherent resources are cornerstones of the BFTC approach. Many of its specific strategies incorporate an attempt to help clients take note of their strengths and intrinsic abilities to overcome their problems. Each strategy proposed by the BFTC, in some way, is an attempt to help clients experience changing by noting the differences between what is occurring when the problem is not happening versus what is happening when the problem is occurring. Several of our suggestions in the ensuing chapters flow from the BFTC view. These strategies will enable you to find new uses for knowledge you already have.

Another derivative of the MRI is the eclectic strategic approach of DIFT.[31] Sharing many commonalities with the two above approaches, proponents of this approach—Barry Duncan, Andy Solovey, and Greg Rusk—advocate the setting up of conditions in people's lives that permit new problem-solving alternatives to occur.

This is accomplished through what the proponents call suggesting a *competing experience* to the client. Competing experiences are essentially suggestions that the therapist makes to the client that compete with or take the place of the usual ways things are done surrounding the client or couple's problem. This, of course, accomplishes an interruption of the solution attempts that are not working. More importantly, competing experiences create the conditions necessary for revisions in meanings that the individuals involved have about the problem and its solution (see Chapter 2 regarding the construction of meaning). Meaning is generated through dynamic social interaction and is a continual process directed by the flow of communication between people. Competing experiences shift the flow of communication in a different direction, allowing the creation of different meanings and, therefore, different solutions. The best part about the use of competing experiences is that people come to realizations about the problem or themselves on their own, independent of their spouses or therapists. Many of the suggestions in the following chapters are useful in part because they permit the opportunity for changes in meaning about the problem under consideration.

In summary, the contributions of the three therapy models are the following: (1) the MRI's focus on failed solution attempts instead of illnesses, deficits, or disorders; (2) the BFTC's focus on exceptions to the problem's occurrence and using the individual or couple's existing strengths; and (3) the DIFT's focus on creating the conditions that enable individuals and couples to change their meanings about themselves and their problems. Each of these contributions will be directly translated into effective strategies for improving your relationship in the chapters that follow. Before moving to the six categories of strategies that emerge from these models, we would like to elaborate upon the normal life cycle. Our intent is to help you understand that problems most often develop from difficulties in adjusting to the inherent struggles of life, rather than from defects of character or mental illness.

Normal Life Cycle

Problems often arise from developmental transitions that individuals experience as they evolve through the life cycle. We would like to briefly introduce you to the important stages of normal development in terms of the individual and the family.

Adult Development

Erik Erickson[32] and three important life-cycle scholars, Roger Gould,[33] Daniel Levinson,[34] and George Vaillant,[35] have reached similar conclusions about adult development. The stages are as follows[36]:

Leaving the Family (16–22): The main developmental task is identity vs. role confusion. Who am I and where do I begin and end are the dominant issues. The peer group becomes paramount in an effort to assert one's individuality and break the hold of the family.

Reaching Out (23–28): Though the search for personal identity continues to be a dominant feature of the twenties, this period is also an age of reaching toward others. The capability to develop intimacy and make commitments is tested and stretched. The growing adult is powerful, expansive and keyed on mastering the world.

Questions, Questions (29–34): Assurance wavers, as life begins to look more difficult and painful around age thirty. Self-reflection churns up new questions: "What is life all about?" "Is this it?" "I thought I would have arrived by now!" There is a wrenching struggle among incompatible drives: for stability, attachments and roots, for freedom from all restraints, for upward mobility at work.

Mid-Life Explosion (35–43): Death will come: time is running out. This is the first emotional awareness of "I will die." Like a second adolescence, all values are open to question, and the midlifer wonders, "Is there time to change?" There is "one last chance to make it big" in one's career. The mid-life crisis does not have to be catastrophic. It does herald a new stage of growth.

Settling Down (44–50): A stable time: the die is cast, decisions must be lived with, and life settles down. A few old values and a few friends become more important. The successful mid-lifer does not stagnate but emerges to help, nurture, teach, and serve the next generation.

Emotional Integration (After 50): Mellowing brings an acceptance of one's one and only life cycle with no substitutions. There is a sense of some world order and meaning, often accompanied by an increasing spiritual awareness. Having taken care of things and people and adapted to triumphs and disappointments, a core of solidness—integrity—is felt. In such final consolidation, death loses its sting. A lack of accrued integration is signified by despair and fear of death.

Family Development

The most widely accepted delineation of the family life cycle is that of Duvall,[37] which has been elaborated upon by Carter and McGoldrich.[38] Duvall separates the family life cycle into stages addressing the events related to the comings and goings of family members: marriage, the birth and raising of children, the departure of children, retirement, and death. Childrearing is emphasized as the organizing element of family life. Each stage requires an emotional adjustment and a change in family status to enable the family to proceed developmentally.

Beginning

In families with young children, the key part of the emotional adjustment is the *acceptance of new members into the family.* Acceptance requires several family status changes, including adjusting the marital relationship to make space for children; joining with spouse in childrearing, financial, and household tasks; and realigning relationships with extended family to include parenting and grandparenting roles.

The shift to this stage of the family life cycle requires that adults now move up a generation and become caretakers of the younger generation. Given that fewer than ten percent of families fit into the traditional norm of working father, stay-at-home mother, and children,[39] the central struggle of this phase in the modern, dual-career marriage is the disposition of child care and domestic responsibilities. The issues of gender and the impact of sex-role expectations weigh heavily, and it may not be surprising that this is the family stage with the highest divorce rate. This is the phase in which Sharon and Jeff (see Chapter 1) were struggling.

Maturing

In families with adolescents, the key part of the emotional adjustment is *increasing flexibility of family boundaries to include children's independence and grandparents' frailties.* Changes required include the shifting of parent–child relationships to permit adolescents more freedom, refocusing of the adults on midlife and career issues, and the beginning shift toward the care of the older generation. Recall the dilemma of Christine and Robert with their daughter, Megan.

The shift to this stage of the family life cycle represents a new era because it marks a redefinition of the children within the family and of the parents' role in relation to the children. Parents must essentially transform their view of themselves to allow for the increasing independence of the new generation while maintaining appropriate boundaries and structure to foster continued family development. The central event in the marital relationship is often the mid-life exploration of one or both spouses of personal, career, and marital satisfactions and dissatisfactions.

Redefining

The next stage of the family life cycle involves the *launching* (leaving the nest) *of children* and a *redefinition of the marital relationship.* The key part of this emotional adjustment is the acceptance of a multitude of exits from and entries into the family system. This stage requires that the rules of the couple be renegotiated and the development of adult relationships between grown children and their parents be recalibrated. The realignment of relationships to include in-laws and grandchildren must also be addressed, and the possible disability and inevitable death of parents endured. The case of Deborah exemplifies the inherent difficulties of this phase.

Because of the low birth rate and long life span of most adults, parents launch children almost twenty years before retirement and therefore must find other life activities. Parents must not only deal with the change in their own status, as they make room for the next generation and prepare to assume grandparent positions, but also deal with a different type of relationship with their own parents, who may become dependent and require caretaking.

We hope it is apparent that life is full of opportunities for problems to develop. One does not have to be mentally flawed or emotionally disordered to experience distress and discomfort with the struggles of development. Neither does one need to be somehow deficient to become stuck at a transition point and need to explore different options for becoming unstuck. In many ways, life is about *experiencing* these life transitions, *struggling* with their meaning, and *adapting* ourselves in such a way that we can make a satisfactory life and continue to enrich and be enriched by the relationships that mean the most to us.

In the chapters that follow, we will present the similarities among the strategies offered in this book so that you can more easily apply them to other problem areas. Six categories flow directly from the three approaches discussed in this chapter and provide a general framework for organizing the strategies presented regarding communication, power, and sex. The six categories are (1) giving up power to gain effectiveness, (2) staying off the defensive, (3) creative interpretation, (4) shifting the focus, (5) going with the flow, and (6) indirect discouragement.

All six categories share a very important commonality, that is, the theme of doing something entirely and noticeably different when faced with a situation in which you feel stuck and that is not improving (remember the nine-dot problem).

Underlying this theme of trying something else is the notion of unpredictability. After patterns develop in relationships, we all become predictable to the point that we know what's going to happen before it happens, and so does everyone else involved. By being predictable, we close down the range of possible responses that could occur in the other person. Research in cognitive psychology has demonstrated that people process information by ignoring that which is usual and customary. For attention to occur, a bit of information must be unusual enough to be registered as different. Predictability breeds a predictable response. Unpredictable responses open the range of possible responses because the other person not only attends to the response, but also is confused by it. He or she must, then, try to make sense of the situation, which often leads to an entirely different way of perceiving it and therefore behaving.

Doing unpredictable behaviors in the face of a problem situation can take as many forms as the creativity of the individual will allow. In the face of a child's temper tantrum, examples include the following:

1. Walking up to the child and handing him or her a penny and walking away without explanation.
2. Encouraging and coaching the child in the correct procedure of throwing a tantrum.
3. Approaching the child and pulling out a notepad and saying calmly, "That's one," and walking away.

In the face of severe criticism, examples in addition to the ones offered in Chapter 5 include the following:

1. Hugging your partner and saying, "It really turns me on when a man (or woman) talks down to me."
2. Responding as if something entirely different has been said and walking away without explanation.

The bottom line, of course, is to enable a different response by doing something entirely different yourself. With this general theme in mind, let's turn now to the six categories of strategies.

Chapter 8

Giving Up Power
to Gain Effectiveness

A key element in many interpersonal transactions is power. As we discussed in Chapter 5, how the power is distributed in any relationship has an effect on how people interact with each other on a day-to-day basis. Power is directly related to control. The person in control of a given situation gets to determine what happens, what is decided, who is "right" in a discussion, and, basically, who "wins."

The ideas of "winning" and competition are relevant to the concept of the struggle for power in a situation or a relationship. We do, of course, live in a competitive society, and many systems thrive on competition. Our economic system is based upon unfettered competition. Competitive sports, in which one team or individual wins and one loses, are favorite pastimes. We compete with other people for promotions at work, for the affection and love of partners or prospective partners, for a good parking space at the mall. Nothing is too big or too little to be the object of a competitive battle. We are used to situations in which someone wins and someone loses. It doesn't surprise or distress us to conceptualize things in terms of who is on top and who is on the bottom.

However, whether the relationship is between lovers, friends, colleagues, or parents and children, a certain amount of cooperation is essential to maintaining a relationship's emotional side. Cooperation involves working together so that both parties win and come away from the interaction with a positive feeling about it.

It is not easy for many of us to step off the competitive treadmill and to engage in the win–win kind of interaction which characterizes cooperation. We are used to seeing things in win–lose terms, and we react instinctively in competitive ways.

Competition, in the form of obvious or subtle struggles for power, shows itself in many forms in interactions between people. It can be fairly direct, such as when one person tells the other what to do or unilaterally makes decisions that affect both people. Less direct attempts to control involve one person's criticizing the other's behavior or decisions, or using guilt to get his or her own way.

The class of strategies we have labeled "giving up power to gain effectiveness" is especially useful in a relationship which is characterized by an ongoing power struggle.[40] In this type of situation, the specific issues that get discussed can change, but the struggle for power underlying the ways those issues get resolved is constant and predictable. You know when you're in a relationship like this because you spend a lot of time on the defensive. Often, you may wind up saying "no" to things you really agree with, just to avoid "losing" or being controlled.

Let's take a brief look at a simple interaction that is made complicated in that it takes place within a relationship characterized by a power struggle. A wife says to her husband, "It's a nice day, why don't you go out and cut the grass?"

He replies, "Quit telling me what to do. I'll cut the grass when I'm good and ready."

She is surprised and says, "I was just making a suggestion. You don't have to jump all over me."

He, still angry, responds, "There you go trying to make me feel guilty. Well, I'm not falling for it this time."

He stalks off, after noticing that she has begun to cry. After a few minutes, muttering to himself, he goes out and cuts the grass, which, by the way, he had been planning to do before his wife suggested it.

This situation illustrates a number of aspects of how people trapped in power struggles tend to react. First of all, the husband chooses a position opposite his wife's and staunchly defends it. In a win–lose scenario, it is critically important to have two opposing sides, or else nobody can lose. So, even though he actually agreed with his wife that it was a good time to cut the grass, he chose to disagree because he didn't want her telling him what to do (being in control of him).

Another characteristic of the power struggle is that both parties get defensive very quickly. People engaged in a battle for control are vigilant for situations that symbolize someone's getting the upper hand, even if that isn't the other person's intention. In these situations it is easy for both people to put up defenses to feel emotionally distant from one another, and to physically become more distant (as happened here when the husband angrily walked away from his wife).

Actually, win–lose situations are very often lose–lose propositions. Even if one person wins the argument, both people feel bad—the husband is angry, and the wife hurt and sad. In addition, the "loser" awaits his or her next opportunity to win and prepares for the next battle. Ironically, the "winner" frequently also loses in a very direct way. In this instance, the husband won the argument, but ended up feeling guilty and cutting the grass anyway. So his wife got what she wanted. This pattern is more common in power struggles than people would expect. The person who wins verbally ends up acquiescing behaviorally. In other words, for many reasons, there tends to be no clear-cut winner in most situations of this type.

The type of strategy explained in this chapter allows one person an effective way to let go of the power struggle. It is analogous to a judo maneuver in which the force and energy of the opponent is used to throw him or her to the ground.[41] The person employing judo uses very little of his or her own energy to accomplish his or her goal; the energy of the attacker is used.

Conversely, competitive situations are more similar to boxing. If you are boxing, and someone throws a punch at you, you block it, which takes energy, and throw a punch of your own, which takes more of your effort. In our culture, we relate more easily to boxing as a metaphor. However, as we shall demonstrate, using judo can be easier and more effective.

It takes two to tangle. If one person ceases to struggle, the struggle is over. A useful analogy in this situation is that of a tug-of-war. If one person lets go of his or her end of the rope, the war is over. Technically, the person who lets go loses. However, the other person is left sitting on his or her backside on the ground holding a limp rope. Who has really won?

In the type of power struggles to which we are alluding, there are two salient aspects: the verbal and the behavioral. An excellent way to remove oneself from the push and pull of the struggle is to give up, *verbally*, your position and agree with the other person. This short-circuits the struggle, since there are no longer two sides in opposition. This dramatically changes the pattern of the interaction and shifts the focus of the two participants, perhaps to a more constructive end. The other person will think he or she has "won" and can let down his or her defenses. This tends to make the person calmer, more agreeable, and more freely communicative.

People are sometimes reluctant to employ this simple strategy, because they see it as giving in, or "losing." Nothing could be further from the truth. It is true that the *verbal* portion of the battle is over, since the other person believes he or she has won and has no reason to continue to fight. However, that says nothing about what happens *behaviorally*. The person who gave in verbally is free to *do* whatever he or she wants. Words and behavior don't have to be consistent. The other person might expect him or her to act in a way that is consistent with what he or she says, but it is completely up to the individual to determine if he or she wants to be consistent or not.

Trying to describe this relatively simple concept can be a little confusing, so let us go back to our earlier example of the husband

and wife arguing about cutting the grass and see how he could have handled the situation differently.

WIFE: "It's a nice day, why don't you go out and cut the grass?"
HUSBAND: "You're right, it is a nice day. I probably should cut the grass. That's a good idea."

The discussion will most likely end there, since they are in verbal agreement. It is still up to the husband whether or not he chooses to cut the grass. There was no argument. She made her point and he agreed with it. No one got angry, and there was no struggle. Of course, if he chooses not to cut the grass that day, she might bring it up again.

WIFE: "I thought you were going to cut the grass."
HUSBAND: "I am."
WIFE: "But I thought you were going to do it today."
HUSBAND: "You're right. I probably should. But you know how I procrastinate sometimes."

Whether she continues to pursue her line of questioning or not is irrelevant at this point, since his strategy is clear. He agrees with what she says, and may even take her position a step further (calls himself a procrastinator), but he won't firmly commit himself to doing anything. He retains his freedom to do as he chooses and doesn't get bogged down in an argument. If she wants to continue to press him, she can, but it is hard to argue if no one argues back.

We need to clarify here that we are only suggesting use of this strategy if a power struggle is involved and a more direct approach would likely be ineffective. It is true that the husband in the previous example could have just said that it was a nice day, but that he didn't want to cut the grass. This works fine if the issue is really the grass. In a power struggle (in which we assume this couple was already engaged), the specific issue can change from the grass, to how to discipline the children, to where to go for dinner. The individual subjects are virtually irrelevant. Who is in charge or who wins is the underlying theme.

Some people to whom this strategy has been presented have said that it is just reverse psychology, meaning that you reverse your field, hoping to manipulate the other person into doing the same. That is not at all the purpose of this strategy. The only goal for the person employing it is to stop struggling for power. The other person might change his or her mind. That would be fine. It is also fine if the person holds to his or her position. If you should decide to use this strategy, do so because you have decided arguing and vying for power is pointless and destructive to the relationship in which it occurs.

There is an interesting, positive side-effect to proceeding in the manner described above. As you become nondefensive and give in verbally, you are better able to listen to the other person, since you are no longer mentally preparing your rebuttal while the other person is speaking. As you listen more, you may find that the other person has a point, or that your positions are not so different. In your struggle not to give the other person control, you may discover that you were trying to defend a position with which you didn't really agree. At the very least, as long as you truly understand the other person's position, you can phrase your ideas in a way that is more acceptable to that person and decrease his or her defensiveness.

In previous chapters, we have presented four variations on "giving up power to gain effectiveness." In Chapter 4, in our discussion of lying, we suggested agreeing with, and exaggerating to a ridiculous degree, an unfounded accusation. In that same chapter, in the section on chronic complaining, the strategy involved accepting, validating, and exaggerating the complainer's position as a way to help the complainer feel less compelled to go on and on. Naturally, our chapter on power (Chapter 5) contained these ideas. We considered agreeing in words, but not in action, as a way to cope with a critical spouse. It was also suggested that one helpful approach with a domineering partner is to agree you're wrong if criticized for doing what you want, but continuing to do it. These applications of "giving up power to gain effectiveness" are similar in their use of words as tools to reduce defensiveness and shift the balance of power by appearing to give it up.

Other applications of this strategy are not difficult to imagine. Many different kinds of relationships allow for the possibility of a power struggle—relationships with colleagues at work, friends, spouses. The two most common situations, apart from couples, that respond well to this approach are power struggles between parents and adolescent children and between adults and their parents (or parents-in-law).

The primary area in which you would not want to try out this strategy is where there is a real, legitimate disparity in power, such as between a boss and an employee, or between a parent and a young child. Using a strategy of agreeing in words, but not in actions, can be quite effective with a peer, but could result in getting fired if it is tried with a superior at work. Similarly, the parent of a young child does have a lot of control since that child is dependent on the parent for most of the essentials of life. More direct methods of control are usually effective and appropriate in that case. However, as a child reaches mid- to late teens, he or she begins to become more independent and can challenge parental control more easily at that stage of development. Let us now look at how that can happen and ways it can be handled.

Power Struggles between Parents and Adolescents

An important task for a teenager to accomplish is to establish independence from his or her parents. Contrary to what many people believe, that process does not have to be conducted via out-and-out rebellion. Most teenagers find relatively nondisruptive means to demonstrate that they are their own people, not just extensions of their parents. Clothing and hair styles, taste in music, choice of friends, and opinions on matters large and small are some areas in which adolescents declare autonomy without dramatic conflict.

There is, however, a significant, and very visible, minority that utilizes more drastic means. These teenagers are relentlessly contrary in both words and actions. They often get into trouble and generate reasonable fear in their parents. No issue is too small for these teens to choose to say "black" just because the parents say "white." And they vociferously defend their positions regardless of how indefensible they may be. Behaviors range from the defiant and annoying—missing curfew, cutting classes—to the genuinely dangerous—drug-taking and drug-selling and stealing.

Parents typically begin their attempts to deal with this rebellion with reason. The activities of the teenagers are so illogical and self-defeating that their parents can't resist the temptation to share their wisdom and the benefits of their experience with their children. Then they get surprised and frustrated when the teenagers don't see the light and mend their ways. What the strategy of reasoning overlooks is that logic and rationality have little or nothing to do with the adolescent's behavior. The goal is to point out differences between them and their parents. They see advice as attempts to control and cling more tenaciously to their positions as the power struggle begins. Parents, please note that innocent and well-meaning attempts to reason are often the starting points for situations that escalate into full-blown power struggles.

After failing in repeated attempts to reason with their teen-aged children, the parents usually resort to threats and/or punishment. With teenagers committed to being contrary, these don't work either. Punishment certainly inconveniences them and is unpleasant. However, it just raises the stakes in the power struggle ("They can't make me do it their way no matter what they do"). Punishment is particularly ineffective in these types of situations if the parents show they are upset. This signals to the teenagers that they have gotten to their parents, which is seen as a victory in the battle for control, as they have forced the parents to lose emotional control.

It is very hard to really "win" a power struggle with a contrary teenager. Even if the parents are able to enforce a punishment, it doesn't often work to change behavior. In fact, if that punishment involves grounding the adolescent, who really suffers? The parents have to be home to enforce it and they are exposed to hostile, sullen attitudes and behaviors.

When a teenager's behavior becomes truly dangerous, or points clearly in that direction, action does need to be taken. The police and juvenile courts are resources that many parents find themselves using, not to punish the teenagers or teach them a lesson, but to protect them from themselves until they can develop better judgment or more control.

In less severe cases, giving up power to gain effectiveness can be very helpful. One strategy alone is unlikely to make a difference, though. In fact, unemotional administration of consequences (punishment) will usually be a part of the package. Complementary approaches will be addressed in subsequent chapters. In the following example, a number of strategies were employed. We will emphasize the use of giving up power to gain effectiveness and the importance of handling the underlying power struggle, as opposed to the individual issues one at a time.

Jean was seeking therapy for her seventeen-year-old son, Todd. Jean was forty-two-years-old at that time. She had been divorced from Todd's father for ten years and was remarried to Bill. Todd's two older sisters were away at college. Jean was a hard-working, conscientious person, who wanted to make sure all her children had the advantages she had missed out on by marrying at a young age. Her two daughters were much like her and were motivated students who got good grades. Her husband, Bill, was an easygoing guy who helped balance Jean's serious approach to most matters. He got along well with all the children.

But, it was Todd who was presenting Jean with a situation in which she felt stuck. He was slow in maturing emotionally and had been mothered by his two sisters. He had been held back a year in elementary school because he was felt to be behind his schoolmates in emotional development. At the time the family entered therapy, Todd was in the tenth grade. He was passing, but his grades were poor—all C's and D's. He had a part-time job after school—except during soccer season, during which he played on the junior varsity team.

In the second semester of his sophomore year, problems arose. It became apparent that he was cutting classes and forging his mother's signature to notes sent home. His mother discovered he was smoking cigarettes, which shocked and appalled her since she was vehemently antismoking. He had a fourteen-year-old girlfriend, and Jean discovered he had been lying about where he was after work and on weekends so he could be alone with his girlfriend. One Sunday morning, after having been out with Bill Saturday night, Jean was stripping Todd's bed in order to wash his sheets when she discovered a pair of girl's panties. Evidently, Todd had been in bed with his girlfriend when Jean was out of the house. This made Jean furious. Not only had he been lying to her, but he had also been having sex with a fourteen-year-old girl under Jean's roof!

Before she reached the end of her rope, Jean tried hard to help Todd. When his grades began to drop, she asked him what the problem was. He talked about missing his father, not having gotten over the divorce, and being worried about girls. She asked if he wanted to see a counselor, but he said he didn't. When things didn't improve, Jean talked to him about the importance of college and that she knew he had the ability to get into college. He said he would buckle down, but matters just got worse.

As Jean began to discover the extent of what he had been doing, she decided he needed more structure and perceived the consequences of his behavior. She gave him a stricter curfew, limited his time on the phone, and grounded him each time a new infraction came to light.

Todd responded badly, many times openly defying her. He would walk out of the house when he was grounded and use the phone when he wasn't supposed to. He also began to blame her for his problems. He said she had worked too much after the divorce and had neglected him. He accused her of favoring his sisters and of picking on him because he reminded her of his father. They frequently yelled and screamed at each other. Bill always backed Jean up when she disciplined Todd, but she wanted to be the one to make all the decisions affecting Todd. Just prior to Jean's calling a therapist, she had become so exasperated with Todd that she had slapped him hard across the face. He pushed her and ran out of the house. When he returned very late that night, Bill confronted him and let him know he would intervene physically if Todd touched his mother again.

Surprisingly, Todd willingly came in to talk to the therapist. He was open and cooperative. He presented a picture of a confused young man who wasn't trying to hurt anyone, but was overwhelmed by the temptations with which he was faced. Not so surprisingly, he neglected to mention a lot of what he was doing and tried very hard to convince the therapist his mother was the problem: "If she would just back off," he could work things out. At the end of the second of the two sessions Todd attended, he said to the therapist, "I really think things would get better if I could use the car more. Maybe you could talk to my mother."

At that point, the therapist decided he was likely to have more of an impact on the situation by meeting with Jean. Jean was desperate enough to try anything; but she quickly realized it would be hard for her not to argue with Todd, because he really knew how to get her upset and confused. She and the therapist came up with a message for her to give to Todd. When issues came up, she tried her best to stick to what she said in the message. When she got home she said to Todd:

> I have just talked to the doctor, and I realized a lot of things. You're right, I have been a bad mother. I didn't spend enough time with you when you needed me, and I'm sure that's why things are tough now. I've been trying to control you and tell you what to do, and I can't. I always think I'm right and that I know what's best for you, and I don't. I am going to try my best to change, but you'll have to be patient with me. I've been this way for a long time. There will still be rules for you around the house, and consequences if you break them. But I realize it's up to you if you want to follow the rules, or put up with the consequences instead.

Jean kept the rules that were important to her, such as a curfew, no smoking or drinking, and his girlfriend not being allowed in the bedroom with him. She eliminated as many trivial rules as possible to avoid opportunities for power struggles. When he did break the rules, she gave him his punishments without much discussion, and did not lecture him on what he did wrong, or what he should have done instead. She stuck to punishments she knew she could enforce. For instance, if she took away his phone privileges, she unplugged and locked up all the phones but the one in her room. She tried her best not to argue with Todd. If he blamed her for something, she usually agreed it was probably her fault. If he said a punishment was undeserved or unreasonable she agreed, but still enforced the punishment. If he got in trouble at school, she told the school to do whatever they thought best and not to show him any special consideration.

At first, Todd tested the limits as he had been doing. He missed curfew, cut classes, and lied about what he was doing. When he got no argument from Jean as he made excuses and blamed her for his problems, he escalated the situation. He accused her of not caring anymore, since she wouldn't talk to him (she did, but not in the way he wanted). He threatened to go live with his father. Fortunately for Jean, Todd did not become totally rebellious, and he did not engage in truly dangerous behaviors. If he had, she was prepared to take him to juvenile court; but her explanation to him would have been that she was too weak a parent to help him.

No miracle occurred, but things did improve. Todd still broke the rules occasionally, but less often. The biggest changes were in how he dealt with Jean and how Jean felt. Todd became a lot more pleasant to her and even began to confide in her again, without trying to be manipulative. Jean felt much less angry at him and a lot calmer overall.

In this example, Jean defused the power struggle by reversing her field in a number of ways. First of all, she stopped telling Todd what he could and couldn't do. She also stopped arguing over who was right and verbally agreed with his criticisms of her without substantially changing her behavior. She continued to employ punishment, but by removing the lectures that used to accompany it, it became matter-of-fact instead of a challenge. The overall tone of her message to Todd was, "You know what's best for you, I don't. You decide." In this way she was able to retain, and actually enhance, her parental authority without creating a struggle for power.

There are a variety of positive outcomes that can result from the use of this strategy with a contrary adolescent. By giving up the verbal struggle, the parents are able to relax more. They feel more in control of themselves and don't overreact to situations. Even if their teenager changes relatively little, they are less angry and desperate.

Another way this strategy can help is by making punishment more effective. If a teenager is being contrary, he or she wants evidence that his or her parents are displeased. Punishment coupled with parental upset is not all bad to the teenager. The punishment is unpleasant, but the parental anger demonstrates that the teenager has "won." Punishment without upset or discussion gives a uniformly negative message and is more likely to end the power struggle.

Believe it or not, the purpose of the adolescent's contrary behavior is not to aggravate the parents. It is his or her way of saying, "You don't control me, I do." The teenager is in a stage between dependence on the parents and independence. An intermediate step for some teens is counterdependence. This occurs when the teenager does not want to be seen as dependent, but does not know yet how to be independent. So, he or she does the opposite of whatever the parents want. By being less clear and insistent about what they expect, parents reduce the number of things the teenager has to react to. This gives the teenager the opportunity to think, "What is good for me?" instead of "What don't they want me to do?"

Power Struggles between Adult Children and Parents

Problems between parents and children don't magically end when the child reaches the age of eighteen. Some parents have a difficult time making the transition from a parent–child relationship to an adult–adult one. Even in the best of cases, this transition takes time. If a parent has trouble letting go of the control that goes along with the parental role, the transition may never occur. Since the adult child no longer lives at home, the ways the parent tries to exert control tend to become less direct. The parent offers to do things the adult child is perfectly capable of doing, tells the child how to do things, and/or is critical of the way the child does things. It can happen in benign ways, such as in the case of the thirty-six-year-old man who was in town visiting his father. One night he was getting ready to leave to visit friends. His father asked, "Do you have your driver's license with you?" His son had been driving for twenty years!

Situations that are more problematic and less amusing occur when a parent (or both parents) stays very involved, to the point of being intrusive, in the adult child's life and does so without invitation. The marriage of the adult child often makes things worse. Now the parent can also criticize his or her child's choice of a mate and that new spouse's behavior and decisions.

The adult child ordinarily tries a number of strategies to deal with a parent who continues to try to dominate his or her life. One is to do things the "right" way, that is, the way the parent thinks they should be done. These attempts are almost always doomed to failure, since the real issue is not how things are done, but who is in control or who has power (or who knows what's best).

Another common approach is to tell the parent that it is none of his or her business, or that his or her help is not needed. These statements are usually met with guilt-inducing responses such as, "I'm just doing it because I care about you," "So now that you're grown up you don't need me anymore," or "I'll remember that when you need a loan or a baby-sitter."

The bottom line is that parents in this situation are not at all comfortable giving up control over their children gracefully. Direct, straightforward attempts to stop these control attempts are therefore met with a great deal of resistance. Many adult children turn to avoidance of their parents as the coping mechanism of choice. This can reduce the stress somewhat since contact is less frequent, but when contact does occur, it is even more strained: "Why don't I ever see you anymore?" or "Your brother calls me every day."

In situations like this, in which there is a power struggle between a parent (or parents) and an adult child, strategies geared toward giving up power are the most effective ones. In the following example, we will look at a couple who are dealing with a struggle on both sides—her mother and his father. Both of these parents continue to exert, in very different ways, a large and unproductive influence on the lives of their adult, married children.

Don and Jill Lewis entered therapy in order to learn how to deal with their parents better. Both were thirty-two years old, and they had been married for twelve years. Don worked as an actuary for an insurance company, and Jill worked part time as a dental receptionist. Jill's father had died when she was fifteen, and her mother, Mrs. Gordon, lived nearby. Don's mother had passed away five years before he entered therapy. His father also lived close to the Lewises.

Jill had two older brothers who worked in the family-owned restaurant. One of the brothers, who was unmarried, lived with his mother. Mrs. Gordon had always favored the boys, and they could still do no wrong in her eyes. She portrayed both her sons as intelligent, happy, and successful. Jill, on the other hand, saw one brother as sullen, reclusive, and depressed, and the other as angry and impossible for people to get along with.

Mrs. Gordon's attitude toward Jill was quite different. While the boys could do no wrong, Jill couldn't do anything right. Mrs. Gordon second-guessed all her decisions and criticized how she did just about everything. Jill did considerably more for her mother than did her brothers (drove her to appointments, took her out to shop, called her daily), but was still accused of being selfish and uncaring. Also, in spite of her apparently low opinion of Jill, Mrs. Gordon still felt Jill could have chosen a better husband than Don. He wasn't ambitious enough and couldn't provide for her well enough. Family get-togethers, which were quite frequent, were a nightmare for Jill. One brother would ignore her, the other would rail on about all the injustices he had recently suffered, and Mrs. Gordon would find fault with Jill in various ways.

Jill tried her best to please, or at least pacify, her mother. She worked hard to do things the "right" way—the "Gordon way," as her mother was fond of calling it. Of course, since Mrs. Gordon had self-proclaimed herself the only judge of what the "right" way was, Jill usually didn't succeed. Jill also went overboard on her attempts to do things for her mother and to keep in touch with her in spite of the fact that these contacts were always unpleasant for Jill. Diplomatically, she tried to point out that her brothers weren't exactly perfect, which shocked and enraged her mother. Jill felt like a failure. She believed she had done all she could and still couldn't get her own mother to accept her.

Don's father presented a very different set of difficulties. He had no interest in telling Don what to do, however he was relentlessly negative and pessimistic. Whenever Don went to visit his father, he could be certain to hear a litany of the things wrong with the government at all levels, with religion, and with Mr. Lewis's friends and neighbors. In addition, he always heard a version of how hopeless and unrewarding life was. Don tended to be pessimistic and somewhat depressed himself, so he found his father very difficult to handle.

Don spent most of his time and energy with his father doing variations of the same theme. He tried to help his father see the brighter side of life. Don was, of course, presented with endless opportunities to try this. It also never worked. His father would mock his naïveté or ignorance and would redouble his efforts to convince Don of the futility of his optimism. Don had years of experience with the frustrations of trying to deal with his father and always felt more depressed and defeated when he left his father's house.

The therapist worked with both Don and Jill to take very different approaches with their parents. Jill began agreeing with her mother's critical assessments of her. Jill not only did not argue with her mother when she told Jill what to do, but she also asked for her mother's advice on a number of occasions. Jill didn't follow the advice or change the behaviors her mother criticized, but she did not challenge her mother at all. Jill made sure to praise her brothers to her mother at every opportunity. She went to fewer family functions, and when she did so she left as soon as she began to feel the least bit uncomfortable. If she was confronted about leaving, she agreed she was being rude and insensitive, but told her mother, "You know how I am. I'm sure you'll understand." Jill began calling her mother less often and volunteering to do less for her. She was still available and responded if pleasantly asked to do something, but she didn't volunteer nearly so often.

Her mother's response was interesting. For a while she became concerned about and solicitous of Jill, probably thinking that Jill was losing her mind. She told Jill she was a good daughter and did a lot of things well. In response to Jill's praise of her brothers, Mrs. Gordon actually began to criticize them occasionally. Jill was careful not to fall into a trap. She continued to point out her own limitations and praise her brothers.

The dramatic changes didn't last too long. Mrs. Gordon did criticize Jill a little less than she used to and criticize Jill's brothers more, but she pretty much reverted to her old pattern. This was disappointing to Jill, but her mother's behavior toward her remained a little better. Jill also felt relatively free of guilt, for the first time in her life, when she didn't dote on her mother and stay in daily contact with her. Jill realized how her mother was and that it would always be difficult for Jill to deal with her. Jill felt all right about having less frequent contact and less resentment toward her mother. She once said to her therapist that she felt as though she had taken the "kick me" sign off of her back and that her self-esteem had never been higher.

The approach Don took with his Dad was very simple. Don treated him in the same way we suggested with the chronic complainer in Chapter 4. He not only agreed with his father's negative evaluations of events, people, and their motives, but he also took these opinions in a more negative direction. Instead of trying to avoid topics he knew his father loved to complain about, he brought them up.

As you might expect, Don's father didn't change a whole lot. He remained a negative, pessimistic person. However, Don felt a great relief once he stopped making it his impossible mission to cheer his father up. He still limited the amount of time he spent at his father's house, because he didn't want all that negativity in his life on a regular basis. Like Jill, though, he felt a lot less guilty when he decided not to visit.

It may be hard to see how the strategies employed by Don and Jill could be called giving up power, since they never really had any control over their parents. What they actually did was give up the verbal struggle for power. In both of their situations, the struggle was a futile and hopeless one. Once they stopped banging their heads against walls, they felt much less frustrated, which allowed them to deal in a more relaxed, less defensive way with their parents.

They also managed to encourage a *slight* decrease in the controlling, criticizing, and/or negative behaviors of their parents that were problematic for themselves. In many cases, a greater change than that which happened in this example occurs. Nevertheless, a small change is much better than an escalation of the struggle, and for Don and Jill this represented the first time either of them had had any success in dealing with their parents' behaviors.

Another benefit Don and Jill derived from giving up power was that their interactions with their parents seemed more like a game than hard-core, serious reality. What they did was no more a game nor any less real than the ineffective methods they used before, but by taking the situations a little less seriously and withdrawing from the power struggle, they changed the feeling tone around their dealings with their parents. That is, they lightened up and felt less desperate and stressed out. It is much easier to cope flexibly with a situation when you feel relaxed than it is when you are feeling pressured.

All the strategies outlined in this chapter involve readily accepting the one-down position (see Chapter 5) as opposed to struggling for power. In addition to lightening up the mood in a previously conflictual situation and preventing escalation of a battle for control, use of these ideas can also produce the beneficial side effect of allowing people to see your side of an issue by not forcing it down their throats. Let's conclude this chapter with an example that illustrates how this can occur.

Gary was thirty-six years old when he entered therapy. He was married with two young children and had been having problems with his family. When Gary was growing up, his mother had been a verbally and physically abusive alcoholic. She went from boyfriend to boyfriend and did little to take care of her children. Gary, as the oldest child, assumed a lot of the responsibility for raising his younger siblings. Money was usually tight, and the family moved yearly, often due to being evicted for nonpayment of rent.

When Gary reached his early twenties, his mother stopped drinking and married a nice man. The family marvelled at the turnaround she had made. However, Gary saw a different side of her. She borrowed money from him, which he couldn't easily afford to lend, and didn't pay it back. She made plans with Gary and his wife and would fail to show up. This irritated Gary, but it didn't make him truly angry until years later, when she began disappointing his children. She promised them gifts and visits and then wouldn't come through. In addition to her old, annoying habits, she began to give Gary and his wife advice and criticism about their childrearing techniques. This really infuriated Gary when he remembered what a poor mother she had been. When he brought up his own childhood, she either didn't remember things unflattering to her, or called him a liar.

Finally, Gary decided to sever contact with his mother. He stopped talking to her and his family no longer spent any time with her. His mother complained about this to all her relatives. Gary began getting calls from his aunts, uncles, and cousins. The conversations went something like this:

AUNT: "So, Gary, I hear you didn't call your mother on Mother's Day, or even send her a card."

GARY: "I've told you before, I've had it with that woman. She hasn't changed. She's still selfish, irresponsible, and dishonest. She's a lousy mother and a worse grandmother."

AUNT: "Oh, Gary, why do you still hold a grudge? She's an old woman who just wants some time with her grandchildren before she dies. I'm really disappointed in you."

GARY: "Goddamn it! She's got you buffaloed too. She's not a frail old woman. She's a lying manipulative pain in the butt, who just likes to stir up trouble."

AUNT: "I must say that I didn't know how vindictive you could be. You were always such a nice, kind boy."

As Gary had more and more conversations similar to this with his relatives, he got increasingly frustrated. He felt he needed to stick with his decision not to deal with his mother, but he couldn't believe that everyone was taking her side and making him out to be the bad guy. After talking with his therapist about agreeing in words, but not necessarily changing his actions, he took a new tack. He developed his own strategy, which he called, "I'm the jerk."

AUNT: "Your mother tells me you're still being mean to her. I suppose you're going to tell me it's all her fault."

GARY: "No, I've got to admit I'm the jerk. I'm holding a grudge and being unreasonable. I know I ought to forgive and forget, but I guess I'm just a stubborn guy."

AUNT: "Well . . . um . . . O.K. How are your boys doing?"

Gary was pleased with the results immediately. Even though he was admitting to being "the jerk," he felt better about himself. He spent less time defending himself and trying to convince everyone his mother was really at fault. He got less upset and his relatives found themselves at a loss for things to say on the subject. Gary said to his therapist one day, "This, 'I'm the jerk' stuff is great. I'm really enjoying it." He then related a recent telephone call he had received from his aunt.

AUNT: "Your mother called today. That woman is getting on my nerves. She started complaining about you and I got tired of hearing about it. When I wouldn't feel sorry for her or bad-mouth you, she turned on me. She told me I had always been jealous of her and that I never missed a chance to put her down. I swear, that woman is crazy."

GARY: "Don't be too hard on her."

AUNT: "Are you kidding? I'm being easy on her. If I were you, I wouldn't have anything to do with her either."

Chapter 9

Staying Off the Defensive

How many times have you found yourself explaining in great detail your reasons for doing something, only to wonder later on, "Why did I feel I had to justify what I did?" Sometimes the explanation comes in response to extensive questioning by another person. Other times it is freely volunteered. In this chapter we will look at situations in which explaining, defending, and/or justifying become problems in a relationship because one person regularly gets *manipulated*, becomes *ineffective*, or feels *inferior*.

Lucy found herself manipulated by her husband, Roger. He accused her incessantly of a variety of sins: infidelity, cruelty, selfishness. Lucy attempted to answer each of Roger's accusations honestly, regardless of their lack of merit. Consequently, she found herself on the defensive a great deal of the time. Meanwhile, Roger was actually doing most of what he accused Lucy of, but his constant attacks on Lucy and her futile attempts to defend herself kept the focus off of him. In this case, Roger's best defense was a good offense.

In Joan's case, she rendered herself ineffective as a parent by explaining too much. Her twelve-year-old daughter, Patty, was a terror. She broke all the rules Joan set and then demanded to know why she was being punished. Trying to be a good and reasonable parent, Joan did her best to explain the reasons for her actions. Patty just argued with Joan's explanations and often either weaseled her way out of punishments, or left Joan feeling guilty and demoralized.

Alison and Lynn were business partners. Lynn routinely questioned Alison regarding how she handled her end of the business and criticized her decisions or offered unsolicited advice. In response, Alison justified her decisions and vigorously defended herself and her abilities. Yet, even though she started out in the business confident of her skills, she began to feel unsure of herself and inferior to Lynn.

These examples have in common relationships in which one person's defensiveness or eagerness to explain is not helpful for that person and the relationship. As the examples demonstrate, a wide variety of relationships are susceptible to this kind of problem: husband and wife, parent and child, colleague and colleague, friend and friend.

As in the situations described in Chapters 5 and 8, power is a key issue, whereby the person doing the explaining gives up a great deal of power. In trying to conceptualize this problem of power, it is helpful to think of who owes an explanation to whom in a given relationship. Generally, where there is a realistic discrepancy in power, the person with less power will often be obligated to explain him- or herself. For instance, if asked, an employee owes a boss an explanation, and a child owes one to a parent. However, a spouse doesn't owe one to a spouse (although he may choose to give one), and a friend doesn't owe one to a friend.

This last point may be a little confusing. A spouse does not owe a spouse an explanation in the sense that a child owes one to a parent. The parent has the power to punish the child if an explanation is absent or unacceptable. Spouses or friends are, theoretically, equals. One does not have the power or the right to punish the other (not that it doesn't happen anyway in power-discrepant relationships). It may be the kind and responsible thing to do to explain in an ambiguous situation, but an explanation can be effectively demanded only by someone in power.

The examples showed two situations in which one member of a pair of equals (Lucy and Roger, and Alison and Lynn) took control by keeping the other on the defensive. In the third example (Joan and Patty) the parent–child power relationship was reversed, or at least confused, by Joan's willingness to overexplain to her child. We will explore how the person who has given up power through defensiveness can restore equality, or a more appropriate distribution of power.

Let us first look at what people do when they take the defensive. When people *explain*, they describe motives for and reasoning behind certain actions. *Justification* involves pointing out the reasons that a course of action was the correct or proper one. *Defending* is justification that occurs when an "attack" or hostile questioning is perceived. Occasionally, this pattern involves *apologizing*, which is an admission of wrongdoing accompanied by an expression of regret for doing so.

There is, of course, nothing wrong with any of these activities done in proper measure in appropriate circumstances. However, in many relationships one person does the lion's share of explaining, defending, and so forth. The explanations and justifications become overly long, and the defensiveness is present in the absence of an "attack" or accusation. Apologizing can be done profusely and without any transgression having been committed.

In such relationships, the person not on the defensive usually spends a great deal of time on the offensive. Offense can take the form of relentless questioning, frequent accusations, criticism of a wide range of behaviors, or advice on how to do just about everything. In other cases, the person on the defensive puts him- or herself in a defensive position, with little help from the other person. Some people are hypersensitive and perceive many ambiguous signals as slights or affronts. Others are very guilty and explain, defend, or apologize long before an accusation of any kind is made.

As we have discussed previously, from a systems perspective it is irrelevant who "causes" the problem. One person might be overly accusatory, the other might be unusually guilty, or both could fall somewhere in between. Regardless, the effects on the person who routinely takes the defensive role are predictable. First of all, that person gives up a great deal of power and becomes vulnerable to manipulation and a decrease in self-confidence and self-esteem. In addition, the focus is on the person who is doing the defending or explaining. That person's behavior is subject to constant, detailed scrutiny, while the other's is not (for example, Lucy and Roger).

It is difficult to describe the general strategy for a defensive person dealing with this situation, since it is not so much a matter of doing something as it is *not* doing a few things. It involves *not* explaining, *not* justifying, *not* defending, and *not* apologizing. Examples of this type of strategy were presented in the Chapter 4 section on lying and the Chapter 5 section on dealing with a dependent but critical partner.

Not responding in ways you have been previously interrupts the old pattern and prevents the imbalance of power and unequal focus. In a relationship that is out of balance, explaining or defending implies that the other person has power and is in control and deserves, or is owed, an explanation whenever it is requested. This becomes reminiscent of the question, "When did you stop beating your wife?" No matter how you answer, you lose. Sometimes the best option is not to answer, or not to volunteer an explanation, justification, or defense.

Unfortunately, it is difficult for many people to just remain silent in situations in which they previously were actively on the defensive. Possible responses or arguments run through their heads and create more and more discomfort, unless other action is taken. Therefore, this strategy of not doing often needs to be accompanied by other, more active approaches. Giving a simple, one-sentence explanation and simply repeating it if pressured is a helpful, straightforward approach. Another useful way to respond to pressure or badgering is to leave the situation. You are not running away when the other person refuses to respect your refusal to take a defensive position. Agreeing verbally without complying behaviorally (see Chapter 8) is also appropriate. With a child who constantly questions his or her parents, appropriate discipline without much explanation can be more effective.

Basically, all these strategies are offshoots of not allowing the other person to set the agenda and put you on the defensive. Since the basic tenet of this general strategy is very simple, it needs relatively little explanation. Demonstration is probably a lot more helpful, so we will expand on the three examples mentioned earlier in this chapter in order to illustrate ways this situation can arise and be handled in very different types of relationships.

Avoiding Ineffectiveness

It is natural and expected of children to test limits and see what they can get away with. And as the child approaches adolescence this behavior becomes even more likely. What Joan had been experiencing with Patty, however, fell well outside the limits of "normal" limit testing. Since she was born, Patty had been a difficult child. She was thought to be colicky as a baby since she seldom slept and cried constantly. As a very active and inquisitive preschooler, she kept Joan busy trying to keep up with her. A younger sister came along when Patty was three and multiplied Joan's management problems with Patty. It didn't help that Joan's husband would not get involved, to any great extent, in child care, and that they divorced when Patty was eight.

In elementary school, Patty was labeled "hyperactive" and was placed on medication. It helped somewhat, but Patty developed side effects and had to be taken off of it. Gradually, Patty acclimated herself to school (she was in special "behaviorally handicapped" classes) and was able to behave well enough to get her work done and be promoted every year.

At home, Jean became increasingly frustrated. She set reasonable limits on Patty and tried to be as flexible as she could in order to meet Patty's special needs. Professionals had advised her that it was important to be both consistent with rules and discipline and to explain to the child the reasons for her being disciplined. What the "experts" didn't seem to realize, from Joan's perspective, was that every fifteen minutes Patty often did something for which she could be disciplined. She did have periods when she was calm and well behaved, but just as often she was out of control, constantly doing something and getting into things she shouldn't get into. She blasted the stereo and always had the television on; and when she couldn't find anything else to amuse her, she picked on her little sister until her sister screamed or cried. Outside the home, she missed curfew, got into fights with neighborhood kids, and even stole small things from her friends' houses.

Ever since she was very young, Patty hadn't seemed to respond well to rewards and punishments. She made the same mistakes over and over again even if the consequences turned out to be unpleasant for her. As she got older, she also learned to question every punishment that was handed out: "Why do I have to be home by six o'clock?" "It's not fair. Debby never has to do the dishes," "Why do I have to stay in my room?" "You're just doing this because you hate me."

It was very important to Joan to be a good mother. This was even more true since she and her husband had divorced; she still felt guilty about this and its possible effects on the children. So she tried as hard as she could to take the time to answer all of Patty's questions and to respond to all of her criticisms. However, between trying to control Patty and explaining and defending her actions, Joan felt completely burned out. She had little patience and found herself shouting at Patty with relatively little provocation. Also, out of frustration and guilt (Patty's accusations played into some of Joan's own concerns about her parenting skills), Joan began to remove or lighten punishments, or sabotage her own efforts by "making it up" to Patty immediately after a fight.

Joan sought therapy because she was afraid she was having a nervous breakdown. Not only were things becoming unbearable at home, but she was also sleeping poorly, having trouble at work, and fighting with her boyfriend. Joan's therapist knew this would be a challenging situation since Patty was a difficult child who would probably always be a challenge for Joan (or any parent).

The initial focus of therapy was to get Joan to stop explaining things to Patty in great detail. Patty wasn't learning from these discussions; she was just finding loopholes in Joan's reasoning, which she tried to use to reduce her consequences. In addition, Joan was just getting more and more frustrated as her attempts to reason with Patty failed repeatedly. It was suggested to Joan that she let as many things slide as possible with Patty and that she save her energy for more important issues. When punishment was necessary, Joan was encouraged to implement it with an absolute minimum of explanation.

Joan understood the new strategy and was eager to use it. But it turned out to be more difficult than she expected. At first, her own guilt led her to begin explaining even when she had resolved not to. Then, as she overcame that tendency, she found Patty to be relentless in her attempts to either get Joan to explain, or engage her in an argument. Joan began to use the "agree, but don't comply" strategy outlined in Chapter 8.

PATTY: "You're not being fair. I was only twenty minutes late, and it wasn't my fault anyway."

JEAN: "You're right. I am being unfair, and I'm probably too strict. Regardless, you still get no TV tonight."

This strategy didn't exactly stop Patty in her tracks, but it did slow her down a little. More importantly, it kept Joan from escalating the argument on her side, and she got much less frustrated.

Once she was better able to handle Patty, Joan was able to look past her guilt and realize that Patty was too much for one person to handle. So she approached her ex-husband and got him more involved with Patty. He had been willing to help for some time, but Joan had been reluctant since he was somewhat irresponsible and temperamental. She finally realized that she wasn't being all that effective with Patty, and he probably couldn't do much worse.

In response to Joan's changes, Patty became noticeably less mouthy and slightly better behaved. To Joan's great surprise, Patty behaved very well with her father. His quick temper and relative irresponsibility seemed to bring out a calmer, more reasonable side of Patty. Joan calmed down a great deal herself once she stopped trying to convince Patty of the wisdom of her disciplinary strategies. She also used the time when Patty was with her father to do some things with her younger daughter and for herself. Life with Patty was still challenging and not easy, but Joan felt much more in control of herself and more confident in her ability to handle her.

In this example, Joan did a good job of getting off the defensive and managed to regain control of a situation in which she had become increasingly ineffective in her role as a parent. She combined not explaining with appropriate discipline, verbal agreement without behavioral compliance, and withdrawing from the situation by getting her ex-husband more involved. Patty did not have to do a 180 degree turnaround in order for Joan to feel considerably better. Some of the changes that occurred were not what Joan or her therapist would have predicted. Nevertheless, Joan's getting off the defensive set those changes in motion and created a positive ripple that helped Joan, Patty, and Joan's ex-husband, who got a lot closer to his daughter and felt like a competent parent for the first time.

Avoiding Inferiority

Before going into business together, Alison and Lynn were friends—not extremely close, but friends. On a few occasions they talked about how tired they were of working for other people, and they shared fantasies with each other about opening their own businesses. After a number of these conversations, they began to take themselves more seriously. Both women had money to invest and had some business experience. Neither woman felt comfortable going into business totally on her own, so they decided to look into going into business together. Alison had researched the idea of opening a gourmet catering business, and Lynn had scouted locations for a boutique.

They decided to pool their resources and operate both businesses jointly. Alison would have primary responsibility for the catering business, and Lynn would operate the boutique. It certainly would have been simpler for each to operate her own business independently, but they felt they could offer each other emotional support, and that neither of them would have to be totally dependent on the success of just one enterprise.

One thing Alison admired about Lynn was her confidence. She was an assertive, take-charge kind of person. Alison, who was very capable, but went with the flow more, thought Lynn's attitude would be a good model for her and good for the business.

It took both businesses a while to get on their feet, but after a few years both were profitable and growing. On a personal level, however, things had become somewhat strained. Lynn's take-charge attitude sometimes appeared to extend to a need to take charge of Alison's side of the business. Lynn's expertise was not in the catering area, but she had a lot of suggestions for Alison on how to improve that aspect of the business. At first, Alison was glad to have Lynn interested and involved, but as time passed Alison's feelings changed. Lynn continued to give Alison advice, which was hardly ever requested. Nor did Lynn leave it at that. She insisted on knowing every aspect of what was going on at all times in the catering business, and she was increasingly critical of Alison in spite of the fact that Alison's catering service was doing somewhat better than Lynn's boutique. Also, Lynn was unhappy with some of the employees Alison had hired and often took it upon herself to give orders to Alison's staff. When Alison disagreed with any of Lynn's suggestions, Lynn engaged Alison in lengthy arguments.

Alison started to feel that Lynn saw herself as the boss and Alison as her assistant. Even though Alison had been confident of her business-related abilities when they entered their partnership, she had trouble dealing with aggressive people and tended to feel a little inferior to people who obviously thought that they were smarter or more skilled than those around them. Consequently, Alison felt very uncomfortable as Lynn's assertiveness began to look more and more like aggressiveness and controlling. She was particularly irked by the fact that Lynn clearly discouraged her from becoming at all involved in what was going on at the boutique.

In response, Alison became very defensive and responded to Lynn's questions and criticisms with lengthy rationales or thinly veiled anger. As Alison got more and more angry, she also felt a great deal of guilt about her anger. She frequently apologized for any anger expressed to Lynn, even if it had been obviously provoked. At one point, when Alison had been having some problems with her marriage, she let Lynn know that her personal problems were making her a little less patient at work. Lynn expressed concern, but also started to question Alison's judgment, saying, "Are you sure your problems with Scott aren't interfering with your ability to run the business?"

The more Alison defended herself, the less confident she felt. She questioned her own judgment in ways she had not done before, and she wondered if she was really pulling her own weight in the business. Alison was depressed, confused, and stressed out when she came in for counseling.

Conversations with her therapist helped Alison to realize how she contributed to the problems with Lynn. The assertiveness that Alison admired in Lynn was something Alison found lacking in herself. Also, she hated to disappoint people and often felt she was disappointing Lynn. As she grew frustrated with her inability to get Lynn to back off, she got angry. She had been raised to believe that anger was not an acceptable feeling for a woman to have. Even though she no longer consciously believed that, she still automatically felt guilty when she felt angry. Understanding these issues helped Alison to see how her problems with Lynn had developed and how she was giving up a lot of power in her relationship with Lynn by asserting a defensive posture.

The strategy Alison and her therapist developed to help her cope more effectively with Lynn involved a combination of getting off the defensive and assertiveness. Alison learned to recognize when she was defensive by paying closer attention to how she felt emotionally (she felt anxious) and physically (she had tense muscles, eye strain, and shallow breathing) interacting with Lynn. As soon as she became aware of defensiveness, she took a minute to take a few slow, timed breaths and collect herself. If she decided at that time that Lynn's question or concern was a legitimate one, she gave a brief, one-sentence explanation. If pressed, she didn't elaborate. If pressed harder, she walked away.

On the other hand, if she believed Lynn's question to be inappropriate or disrespectful to her, Alison expressed this belief and how it made her feel. On such occasions, Lynn's questions went unanswered and her criticisms were not directly responded to. Alison also became more assertive in initiating conversations about more clearly delineating areas of responsibility and making sure that they applied to both partners.

Lynn's initial response to Alison's changed behavior was to escalate her questioning and criticism. But, as Alison showed that she was going to stick to her guns, Lynn did begin to back off, and she learned to respect the limits Alison set. As these changes proceeded, Alison felt more confident and in control of herself. Interestingly, not long after Alison concluded her therapy, the women mutually agreed to go their separate ways. Both businesses were doing well, and both women felt the need for more autonomy. Alison was pleased that they were able to part on good terms.

This case illustrates a couple of important points. One is the way in which staying off the defensive and assertiveness can be combined. Alison thought she was already being assertive when she stood up for herself with Lynn. That was not the case. By letting Lynn set the agenda and responding with lengthy defenses of her position, Alison was reactive and seldom in control of the direction of the interaction. By responding to Lynn's agenda only when she felt it was appropriate and proactively setting her own agenda more often, Alison was better able to act assertively in her own best interest. She couldn't do that until she first got her own defensiveness under control.

The second point brought out by this example is that the initial response to a change is often a worsening of the problem.

The person who does not initiate the change (Lynn, in this case) tends to do more of whatever he or she was doing prior to the change in an effort to restore the status quo. The person who decides to change how he or she is handling a situation needs to be prepared for this initial worsening of the problem. This worsening is predictable and usually temporary.

Avoiding Manipulation

Marriage is frequently described as being a matter of give-and-take, and to a large extent that is true. Seldom does a 50–50 arrangement work out in which each person both gives and takes half the time, but an important part of an intimate relationship is the ability of the partners to work out ways to balance sacrifice and gratification. Some people, however, have a very difficult time giving in or sacrificing. They have difficulty in delaying gratification, being patient, and seeing other people's points of view. People like this are often described as spoiled, selfish, or controlling.

For some reason, therapists often discover situations in which a person like the one just described is in a relationship with someone who is more than willing to give more than he or she takes. It is not clear whether the relatively unselfish person entered the relationship that way, or adjusted to the relationship, in which his or her partner takes significantly more, by becoming more giving. Regardless, many relationship systems function quite well until the giving partner becomes distressed with the lack of reciprocity in the relationship. Then, it is usually the more giving partner who comes in for help.

Lucy found herself in such a situation, although she didn't always perceive it that way. She and Roger met while they were in high school and, shortly after they graduated, got married because she was pregnant. Roger had always been somewhat demanding and critical, but Lucy had adjusted to that during their forty-two years of marriage. The couple didn't have too many friends because Roger insisted on having things his way—where they went, who drove, what route the driver took—and made scenes when he couldn't. Lucy was used to this as well. She had her own friends and spent time with them while Roger was at work.

Things seemed to get out of control for Lucy after Roger retired. They both enjoyed dancing to country and western music and had even entered a couple of competitions. Once Roger retired, he wanted to pursue this interest more seriously. However, he was a more skilled dancer than Lucy. So he decided it would be a good idea for him to find a different dance partner with whom he could enter into more contests. Lucy did not object.

It did not take Roger long to find a partner. She turned out to be an attractive divorced woman about twenty years Roger's junior. At first they spent a lot of time practicing and competing. During this time, Lucy also found a dance partner of her own—with Roger's permission. He was a married man about her age. They danced together one or two nights a week, always where Roger was competing or practicing.

Roger began spending more and more time with his new dance partner. They went to lunch together and sometimes went to movies or sporting events together. Lucy's friends and children, and even Roger's siblings, suggested he was having an affair. Lucy did not believe that he was.

Meanwhile, she also became more friendly with her dance partner. They talked on the phone occasionally and Lucy spent time with him and his wife. Then, Roger began making accusations about Lucy and her dance partner. He told her he believed she was having an affair, calling her a slut, a tramp, and a liar. He displayed emotional outbursts in front of family and friends, yelling at Lucy, calling her names, and generally degrading her. On rare occasions, she stood up to him and pointed out that he was spending more time alone with his dance partner than she was with hers. He ignored her statements, or called them a lame attempt to cover up her own infidelity. Finally, one night he accosted Lucy's dance partner in a crowded bar. Roger grabbed him by the shirt and threatened to kill him if he came near Lucy again.

He then screamed at Lucy while they were still in front of a crowd and told her she wasn't allowed to go dancing anymore since he couldn't trust her to "keep [her] pants on."

Prior to this time, when they were alone and he was accusing her, she explained her actions and defended her innocence in great detail. She apologized to him if what she did looked suspicious to him, and she did all she could to keep her contact with her dance partner as public and as tame as possible. When she came in for therapy, she was angry at him for humiliating her in public, but felt she probably was at fault in some way. She was also very confused and anxious because he had moved out and was living alone in an apartment.

Lucy had spent so much time on the defensive during her relationship with Roger that she did not see his involvement with the dance partner as particularly out of the ordinary. She did know that things had escalated to the point at which she could no longer handle them. As Lucy described the situation to her therapist, she was reluctant to say anything at all critical about Roger and said that she always went to great lengths to defend him when anyone else criticized him. However, once he moved out, many different people began to tell her that they had barely tolerated him for years only because they liked her so much. Two of Lucy and Roger's grown children and Roger's sister called Lucy's therapist to underscore how badly Roger had always treated Lucy and how much worse his behavior had gotten lately.

The strategy Lucy and her therapist devised was very simple. She was to try to stop defending herself and apologizing when Roger verbally assaulted her. Instead, she was to pay attention to what he was saying in order to determine if it sounded reasonable to her. She decided to limit her contact with Roger, at first, to phone calls. In that way, if he became too abusive she could hang up.

Initially, it was very difficult for Lucy not to speak at length in her own defense. As she got better at not doing this, she was able to step back and look at what Roger was saying from a different perspective. She had prevented herself from doing that by keeping her mind so focused on explaining her own position that she never thought to question Roger's.

She soon realized that Roger's accusations were completely unreasonable, and that he showed no respect for her in the way he expressed them. On the other hand, he didn't make light of the fact that he still spent a lot of time with his dance partner, including time spent alone with her in his apartment. He didn't bother to explain further, only saying that, unlike Lucy, his dance partner was good to him and honest with him.

Lucy gradually noticed that her guilt was being replaced with anger and resentment. She started to see Roger's actions as selfish, manipulative, and often irrational. She felt foolish for putting up with him for as long as she had and was determined not to give in to her previous way of responding to him any longer.

It didn't take long for Lucy to get the opportunity to test that determination. Roger called her one day and told her he was ready to give her another chance, even though she probably didn't deserve it. He and his dance partner had had a falling out and he was willing to come back home. However, Lucy would be "on probation," and if she reverted to her old form, he would leave again.

Lucy let him know, somewhat angrily, that she wasn't sure she wanted him back. She did know she didn't want him back right away and that his terms were unacceptable. If he wanted to return, he would have to apologize to her and show her that he would treat her with more respect. He was shocked and then enraged. When he began to yell and curse at her, she hung up the phone and left to visit her son.

Lucy surprised herself, her husband, her family, and her therapist with the dramatic reversal of her behavior in response to Roger. She had moments of uncertainty, but her anger gave her the strength to stand her ground. When she last saw her therapist, she and Roger were still estranged, and he showed no signs of changing his behavior. Lucy was prepared to divorce him if she needed to and felt stronger and better about herself than she had in a long time.

Hopefully, the examples just presented have demonstrated the wide variety of relationships to which "staying off the defensive" can be applied. The general idea behind this type of strategy is that as one stops pouring one's energy into trying to explain one's position, behavior, or motives, one can get a clearer perspective on the relationship pattern and establish equal footing, rather than an inferior position, with the other. This strategy is often used prior to the implementation of other change strategies described elsewhere in this book, since it serves to break old patterns and allow a person to step back and collect him- or herself before employing more active changes in behavior. In other words, this helps one to stop, observe, and think before pressing ahead in more productive ways.

Chapter 10
Creative Interpretation

An old saying suggests that an optimist is a person who says of a bottle that it is half full, while a pessimist laments that it is half empty; yet both are describing the same bottle and the same amount of liquid. The difference, of course, lies in their different views of the same reality; neither view is more correct than the other. Both descriptions accurately account for the facts of the situation: a container of liquid holding fifty percent of its capacity.

Whether the bottle is seen as half full or half empty has nothing to do with the bottle or the objective facts as such, but with the *interpretation* of the bottle and those objective facts.[42] The interpretation of the facts speaks of not only things like the bottle, but also of interpersonal events and our relationships.

Recall our discussion of constructivism (how we construct reality) in Chapter 2 and the notion of multiple truths in Chapter 3. We suggested that the ascription of meaning occurs in relationships continuously through ongoing communication. We also suggested that there is usually no one right way or absolute truth, particularly regarding relationship difficulties. There are multiple truths or realities that can be asserted to accurately describe the facts of a given situation. When we are stuck in a problem, we generally pick a particular way of viewing the problem, and we get locked into whatever solution attempts flow from our view. That view or the meaning we attribute to the problem situation may not only prevent problem resolution, but may also actually *account for* our distress.[43]

Gary found himself very distressed by Anita's propensity to work a lot of hours. He expressed his concerns openly, but Anita didn't change and felt as if Gary didn't understand the difficulties inherent to success in a competitive business environment. Gary complained, warned Anita about the health implications of over-work, and admonished her for neglecting their child. Gary ulti-mately concluded that Anita loved her job more than him or her family.

Greg was at the end of his rope with his sixteen-year-old son, Paul. Paul was an underachiever who jumped at every opportun-ity to argue with his teachers and the vice principal, who was in charge of discipline. The results were consistent: arguing led to detentions, in-school suspensions, and gradually longer periods of out-of-school suspensions. Paul's grades spiraled downward. Greg punished Paul in every conceivable way. Greg also con-tinually lectured Paul about the ultimately self-defeating nature of his behavior. Greg believed that the school officials were only doing their job and that Paul needed to accept their authority, like it or not. Greg also felt quite miserable; Paul seemed to feel only hostility.

Linda was worried sick about her best friend, Mandy, who had recently divorced herself from a very unsatisfactory marriage. Linda was concerned because Mandy often appeared unhappy and complained of sadness and loneliness. Linda attempted to help Mandy by suggesting things to do and inviting her participa-tion in singles activities with her. Linda was also very supportive and spent much of her free time consoling Mandy. It seemed that Mandy always had a reason not to participate or do anything outside of working and grocery shopping. Linda, although con-tinuing her support, began to feel annoyed as well as concerned. Linda believed that Mandy needed to stop feeling sorry for her-self, accept her situation, and start doing something about it.

These examples share a relationship in which one person is attempting to change the other based upon a particular view of reality or belief about the problem under concern. The particular view of reality, in each case, is leading to continued unsuccessful solution attempts. Remember that any way of describing the world represents but a single view or perspective, although some perspectives may be more accurate or helpful than others. Regardless, though, a given view provides just *one* way—not *the* way—of describing the world and, therefore, limits problem solving to that one specific description.

The general strategy of creative interpretation directly challenges the notion that there is only one way of perceiving a given situation. Creative interpretation entails perceiving a problem circumstance in an entirely different light and verbalizing your new perceptions to the other person involved. This strategy often involves creatively interpreting *negative* situations that you would like to see changed as *positive* or beneficial for you or the other person.[44] It also involves redefining a given situation in such a way that it acquires a totally different meaning without changing the facts of the situation (remember the half-full/half-empty bottle).[45]

Examples of creative interpretation were offered in Chapter 4 regarding a noncommunicative spouse, and in Chapter 5 regarding a critical, but dependent partner. In Chapter 4 we suggested, "interpret the silence of your partner in a positive way." This strategy removes pressure, negates possible power struggles, and to the silence attributes a new meaning that may allow different problem-solving action by all involved. In Chapter 5, we suggested, "interpret the message the person is giving you in a way that allows you to stop receiving the criticism for attempting to help." Similarly, this strategy changes the meaning of the criticism, which permits different actions by both individuals.

Interpreting negative situations in positive ways may sound off base, but it isn't as difficult as you may suspect. Problems are rarely white or black: Problems are not *all* bad, and everything will not be *all* good when the problem is gone. There are usually several shades of gray to each problem, including both positive and negative features or both advantages and disadvantages. Take, for example, a promotion at work, which is typically considered an overwhelmingly positive situation. A promotion may mean a better salary, more prestige, and another career goal accomplished. It may also mean more hours, more responsibility, and less time spent with family and friends. Problems and events in relationships can similarly be described in terms of their advantages and disadvantages. Even the most negative of circumstances can be analyzed and determined to contain some benefit for someone involved in the problem.

Problems can also be redefined in many ways. Consider the different implications of the following sample of brief redefinitions:

Arguing: sharing emotional intensity
Controlling: structuring one's environment, taking charge
Defiance: having one's own way of doing things
Immaturity: aggressive exploration
Impulsiveness: creative spontaneity
Reclusiveness, withdrawn: introspection, contemplation, taking care of oneself
Passivity: ability to accept things as they are
Rigidity: steadfast purpose

Each of the above negative labels is redefined in ways that address the positive side of the behavior. The redefinitions may permit the consideration of solutions that the original definitions do not.

Thinking of the advantages and disadvantages of problems as well as other definitions that fit the facts are simply the useful *relabeling* of the problem. People often interpret their own behavior or that of others in ways that make for continuing difficulties. If we can redefine the meaning attributed to a problem behavior, this itself may have a powerful effect on attitudes, responses, and ultimately the relationship. If the meaning attributed to the troubling situation is altered, then the consequences of the situation will change as well.

Creative interpretation attempts to change your partner's, child's, or friend's subjective experience of the given problem in such a way that the original motivations and beliefs of the person now lead toward quite different behavior.[46] The new interpretation provides a different way of thinking, feeling, and acting about the issue under concern. Creative interpretation emphasizes that what we say is not necessarily what reality *really* is; words do not unqualifyingly represent a concrete reality, because words have different meanings for different people. How we describe it affects how we behave in a given circumstance. Different descriptions allow for alternative and, perhaps, more useful or relationship enhancing solutions.

If this seems nonsensical, don't worry. It will make more sense as we discuss the application of creative interpretation in the earlier examples. There are three types of creative interpretation: (1) the advantages of the problem for you, (2) redefinition of the problem,[47] and (3) the disadvantages of changing the problem for the other person.[48]

Advantages of the Problem

Gary and Anita were in their late thirties and in their second marriage. An ongoing problem between them originated almost from day one of their four-year relationship, namely, Anita's drive for career success and devotion to her job. She was a district sales manager of a large computer company and was still on her way up. Gary reluctantly accepted her ambition, but felt rejected from time to time. He was an accountant in a small firm and described himself as a person who derives greater pleasure from life outside of his job. What Gary enjoyed most was spending time with Anita and their baby son.

The recent birth of their son brought the issue of Anita's working habits to a head (remember the stages of the family life cycle). Gary had secretly hoped that the pregnancy and the baby would change Anita, making it more difficult for her to work long hours. Gary fantasized about Anita taking a leave of absence after the baby was born and ultimately deciding to take a job that allowed for a more reasonable work week. In his most "delusional" state, he imagined Anita working part time so she could be home with baby even more. But the reality was that Anita continued her working patterns. She enjoyed a trouble-free pregnancy and continued to work up to the day she gave birth. She stayed at home for a month, but worked on her computer every day. Then, she returned to work and resumed her regular schedule.

Gary frequently brought up the work issue, but Anita was quick to point out to him that he knew she was invested in her career before he married her, and that she had been very explicit in telling him that her career broke up her first marriage. Gary, over time, grew more and more resentful and began regularly referring to Anita sarcastically as "Ms. Workaholic." Although he was sincerely concerned about her health and the effects of her work on the relationship, what generally came across was his anger. He began to routinely criticize Anita for her misguided priorities.

In defense to Gary's barrage of hostility and guilt induction, Anita said again and again that he didn't understand what it was like to succeed in the competitive environment in which she worked. She believed that he was insensitive to how important it was for her to meet her career goals in an all-male environment. Anita had been a ground-breaker in her company, accomplishing two firsts for her women co-workers; her last two promotions each represented the first time a woman had held such a position within the company.

Gary confirmed Anita's belief regarding his lack of sensitivity and understanding by escalating the discussion into fights. He accused her of loving her career more than him and the baby. Such a pattern of discussions leading to fights began to characterize much of their interaction, so that what little time they did have was spent fighting or was tension-filled.

Before we discuss how creative interpretation can be applied to this situation, let's consider how the nine-dot puzzle relates to Gary's perspective and his ineffective solutions. Gary's point of view was limited in that he saw only the negatives associated with Anita's work habits and envisioned that positives would only happen if her work habits changed. This view ultimately led Gary to the conclusion that Anita loved her job more than her family. Such a meaning or value attributed to his situation naturally led to distress and hostility. It also led to repeated attempts to browbeat Anita out of her work habits. These methods not only helped to perpetuate Anita's work habits, but also created tension in other areas of the relationship.

After having a particularly bad week and feeling quite hopeless about his marriage, Gary consulted a therapist. He loved Anita very much and was fearful about the possibility of their marriage failing. The therapist recognized the difficulty of the problem and believed that Gary's acceptance of at least part of the problem would benefit both him and Anita.

The therapist suggested to Gary the form of creative interpretation that looks at the advantages of the problem. This strategy is effective in situations like Gary and Anita's, in which one individual wants another to change and attempts over and over to convince the person of the ills of their ways, while the person on the receiving end tends to feel pressured and misunderstood. This method of creative interpretation involves thinking of your advantages in the situation and then verbalizing those advantages to the other person. You creatively interpret situations that you would like to see changed as actually beneficial for you in some ways. We are *not*, however, advocating lying. We are suggesting that you look at the problematic situation and brainstorm *plausible* benefits that the problem includes for you. If you cannot think of any legitimate advantages to the issue under concern, then this strategy is not for you.

A possible outcome of this strategy is that it allows us to see the advantages of the situation the way it really is, thereby changing our own self-restricting mind set and opening up other potential avenues for solution. At the very least, acceptance of the situation is promoted, which can be quite helpful in and of itself. As we will see, many other outcomes are possible.

The therapist suggested that Gary seriously consider the outright advantages of Anita's work habits and commitment to her career. At first pass, the therapist's suggestion seemed ridiculous; but as Gary thought beyond his obvious dissatisfaction with the situation, several plausible benefits emerged: (1) Gary was extremely proud of Anita's accomplishments as a ground-breaker for women's rights in a corporate environment; (2) Anita was paid very well and frequently received bonuses and free trips, enabling a very comfortable lifestyle; (3) Gary had plenty of time for himself and for socializing with friends; (4) Gary was developing a very special relationship with his son because he was his primary caregiver; (5) Anita was not looking over his shoulder and telling him what to do all of the time; and (6) Gary felt reasonably sure that Anita was working and not fooling around, which hadn't been the case with his first marriage.

Creative interpretation can enable several positive outcomes. If any power issues are involved, they are undercut, because now you are not pushing for change, but rather are conveying that you are accepting and understanding that things will stay the same. With the pressure removed, the other person now has the freedom to change by his or her own choice and determination. If the person freely changes by his or her own will, this will reflect a meaning change that will likely be enduring and not just a response to coercion. This strategy, like all the others presented in this book, represents doing something different to enable a different response in your partner, thereby interrupting the problematic patterns of interaction. Once the person you are attempting to influence is made aware that you understand there is benefit to the situation the way it is, that person can then begin to see the disadvantages. Also, once you allow yourself to see the advantages, you may feel a little better if nothing changes; at least you'll know that you are not negatively contributing to the problem because of pressure and power issues.

Gary enacted the therapist's suggestion and did not bring up the problem of Anita's work habits. When Anita opened discussion on the topic, Gary expressed one of the benefits of her work habits for him as well as how proud he was of her accomplishments. When they socialized with family and friends, Anita frequently heard Gary expressing his pride and his contentment with the life style he was living.

The overall tension surrounding the relationship significantly diminished, and the time they did spend together became enjoyable again. Anita often thanked Gary for his understanding and support. After a few months and seemingly out of the blue, Anita told Gary she had something she wanted to discuss. She said that she had been thinking a lot about her priorities lately and that she had made a decision to strive for more balance in her life. Anita said that she had been troubled for some time about the struggle between work and home commitments, but that recently she had realized that Gary and the baby were the most important aspect of her life. Anita proposed a new work schedule that would have her home by six on two nights and would include no work past two o'clock on Saturday. Gary was delighted and Anita felt good about her decision.

An important component to the changes that occurred is that Anita felt understood and that Gary accepted the importance of her work to her self-image. As we have said many times in this book, understanding the other person's frame of reference or point of view and accepting/validating it as totally justified often produces significant change in and of itself. Anita no longer needed to convince Gary about the validity of her position and, therefore, could evaluate her position independently. Gary's use of creative interpretation allowed him to stop being an impediment to Anita's reconsideration of her work and home life. His recognition and verbalization of the benefits for him enabled Anita to arrive at a new meaning that permitted her to strive for more balance between work and the home.

Redefinition of the Problem

Greg had become a single parent when his son, Paul, was seven and when his wife filed for divorce. Paul had little contact with his mother who lived in another state, where she was pursuing a graduate degree. Greg and Paul had always gotten along famously and enjoyed a very close relationship. Greg valued the ideals of self-expression and throughout Paul's childhood encouraged him to share his opinions. People often commented on the ease at which Paul conversed about a variety of topics with adults.

At age sixteen, Paul became somewhat disinterested in school and tended to slide by with B's and C's, although he was able to do much better. Greg reluctantly accepted Paul's grades and typically did not make them an issue until the grades started falling because of multiple suspensions for arguing and disrespectful behavior. Paul had particular difficulty with the vice principal in charge of discipline, Mr. Norman Q. What would usually happen was that Paul would receive a detention for some minor infraction of the rules and would attempt to protest its fairness with the teacher. Paul would then be sent to Mr. Q's office and an argument would ensue that predictably led to suspension.

Greg attempted to correct Paul with a variety of methods, largely revolving around punishment and lectures about the self-defeating nature of Paul's behavior. Paul responded that he didn't care about how self-destructive he was; nothing would make him accept the unfairness of the situation and nothing would make him buckle under to "Stormin' Norman," the "Nazi" vice principal.

Paul's grades continued to plummet as more and more suspensions added up; he was now failing in two subjects. Greg went to a conference with Mr. Q and the school counselor. Mr. Q advised Greg that the next occurrence of disrespect would result in expulsion. He also added that sometimes it takes expulsion to get to rebellious kids like Paul, because only then would he be forced to face the consequences of his disrespect for authority. Although Greg recognized that Mr. Q was only doing his job as disciplinary leader of the school, Greg felt uncomfortable with him. In spite of the fact that he couldn't quite explain why, Greg thought that Mr. Q seemed a bit too enthusiastic about Paul's expulsion and perhaps *wanted* Paul to screw up. Greg talked Mr. Q into allowing Paul to complete homework assignments while suspended. The school counselor recommended that Greg and Paul seek a therapist.

Greg came alone to see the therapist; Paul refused to attend because the idea came from the school. Paul said it was just another attempt by the "Kangaroo Court" to make him look like the guilty one. Greg's efforts at influencing him were always met by Paul's belief (meaning) system of total hostility against Mr. Q and complete defiance of anything that looked like giving in to authority.

The therapist suggested creative interpretation in the form of redefinition of the problem. Redefinition of the problem entails listening to the views, expectations, reasons, and motivations of the person you are attempting to influence and using that information to redefine the problem under concern. Based upon the idiosyncracies and motivations of the person, a redefinition can occur without changing the facts of the situation, but that leads to an entirely different solution. If the meaning of the facts is changed, the consequences of the meaning will change as well. So Greg's task was to change Paul's experience of Mr. Q's disciplinary actions in such a way that Paul's beliefs and motivation, his hostility and defiance, would lead to quite different behavior. Changing Paul's meaning attributed to Mr. Q's actions could lead to more adaptive ways for Paul to respond.

After discussing the situation with Greg, the therapist thought that maybe Paul's disdain for Mr. Q could afford a lever for change if it could be directed in a constructive way. Recalling Greg's perception of Mr. Q from the meeting, another way of looking at the facts of Paul's situation was that Mr. Q was out to get Paul either by failing him or expelling him for misconduct. Greg remembered that Mr. Q was somewhat pompous and seemed to derive some pleasure from the idea of Paul facing expulsion. It was almost as if it were a "set-up" to make Paul an example to the students and that Paul would be playing right into Mr. Q's hands if he persisted in his present course. Additional relevant information was that Paul's plight with Mr. Q had become a favorite gossip topic throughout the school. Continuing this different interpretation of the facts, it could be that the only way for Mr. Q to save face and win would be to expel Paul for questioning his authority. As long as Paul naïvely played into his hands, Paul looked like just another defiant teenager, not to be taken seriously. If Paul really wanted to make his point and demonstrate what a jerk Mr. Q really was, he would embarrass Mr. Q by succeeding academically and pursuing his grievances in a way that would force Mr. Q to take notice.

The facts of Paul's problem had not changed; Paul's arguments with Mr. Q had led to progressive disciplinary steps. Paul's contempt for Mr. Q had also not changed. The meaning attached to the situation was altered from courageously standing up to a jerk in authority (Paul's meaning) to naïvely playing into that jerk's plan to make Paul an example and save face in the school. The problem, now redefined using the beliefs and motivations of Paul, could lead to quite a different response and solution.

After Greg repeated variations of the above redefinition of the problem, Paul began doing his homework and grades improved to their previous level of B's and C's. Moreover, Paul became a constant thorn in Mr. Q's side by filing petitions against certain school rules, writing letters to the school board, and even calling local media. Paul pushed for and eventually got a student grievance procedure implemented. Greg didn't share his strategy with Mr. Q, but Mr. Q acted as if he were doing everything he could to reaffirm Greg's redefinition of the problem. Mr. Q continued to pompously engender defiance in Paul by strongly criticizing his efforts to change the rules. Paul met the criticisms with a smile and even more resolve to challenge Mr. Q, which, on many occasions, he did and won.

The redefinition, or alternative explanation of the facts, led to new problem-solving possibilities. Again, note how Greg's acceptance and validation of Paul's point of view about the principal played a key role in the success of the creative interpretation strategy. Also note that Greg was not making up the alternative explanation out of the blue. The redefinition was a plausible and credible view of the problem that was as valid as any other. The redefinition not only fit the facts of the situation, it also fit Paul's beliefs and utilized his disdain for Mr. Q in a positive way. Changing the meaning of Paul's experience allowed Paul to change what he did in response to Mr. Q and thereby enabled many new solution options.

The Disadvantages of Change

Linda and Mandy had been best friends since they started working together some ten years ago. They grew particularly close when Linda went through the illness and death of her husband. That experience created a strong bond between them that had endured many ups and downs of life. Linda had remained single after the death of her husband for about five years and was very active in various singles organizations. She dated frequently and was satisfied with her life, except for her relationship with Mandy.

Mandy had always been a source of her strength and inspiration until recently, when Mandy had finally gotten herself out of a relationship in which she had felt stuck for many years. Mandy's husband had traveled extensively throughout the marriage and had had several affairs. There had been no emotional ties between them for many years, but Mandy had felt obligated to remain married until the children left home.

The divorce was quite adversarial and it dragged on for two years. During that time, Mandy seemed to become more and more unhappy. Linda made frequent contact with Mandy and often invited her to singles activities. Mandy always declined for one reason or another. Linda was hopeful that when the divorce was final, Mandy would close the book on her marriage and start a new life for herself.

Unfortunately, Mandy seemed to get worse rather than better. Linda continued making frequent contact and encouraged Mandy at every opportunity to become involved and get active in singles organizations. As you might suspect by now, Mandy predictably declined: She was too tired, she wasn't ready for that yet, she wouldn't know how to act, the people in those places are losers, and so on.

Linda was very concerned about Mandy, but now she was getting a little annoyed and her irritation came across occasionally. One night after Mandy called complaining about her loneliness, Linda scolded her for feeling sorry for herself and admonished her for not getting out of her apartment. She lectured Mandy and suggested that she see a therapist.

After this unpleasant exchange, Linda felt terribly guilty and decided to see a therapist herself since Mandy angrily refused. Consider the nine-dot puzzle in which Linda found herself. The assumption she made or the meaning she attributed to the situation was that Mandy needed to go out and be involved with others in order to feel better. Linda's solutions flowed from that meaning. Linda encouraged and invited participation until she was blue in the face, but Mandy seemed only to feel worse. While Linda's strategy for feeling better clearly worked for her when she lost her husband, trying to influence Mandy to act similarly was not proving to be useful.

The therapist suggested creative interpretation in the form of looking for the disadvantages of changing the problem. This strategy is effective in situations where there seems to be something unacknowledged holding back the person you are attempting to influence from trying things that may be helpful. Mandy knew she felt sad and lonely and recognized that she needed to get out of her apartment, yet she avoided situations that probably would help her loneliness and feelings of sadness. It seemed that Mandy knew what would make her feel better, but was reluctant for some unknown reason to follow through with action.

This form of creative interpretation entails thinking of the disadvantages of changing the situation for the other person and verbalizing those disadvantages to him or her. You creatively interpret the change that you would like to see as possibly detrimental to the other person. Once again, we are *not* advocating lying or making up wild stories, but rather looking at the situation and brainstorming plausible drawbacks for the other person of the very change you would like to see.

Disadvantages of change directly addresses the ambivalence that people have about changing their behavior. People usually have every intention to try and change their problem (Mandy wanted to feel better), but they are quite ambivalent and may be even fearful of the loss of security or permanence involved in the change. No matter how much pain is currently experienced, the draw toward the familiar and hesitancy to confront the unknown seem always present to some degree. The "disadvantages" strategy directly addresses this ambivalence and aligns with that part of the individual that may be afraid or reluctant to change. This form of creative interpretation helps clarify the feared consequences of change in the hope of motivating the person toward action regarding the problem.

The therapist suggested that Linda seriously consider the legitimate disadvantages of Mandy's getting involved in the singles club. Although it seemed ludicrous at first, Linda hung in there and several potential disadvantages emerged: (1) Mandy may not have worked through her divorce completely and would be setting herself up for failure; (2) Mandy may find that men are not as attracted to her as she had thought, and she may be rejected; (3) Mandy may find that men are very attracted to her and feel overwhelmed; (4) in her vulnerable state, she may meet someone special and be hurt deeply if their relationship didn't work, which could make her even more depressed than she is now; and (5) even if things went well for her in a new relationship, there would be lots of work and effort required to maintain it.

Several positive outcomes can occur from this form of creative interpretation. By aligning with the side of the person that is afraid of change, you undercut any power issues if there are any. You are no longer saying, "You must change," but rather, "I understand why you are not changing." By accepting the inherent difficulty of the situation for the other person, you allow them the opportunity to move beyond the ambivalence. They no longer have to convince you how difficult it is by remaining stuck in the situation. Sometimes verbalizing the disadvantages of change leads to a productive discussion about the person's fears of change and what can be done to alleviate or reduce those fears. Sometimes the disadvantages of change results in the person's refuting each disadvantage as not a good enough reason not to change, thereby gaining more resolve to attempt change as the discussion unfolds. In any event, the dynamics of the interaction change, which permits new and perhaps more helpful meanings and solutions to be considered.

Linda enacted this strategy and stopped suggesting things for Mandy to do. Linda initiated discussions about the drawbacks of being single and how phoney people seem at times. Linda expressed openly the possible disadvantages of Mandy's accompanying her to the singles club and a long discussion ensued. Linda shared that she was most fearful of being hurt again and saw her own lonely situation as preferable to the hurt of another bad relationship. For the first time, Mandy felt that Linda understood her fear and accepted it as valid.

Linda continued the discussion of disadvantages of change from time to time, as well as not pushing Mandy to do anything, and, once again, felt close to her. Mandy started going out to dinner with Linda and visiting her family more frequently. Mandy never joined the singles club, but began dating a man she met at church. Mandy and Linda often double-dated together. The disadvantages of change seemed to not only align Linda with Mandy's ambivalence and therefore enable her to move beyond it, but seemed to also convey understanding and validation that permitted Mandy to discuss her fears openly with Linda. In addition, if power or control factors were beginning to cloud the issue, the disadvantages of change effectively undercut their impact by changing Linda's conveyed message from "you must change" to "you have good reason not to change." Mandy responded by working through her fears and solving her problem on her own terms.

We hope you find creative interpretation a helpful strategy in many situations. The key point to keep in mind is that the concrete facts of the situation are never as important as the meaning that people are attributing to them. If you can change the meaning of the facts by considering advantages of the problem, a redefinition of the problem, or the disadvantages of changing the problem, you can open a new vista of alternative solutions.

Chapter 11

Shifting the Focus

We are taught throughout our lives to solve problems by tackling them directly and staying with them until we've worked them out. Tenacity and persistence are sacredly held American values. Unfortunately, a problem-solving style that involves continual intense attention can often escalate the problem so that it affects nonproblematic issues, as we have seen over and over in the vignettes presented in this book. Sometimes, just figuring out ways to break the intense attention that is paid to the problem and to redirect attention toward what is happening other than the problem circumstance can result in problem improvement.

The strategy of *shifting the focus* generally entails focusing *less* on the problem and its experience and *more* on what's happening when the problem *isn't* occurring and the experience of *not* having the problem.[49] All shifting-the-focus strategies have one quality in common: Each attempts in some way to help you, your spouse, your friends, your children experience change by emphasizing existing strengths and resources in areas in which there is more control and competence.

Shifting focus and experiencing the changes that are continuously happening apart from the problem can accomplish several positive outcomes. First, tension and "eggshell walking" are reduced, and the feeling tone (emotional context) of hopelessness and/or hostility associated with the problem is changed, thereby opening the possibility of different problem-solving actions for each person participating in the problem. Undercutting tension allows people to draw upon their own inherent capacities for making changes. Feelings of defensiveness, hopelessness, and hostility undermine and inhibit proactive behavior. Focusing on existing strengths and areas of control tends to increase confidence and feelings of self-esteem and competence. Feeling in control and good about ourselves powerfully influences our ability to consider different solution alternatives as well as different perspectives of the problem. Finally, by leaving the problem alone and relaxing our problem-solving attempts, it may recede to a diminished role in the overall context of the rest of our lives, and other areas may become more salient.

This strategy was exemplified in Chapters 4 and 6 of the book. In the section on lack of communication, it was presented as focusing less on getting the other person to talk and focusing more on one's own life and interests. When we discussed problems with sexual frequency, one option we considered was placing less emphasis on sex and more on more satisfactory aspects of the relationship.

Shifting the focus is based on two assumptions intimately related to many of the concepts discussed and applied in this book. The first assumption is that change is inevitable and continuous apart from our observation of it.[50] Change is always happening, but we are not aware of it and do not experience its occurrence. We prevent our experience of the ongoing process of change by our intense focus on the problem and the experience of its *not* changing. By concentrating on the problem circumstances staying the same, we are inhibiting the possibility of the problem not staying the same.

What we are leading to is the second assumption, which is that our observation alters the nature of what we observe.[51] By virtue of merely *observing* something, we actually *influence* that which is observed. This is the Heisenberg Principle. Probably the best illustration of the Heisenberg Principle is the self-fulfilling prophecy, which suggests that an assumption or prediction, purely as a result of having been made, causes the expected event to occur, thereby confirming its own accuracy.[52] Perhaps you are already getting the flavor of what shifting-the-focus strategies are at least partially attempting to do; that is, they attempt to construct the conditions necessary through observation and expectation that will encourage change in the problem circumstance. Some of the most compelling reports of self-fulfilling prophecies in the area of interpersonal communication are associated with psychologist Robert Rosenthal. In his book, *Pygmalion in the Classroom,* Rosenthal describes the results of experiments in a primary school with 18 teachers and 650 students.[53]

The self-fulfilling prophecy was introduced to the teachers at the beginning of the school year. After an intelligence test was given, the teachers were intentionally misled to believe that the test could identify those twenty percent of the students who would make rapid and above-average intellectual progress in the coming school year. Before the teachers had met their new students, they received the names, which were randomly picked from the student list, of those students who, on the basis of the test results, could be expected with certainty to perform unusually well.

It is important to recognize that the difference between these students and the others existed solely in the minds of their teachers. No one else was given the test results. The same intelligence test was given again at the end of the school year and showed *actual* above-average increases in the intelligence and achievements of these "special" students, and the reports of the teachers demonstrated that these children also distinguished themselves by their behavior, intellectual curiosity, friendliness, and other indicators of performance.

Rosenthal's experiment provides an especially clear illustration of how other people are influenced by our observation, expectations, prejudices, and wishful thinking. All, of course, are constructions of our own minds and not reflections of one true reality. By virtue of our observations and expectations, we, in essence, construct a reality and, therefore, influence those around us to confirm that constructed reality. By shifting the focus from the experience of the problem and observing the reality of what we are experiencing apart from the problem, we create, construct, or influence change and open up new possibilities for solution. Once again, if this is beginning to sound like gobbledygook, bear with us. The ideas are very complex, but their application is not. Consider the following vignettes with the two assumptions (change is continuous and self-fulfilling prophecy) in mind.

Renee was distressed about her sixteen-year-old daughter, Jessica, particularly about her F in math on her recent report card. Like most good parents, Renee tried to address Jessica's grade problem directly. Renee helped Jessica with her homework, structured mandatory study times, had regular contact with her teacher, and punished Jessica when her weekly progress reports were unsatisfactory. These strategies, however sound in theory, were ineffective in application. Jessica's grades did not improve. Conflict surrounding the grades grew and seemed to dominate their conversation. Jessica felt alienated and persecuted, while Renee felt guilty and frustrated.

Kim and Nathan were distraught about their fourteen-year-old son, Brent, who had put his fist through a window and ran away after an argument with his parents. Kim and Nathan were very concerned about Brent and were keeping him under close scrutiny. They described him as overemotional and very different from his older brothers, who were academically more successful and very popular and were star athletes. The parents' concern grew into anger and frustration, and arguments with Brent seemed to be the norm in the house. The arguments usually culminated in Brent's screaming about being misunderstood and his stomping off loudly to his room.

Alan and Pamela were concerned about Alan's eleven-year-old son, Michael, and his poor grades. They were more concerned, however, with the effects of the poor grades on their relationship. Alan and Pamela had radically different approaches to the grade problem and began arguing regularly and criticizing each other's approach. Alan seemed to subscribe to a laissez-faire method of parenting, while Pamela was known for her drill-instructor tactics. The fact that this was a remarried family, which is often fraught with inherent difficulties, did not help. The more involved Alan and Pamela became with the grade problem, the more they argued. They realized that their disagreement didn't help the grade problem, but were unsure about how to resolve the problem. The level of tension continued to rise, and each situation felt like an argument just waiting to happen.

Each of the above examples has in common an intense and direct involvement in the problem itself or what is happening when the problem occurs. The problem has, therefore, become the center of attention, around which all other activity revolves. Said another way, the problem and its experience have been elevated to a position of such importance that the problem essentially *defines* the family's reality. Although well meaning, such intensity of focus on the problem to the degree that it becomes the major point of reference to daily interaction rarely results in finding new and creative methods of solution.

Shifting the focus offers alternatives to those problem situations in which it seems that problem resolution is stymied by too much involvement. Each shifting-the-focus strategy seeks to remove the problem from its position of the center of the universe and to redefine the family's reality to *not* include the problem. Shifting the focus also intends to set the context for solution to the problem by allowing the experience of continuous change (assumption 1) and promoting the effect of the self-fulfilling prophecy (assumption 2). There are three methods of shifting the focus: (1) intentional inattention,[54] (2) noting things you would like to see continue,[55] and (3) observing what works.[56]

Intentional inattention involves the conscious removal of attention from the problem situation and redirecting that attention toward yourself, your relationships, and other interests. The major idea is that the degree of attention that people pay to one another is an important part of the nature of the relationship and can easily become the source of the problem. Intentional inattention seems to open up many alternatives for problem resolution that were previously unrecognized. Although it sounds very simple—and it is in concept—it is very difficult to actually implement. This shifting-the-focus strategy sets the stage for the other person involved in the problem to take action independent of the person employing the strategy.

Intentional inattention to promote action by another person is the central theme of a short story by the Viennese humorist, Roda Roda.[57] The young officers of an Austrian cavalry regiment were stationed in a remote little town in Galicia. It seems that their only source of hope and entertainment was the cashier in the only cafe in town, who was a very attractive and desirable young woman. In the cafe, the charming young woman is the source of continual attention and affection of a crowd of eager, dashing officers. She responds to the barrage of romantic entreaties by holding court and coyly rejecting all their advances. The hero of the story is madly in love with the cashier, but knows that his chances are slim if he chooses to compete with his fellow officers on their terms. He also knows that, although handsome and witty, his comrades have persistently failed to win the affection of the cashier. Our hero, therefore, adopts the method of intentional inattention. He goes to the cafe frequently, but sits alone at his table, with his back toward her and is only interested in talking to those near him or simply enjoying his coffee. When he leaves, our hero pays his bill with studied indifference or while talking to a fellow officer. This strategy, therefore, makes him the only officer who is not pursuing her and significantly arouses her interest. Ultimately, she goes after him, to the utter amazement of his fellow officers. Intentional inattention proved to be far more powerful than the other means of seduction employed by our hero's comrades. It can similarly be powerful in application to other relationship difficulties in which overinvolvement seems to be perpetuating the problem.

The second method of shifting the focus is noting things that you would like to continue.[58] This strategy entails *observing* what is happening that you would like to see continue and making note of those things. This method is designed to shift your perspective or focus from the past and its negative depiction of the problem to present and future events. It is also designed to promote *expectations* of change such that a self-fulfilling prophecy can occur. In this instance, the prophecy is that something worthwhile is going to be noticed and many times, the likelihood is that, indeed, that will be the case.

Noting the good things requires attending to the aspects of daily life that are pleasing and that are not a part of the problem under concern. This permits the observation and recognition of positive things that are happening and focuses the people involved toward one another's strengths and resources. Noting the good things enables one to experience the satisfying aspects that are happening (or that could happen), but are unnoticed or inhibited, and promotes those satisfying aspects by encouraging people to look for just them. This method of shifting the focus is good for situations in which it seems that the individuals involved are only seeing the negative attributes of one another and are not experiencing positive interactions, that is, it is primarily for quality of relationship problems. It allows for the construction of a more positive relationship reality. After a period of noting the good things, but not sharing those things with each other, the persons involved should meet and discuss what they have observed. Discussion should be limited to only those things observed that each wants to see continue. Sometimes this discussion may not seem relevant because the problem itself may have already improved. That's okay; in fact, that's exactly what we expect will occur.

Attention, inattention, and creating positive realities between people through observation is nicely illustrated by the matchmaking routine in eastern European family tradition.[59] Marriages were arranged by the parents, and you can imagine that their choices of mates for their children were rarely met with unbridled enthusiasm by the two prospective spouses. In such cases where the two prospective lovers were not thrilled with their fates, the parents would hire the services of a professional matchmaker. The matchmaker would proceed in the following way. First, he would take one of the two aside, let's say the young man, and ask him whether or not he had noticed how intently the young woman was watching him whenever he did not look at her. Of course the answer was likely no, so the matchmaker instructed the young man to observe carefully, but unobtrusively, and he would see for himself. The young woman, the prospective bride, was then similarly instructed. Soon, the two young people were quite interested in each other, gazing into one another's eyes for long periods of time. Remember the Rosenthal study and how the "special" children actually became special. The power of expectation and observation cannot be overstated.

The final method of shifting the focus, which includes aspects of the other two methods, is called observing what works.[60] Observing what works entails adopting the role of a participant observer and noting which strategies employed to help the problem are attaining the desired goals. Special observation should be given to *how* the strategy observed to be effective is working. What aspects are helpful and how the effective methods can be replicated are the questions to be considered.

This strategy is particularly appropriate for situations in which there is disagreement about the methods to be used to address a problem situation. Observing what works requires that the two parties in disagreement over a particular issue agree to continue to disagree until objective data has gathered that point toward one method of addressing the problem over the other. Then, on odd days of the week, one of the parties to the disagreement handles the problem as he or she sees fit without any interference from the other person. Both individuals observe the outcome and note what was helpful about the strategy and how it was helpful. On even days of the week, the other party to the disagreement handles the problem as he or she desires, without interference, and likewise both individuals observe and note the results. On the seventh day of the week, neither party should do anything about the problem.[61]

If there is a third person involved, as in our example of a child problem, that person is also included in this method of shifting focus. The child or third party's task is to monitor adherence to the odd/even day rule and report infractions at a meeting. The third person also observes what strategy works and notes how it is helpful.

At the end of a predetermined period of time—a couple of weeks is usually adequate—the parties meet and discuss their observations. Each person reports only what he or she observed was helpful. Discussion should focus on how the helpful strategies promoted improvement and how they were contributed to by each individual involved. Often, such discussions lead to a collaborative formulation of the strategies to be employed in problem resolution. Sometimes the solution is apparent so that no discussion is necessary.

Observing what works is relevant when the problem itself is either not being addressed or is sabotaged because of a disagreement about what to do about the problem. This strategy shifts the focus by redirecting attention away from the disagreement about what to do and toward what can be done about it. Looking for what works rather than looking for the limitations of the other person's point of view seems to set the context for alternative strategies to emerge. Once focus is shifted from the conflict and tension, a more relaxed problem-solving approach can be formulated. Not experiencing a disagreement (or any other problem) allows you to experience other more satisfying elements of life and more fruitful approaches to problem resolution.

Intentional Inattention

Renee was a thirty-eight-year-old single parent who had custody of her sixteen-year-old daughter, Jessica, since her divorce four years previously. Jessica's father lived out of town and had little contact with her beyond holidays and special occasions. Renee was an office manager at a medical office and was very dedicated to her job. She felt guilty about the divorce and "breaking up the family." It seemed that she dealt with guilt by trying to be the perfect parent. Renee routinely put Jessica's needs first in nearly every situation and believed that no sacrifice was too big for her to make for Jessica's well-being. Renee watched her budget closely and did not pursue interests that involved any expense because she wanted Jessica to attend a private high school with a good academic reputation. Renee did without new clothes herself so that Jessica could dress fashionably.

Jessica was the center of Renee's universe, and the grade issue was an example of this. Jessica had never been a good student of math, but only recently had fallen to an F. Her other grades were also slightly down. Renee suggested to Jessica every possible way of helping her perform better in math. Renee worked out a study plan, spent time every night with Jessica working on math, hired a tutor, took time off work to meet with the school counselor, and talked to the teacher. At the teacher's suggestion, she began punishing Jessica for missed assignments.

Matters went from bad to worse. Jessica argued with Renee regularly about the removal of privileges, and the assignments continued to be missed. Every night seemed to evolve into a gut-wrenching ordeal. The school counselor suggested that perhaps the divorce was behind all this and that Jessica needed to see a therapist to allow her to work through her feelings. This, of course, was all Renee needed to hear to mercilessly flog herself with guilt.

Renee's major solution attempt involved paying intense attention to Jessica's grade problem and taking almost complete responsibility for it. Although this strategy probably helped her deal with her guilt, it was quite ineffective in motivating Jessica to improve her math performance.

Renee consulted a therapist. Jessica refused to attend the session. Renee and the therapist discussed the grade problem, Renee's solution attempts, and her thoughts and feelings about the divorce. The therapist believed that intentional inattention seemed worth a try because all of Renee's attempts to influence Jessica involved the continual paying of intense attention to the grade problem. The therapist suggested that, on a trial basis, Renee deliberately ignore the grade issue and begin taking care of herself. This would entail not discussing the grades with Jessica or helping her in any way, but rather doing things specifically for herself and only interacting with Jessica around topics unrelated to grades. The therapist asked Renee to think of as many ways as possible to focus less on the grades and more on herself and activities with Jessica unrelated to grades. Both Renee and the therapist agreed that the consequences of missing assignments should remain, but that explanations and discussion of the consequences be eliminated.

Renee implemented the intentional inattention strategy and apologized to Jessica for treating her like a child (see Chapter 8). It was difficult for Renee to think of herself first because she didn't have much practice at it, but she experimented and tried a few things. Occasionally, Renee began meeting with friends after work. She also started a jazzercise class, which met a couple of times per week. Although she had dated since the divorce, Renee had almost completely stopped dating in response to the grade problem. She began dating once again. Renee spent time with Jessica discussing what was going on in her life as well as what was important to Jessica. The tension dropped significantly and the quality of interaction improved.

Renee's interaction with Jessica had become over-focused on the math grade, which emphasized a negative aspect of Jessica's behavior and resulted in a strain in their relationship and a feeling of guilt in Renee. The shift-of-focus strategy of intentional inattention took the pressure off both Renee and Jessica and allowed both to pursue other alternatives. A change in the quality of the relationship happened first and Renee noticed it, which helped her continue taking care of herself and avoiding the conflictual grade discussions. Renee also noticed that she felt better both physically and emotionally. Jessica began initiating discussion about the grades. Renee listened and was supportive, but did not offer any suggestions. Finally, Jessica asked Renee if she could again hire a tutor in math. Renee agreed, but only on a trial basis. Jessica arranged for the tutor herself and consequently improved her math grade to a C.

Instead of giving Jessica the message that Renee was responsible for fixing the grade problem and that it was a catastrophe if it didn't improve, Renee's inattention to the problem gave Jessica the message that it was Jessica's problem and that Renee's life would continue regardless of the outcome of the grade situation. Renee accomplished one of the most difficult things that a parent can do: backing off of an adolescent and allowing her to make mistakes and learn from them. Renee enabled the problem to improve by putting herself, rather than the grades, first.

If you need another rationale to try this method of shifting the focus and you happen to be divorced, consider the following. There is mounting evidence to support the conclusion that the most significant indicator of a child's adjustment to divorce is the *adjustment of the parents* to the divorce. If the parents do not do well with divorce, then the kids don't either, generally speaking. If a parent is dissatisfied or unhappy after divorce, that unhappiness is communicated to the children, which makes it more likely for the children to experience adjustment problems. This evidence points to the importance of parental adjustments and the successful transition to a productive, single life. When you take care of yourself and make yourself happy, you are teaching your children a valuable lesson in life regarding personal responsibility for one's emotions and one's happiness. Parenting is, by necessity, self-sacrificing at times. However, ongoing self-sacrifice at the expense of personal satisfaction is not a particularly good model for children to observe.

If you find yourself in a situation in which your life seems to revolve around a problem, and the more attention you give it the worse it gets, you may want to consider intentional inattention. It simply requires you to focus less on the problem and more on yourself and the quality of your relationship. However, it communicates a far more complex message that often results in problem improvement.

Noting Things You Would Like to See Continue

Kim and Nathan had been married for eighteen years and had three children, all boys, ages seventeen, sixteen, and fourteen. They considered themselves happily married and very proud of their family—at least until recently, when loud arguments and emotional outbursts were occurring with frightening regularity. The impetus for the arguments always seemed to arise from their youngest son, Brent. Kim and Nathan had always known that Brent was very different from his older brothers. The older boys were sports fanatics and seemed to be involved in sports all year round. Brent never acquired a taste for sports, preferring instead to put his energies into music, particularly playing the piano and composing. The older boys worked hard academically and enjoyed competing with each other about who would get into the better college. Brent could care less about school, although he maintained a C average. Brent preferred to contemplate the universe and critique his jock brothers. But secretly, he envied his brothers' popularity and the ease with which they seemed to handle life.

Kim and Nathan did not know what to do about Brent's angry outbursts, because they had never encountered a similar situation with the two older boys. Any time that one of them confronted Brent about anything, Brent would scream and stomp off. Sometimes, he would run out of the house, and on one occasion he put his fist through a window in what appeared to be uncontrollable rage. This, of course, scared Kim and Nathan, and they began closely monitoring everything they said for fear it would cause a blow-up. Tension mounted with each interaction as it became more and more obvious that something was wrong. Kim and Nathan asked the older boys to keep an eye on Brent and report anything unusual.

Things continued to get worse. Trying to say everything diplomatically with regard to Brent's sensitivity just made things worse. Everyone became frustrated with Brent, and much of family interaction was characterized by veiled criticisms of Brent or tense conversation described best as "eggshell walking." It seemed that no one could do anything right, especially Brent. The whole situation culminated in an explosive argument one night in which Nathan accused Brent of ruining the family with his "mental" problems.

The family sought therapy and shared their troubling experiences and attempted solutions with the therapist. The therapist suggested that Nathan, Kim, and the older boys observe Brent and note the things that they would like to see continue. It seemed to the therapist that everyone in the family was locked into looking at the negativity of the past situations, which was preventing the possibility of a solution by creating a negative self-fulfilling prophecy. Brent was under the closest scrutiny, and everyone expected the worst from him. Not surprisingly, the worst often happened. It also seemed to the therapist that Brent's resources and strengths were going unnoticed and, therefore, were not being utilized to enhance change in the problem process. Noting down the good things enables a shift of focus to present and future events so that a positive self-fulfilling prophecy is set into motion. In the case of this family, the positive prophecy was that Brent would do many worthwhile things that would be noticed by his family.

Nathan, Kim, and the older boys began a three-week commitment to observe Brent without comment and to note what they wanted to continue. At the next meeting, the therapist asked what they had noted. A long list of positive attributes, events, and examples ensued and a lengthy discussion developed about how all these things could possibly happen, given the circumstances described previously. Kim discussed how helpful Brent had been around the house and how well he had accepted her refusal to allow him to attend a rock concert. Nathan discussed Brent's refreshing lack of interest in fashionable clothes and the concern he often demonstrated for his friends' problems. One of Brent's older brothers discussed an instance in which Brent comforted him after a particularly bad performance in a basketball game.

Brent joined the discussion and commented on how much better he felt lately and how he believed that he was finally being accepted for who he was. Everyone noted how the overall tension had been eliminated, and things seemed to be back to normal.

Noting the good things seemed to permit the recognition of positive events within the family and focused Kim, Nathan, and the boys on Brent's strengths and resources. Such a shifting-the-focus strategy permitted Brent to change his troublesome behavior and to feel more accepted by the family, which in turn enabled the family to find more positives. A change in one person in the family enables changes in each family member and a change in the family overall.

This method of shifting the focus is helpful in situations in which it appears that a negative self-fulfilling prophecy is restricting solution alternatives. It is especially good to use in quality of relationship problems. Noting the good things requires three steps: (1) gathering the individual(s) involved and asking them to note without comment the things they would like to see continue; (2) setting a period of time for the observation; and (3) meeting after that period of time to discuss the results, focusing only on those things that were noted. Often times, new solution alternatives occur spontaneously and new meanings are arrived at. Brent learned that blowing up didn't get him what he wanted, and Kim and Nathan learned to appreciate Brent's differences from his brothers. People are capable of significant change and great insight if only given the opportunity. Noting the good things provides such an opportunity by enabling the experience of positive aspects via their mere observation.

Observing What Works

Alan and Pamela had been married just three years, and both were in their second marriage. Michael was Alan's eleven-year-old son from his first marriage, who had recently come to live with Alan and his new step-mom after Michael's mother and step-dad decided to move to another state. All were in agreement that it was best for Michael to be in his father's custody.

When Michael's mother had custody and he only visited

every other weekend, there were minimal problems. But as time passed under the new custody arrangement, problems related to Alan and Pamela's different styles of parenting quickly ensued. To Alan, Pamela seemed overly harsh and negative toward Michael. To Pamela, Alan seemed overly permissive and naïve. Alan and Pamela began to disagree frequently about what to do about anything regarding Michael. Often the disagreements resulted in arguments.

Michael's grades became the central issue that reflected the parenting differences and led to an increased intensity and frequency of arguments. Many times the arguments escalated to screaming matches and the resentments seemed to linger for days. Pamela believed emphatically that what Michael needed was structure, firm guidance, and rapid punishment for poor performance. She insisted that Michael complete his homework before doing anything else and made him copy from a dictionary if he didn't bring his homework from school. She also corrected Michael's work and required him to do assignments over completely if there were too many wrong answers. Alan believed that Pamela was far too critical and needed to back off. Alan allowed Michael to go out to play after school, believing that he needed a break after being in school all day. He would remind Michael to do his homework, but would often not follow up or check the homework's accuracy.

In many ways, it looked like one attempted to compensate for the other, and that they couldn't agree about anything. The smallest, most insignificant issue was blown into a major fight, as tension surrounding parenting and the grade problem grew and grew. The tension spread to unrelated issues and a sense of dread and resentment characterized Alan and Pamela's relationship.

Alan and Pamela sought therapy after a long period of not speaking to one another. Both recognized that the problem was their disagreement about how to handle Michael's grades, as well as other parenting issues. After a thorough discussion of the problem, the therapist believed that the solution could probably be found in some combination of their very different points of view.

The therapist suggested observing what works in order to discover the ideal combination. Alan and Pamela agreed it sounded like a good thing to try. The therapist suggested that on odd days, Pamela should handle the grade problem however she desired, with positively no input or interference from Alan. On even days, Alan should address the grade problem as he saw fit. On the seventh day, both were instructed to do nothing about the grade problem. Michael was asked to keep track of whose day it was and whether or not any infractions of rules occurred. If someone attempted to address the grade issue on the wrong day, Michael was to politely point it out. (And he was delighted to do so.) All three individuals were asked to observe the methods that worked best and to figure out what was most helpful as it related to the grade issue.

As you might suspect, without the grade issue to argue about, tension decreased between Alan and Pamela almost overnight. The reduction in tension allowed the entire family to experience satisfying aspects of their lives and enabled a fresh perspective regarding the grade problem. Pamela continued her own parenting style, but softened considerably as the week progressed. She allowed Michael to play after school for one hour before starting his homework. She seemed much "looser" and "lighter" with him. She included in her nights of responsibility a reward for him for successful completion of his homework.

Alan was very pleased with the changes he observed between Michael and her and responded by resolving to be better at following up on Michael's homework. On his nights of responsibility, he thoroughly checked the homework problems and on one occasion required Michael to completely redo an English assignment because it was sloppily done.

At the next meeting with the therapist, it was apparent that the feeling tone had changed. The discussion of the session focused on what specifically was done that was helpful in addressing the grade problem and how it seemed to help. Pamela shared that when she allowed herself to pay more attention to her relationship with Michael, he seemed to be more cooperative, not only with his homework, but in general. Alan reported that making Michael accountable by checking his work seemed to be the key element in his observations. Finally, Michael said that he didn't know what exactly was helpful, but that there seemed to be a lot less "hassle" around the house.

Alan and Pamela agreed on a plan based upon their observations. The plan itself was not really as important as the fact that they agreed on a plan. Observing what works seemed to redirect attention away from their differences regarding parenting and toward what they could do about Michael's grades. The odd/even suggestion set the context that enabled both Alan and Pamela to stop criticizing one another and look for alternative ways to approach Michael's academic problems. By diverting attention from their conflict and tension, both could relax and creatively address the problem. Observing what works shifted the focus from the experience of failure in the past to looking for the successful aspects of both the strategies used and Michael's performance.

Observing what works is especially useful in situations in which a disagreement exists that is preventing productive problem solving. This method of shifting the focus entails: (1) assigning one person the responsibility of the problem on odd days and the other person on even days; (2) no input or interference from the person who is not in charge that day (can be monitored by a third person); (3) observing what specifically is helpful to the problem; and (4) discussing the observations and formulating a collaborative plan. As in noting down good things, solutions may occur spontaneously, and new meanings may be generated by this strategy. Setting the context for change to occur is often all that is needed for many individuals to tap their own inherent capacity to resolve problems.

Chapter 12

Going with the Flow

When you are stuck in a rut, it is important to make a change that is noticeably different from what you have been doing. This seems quite obvious, but as we have seen over and over again, people tend to persist in variations on a theme of a particular way to approach a problem. Often, the theme is one of directly trying to change another person to fit our own view of the circumstance under concern. We view such direct attempts at changing others as analogous to swimming upstream or against the flow of the current. You may ultimately reach your destination, or you may not, but you will likely be quite fatigued and feel considerably worse after making the effort. Attempting to induce another person to change can be just as exhausting and, ultimately, unrewarding. Sometimes, the brainstorming of ways to go along with the other person's point of view or behavior can be conducive to problem resolution. We call these creative methods of approaching relationship difficulties "going with the flow."

The strategy of going with the flow entails listening to and accepting the other person's statements, recognizing the values and beliefs that the person holds, and avoiding taking a position that opposes that person's beliefs and actions. Successful implementation of going with the flow requires you to overcome the temptation to confront, reason, or argue with the other person. Restraint from attempting to help by direct educative or persuasive methods reduces opposition by not creating an unnecessary value conflict. After recognition of the other person's point of view, the task of going with the flow is to actually encourage or promote that point of view and the actions that come from it.[62]

The problem scenario that going with the flow addresses involves a situation in which one person wants another person to change what he or she is doing. So, the person desiring the change tries again and again to change the other person's behavior. The person who is trying to be changed feels forced and pressured and, often, threatened. People tend to respond to the perceived pressure and the threatened loss of independence by clinging to their points of view so intensely that it appears they are deliberately doing the opposite of what is asked or demanded.

One way to look at this situation is that a power struggle emerges such that the person who feels forced responds with an escalating move and gives the message, "I'll show you I can't be pushed around." Another way to look at it suggests that when people feel pressured, they tend to retreat to a more extreme position to counteract the pressure. The pressure, therefore, prevents those individuals from considering the alternatives and possibly from changing the problem of their own volition.

Going with the flow requires the person attempting to get the other to change to do a reversal and say in words and in action, "You don't have to change; it's O.K. with me the way things are. I'll even help you stay the same." If done effectively and genuinely, this strategy makes it clear that the pressure is off and enables the other person to evaluate the situation and explore the options. He or she can step from the extreme counterposition of not changing and freely choose to change the problem behavior. If there are any oppositional tendencies left once the pressure is removed, the only way it can now be expressed is by doing what you initially wanted. By reversing your request or promoting things to stay the same, you can utilize the other person's opposition if it indeed exists. More often, however, going with the flow is effective because it promotes the conditions necessary for the other person to exercise his or her own good judgment.

Many examples presented in the book represent variations of going with the flow. In the section on lack of communication, we suggested making oneself less available for communication, which, in effect, says behaviorally, "It's O.K. if we don't talk. I'll make it even easier not to talk by not being around as much." This serves as a dramatic contrast to attempts to plead with and persuade the other person to talk. For sexual frequency problems, our suggestion of making oneself less available gave a similar message, which removed pressure and allowed the pursuer to become the pursued.

Initiating discussion of a chronic complainer's complaints—inviting what you dread—is another form of going with the flow. Instead of opposing the expression of the complaints and swimming upstream, we suggested that you initiate discussion of the complaints and encourage their expression at every opportunity. Finally, bringing up a past affair with a hurt, angry, or jealous spouse rather than attempting to avoid it or shut conversation down similarly can be seen as an illustration of going with the flow. Each of the above examples reflects an attempt to accept things the way they are and even encourage that state of affairs. Such a position sets the context for change to occur.

This strategy can be particularly useful with children of all ages, since it seems that children often appear bent on doing the opposite of what their parents want. Probably the concept of the power struggle is best understood in the context of child rearing. Consider a young boy who throws temper tantrums. Parents use a variety of direct attempts to resolve this difficulty including reason, ignoring, and punishment. Sometimes these work (especially ignoring), but other times they fail or make it worse. Our solution, in that instance, is to encourage the tantrum in words ("You're not getting what you want. This would be a good time to throw a tantrum . . . Come on, you can yell louder than that") or behavior (roll on the floor and kick and scream along with him).

As silly as this strategy sounds, it has a number of beneficial effects. First of all, if the tantrum was geared toward getting a certain reaction, it now gets a very different one. If the child wanted to displease his parents with the tantrum, he is now following their wishes. So, if a tantrum does happen, the parents aren't being defied, they don't get as upset, and the power struggle is diminished. Also, the feeling tone of the interaction changes. Rather than having a serious battle for control, have it become a somewhat goofy spectacle (imagine a young child watching his mother or father rolling around screaming).

Going with the flow can take as many different forms as there are situations in which one person is attempting change through direct confrontational methods and meeting with either stiff opposition or no response at all. By virtue of encouraging things to stay the same, the context in which the problem behavior occurs is dramatically changed. The goal of going with the flow is to set up an experience that interrupts or replaces your current ineffective solution attempts that are helping maintain the problem and to enable all of the people involved in the problem to perhaps see things differently.[63] Remember constructivism and how people generate new meaning from their behavioral interaction in the social context. Changing your behavioral interaction enables others in the system to change and creates the conditions necessary for new meanings to arise. These new meanings can lead to more productive and adaptive ways to handle relationship difficulties.

Three more variations on the theme of going with the flow are presented below. Each example represents the acceptance of the other person's point of view and the genuine encouragement of the very problem previously desired to be changed. The first example, which we call the "Romeo and Juliet" phenomenon, involves a situation in which concerned parents strongly disapprove of their daughter's boyfriend and inadvertently create a melodramatic love affair. The second application of going with the flow involves a worried husband who is willing to do anything—even threaten his marriage—to get his wife to stop smoking. The final example brings us full circle, back to Sharon and Jeff, the couple we introduced to you in Chapter 1. Recall that Sharon initially wanted Jeff to hold his advice in abeyance until she asked for it, but the situation escalated to Sharon's accusing Jeff of chauvinism and Jeff's closing down communication.

The Romeo and Juliet Phenomenon

Evelyn and William had been married for twenty-five years and had raised five children. The sixth child, seventeen-year-old Erica, was a senior in high school. Evelyn and William had enjoyed a relatively trouble-free parenting life and prided themselves on the good environment and strong values they provided for the children. Erica was no exception and had pretty much led a charmed existence in high school. She was an honor student and a fine soccer player. She was a youth counselor in church and dated the boys from her church regularly.

Then, as far as Evelyn and William were concerned, the roof fell in. Erica met a boy, Jesse, at an outdoor rock concert. Normally, Erica would not have given Jesse the time of day, because of his punk-like appearance. Erica looked beyond Jesse's appearance because a friend told her that Jesse's father had died recently. She felt great sympathy for him and, therefore, chose to talk to him when he initiated conversation.

Even though Jesse was different from Erica in almost every conceivable way, they hit it off famously. Erica really enjoyed how they could talk for hours at a time. She felt that Jesse was far more sensitive than other boys she had been dating. All of Erica's friends were surprised at the growing relationship, because Jesse had somewhat of a bad reputation. He smoked cigarettes and hung out with a group usually referred to as "hoods." Jesse was known as a suspected pot smoker and hell raiser. To make matters worse (in Erica's parents' eyes), he lived in a government subsidized apartment complex, which was a problem only in the sense that it placed him in an economic level far below the norm of the school and well below Erica's socioeconomic status. At this point, Erica considered their relationship to be one between friends.

Erica began dating Jesse and her parents finally met him. William and Evelyn could hardly believe it when they saw Jesse. They were displeased with his appearance and did not try to hide it. Erica shared how disappointed she was that her parents couldn't judge Jesse on the basis of something other than dyed black hair and an earring. She told her parents that Jesse was a good person and that she believed she was helping him with his problems. She said that he already promised her that he would stop smoking pot. This did not comfort Evelyn and William. Erica began dating only Jesse.

Jesse became a regular topic of discussion and argument. Evelyn received more information about him from the schools, as well as from her friends. Unfortunately, she didn't hear too much that was complimentary. Both Evelyn and William started a campaign to discourage Erica from seeing Jesse. They pointed out his flaws as often as his name was mentioned. Erica usually responded by reminding them that their comments were not reflective of a Christian attitude.

William and Evelyn also talked highly of boys of whom they approved and invited boys from church over for Sunday dinner. Conflict escalated and discussions about Jesse usually became mudslinging arguments. William began casually referring to Jesse as the "slimebag from the welfare apartments." Finally, in an argument, Erica announced that she loved Jesse and that nothing they could say could change her mind about him.

Things became very tense and conversation was limited. Erica seemed to change overnight. Her attitude was negative, and she began to dress a little differently. She made sarcastic comments and withdrew into her room as much as possible. She also began listening to a much "heavier" version of rock and roll. Evelyn and William noticed all these changes and decided to forbid her from seeing Jesse.

This only heightened the melodrama and Erica responded in a fury that they had never seen before. She screamed at William and Evelyn for the first time that they could remember and threatened that if they tried to keep them apart, she would run away; after all, she was not going to let them tell her whom she could love. After discovering that she was secretly seeing Jesse by lying about her whereabouts, William and Evelyn decided to seek therapy.

Let's consider the nine-dot puzzle aspects of the Romeo and Juliet phenomenon. William and Evelyn's solution attempts ranged from discouraging the relationship to forbidding it, but all were variations on direct confrontation and persuasion. William and Evelyn ignored Erica's viewpoint about the relationship, which in the process served to add fuel to the fire. Erica just began the relationship by talking to Jesse; it only grew to "love" status after William and Evelyn intervened to convince her that Jesse was not for her.

Unfortunately, the element of power also became an issue. Never before was Erica rebellious, but now she had just cause: her parents were forbidding her to see the person she loved. She had every right to do whatever it took to see him and to show them that they had no right, or ability, to control her. Erica began demonstrating her power in other ways such as in sarcastic comments, withdrawal, lying, and changes in music preference and dress. If the pattern of escalation had continued, then it could have led to more drastic forms of rebellion, such as lowered school performance, sexual acting out, or other similarly serious events.

The therapist suggested going with the flow. In this instance, it entailed the parents' making a total reversal in their position and accepting Erica's position about her desire to see Jesse. Specifically, going with the flow required that Evelyn and William look for, find, and comment on the strengths and positives that Jesse possessed; encourage Erica to see him; and even invite Jesse to participate in family activities whenever possible. The therapist also suggested that a genuine rationale be given to Erica for the reversal in their position (e.g., they tell her that after talking it over with the therapist and their friends, they see how wrong they have been).

At first, William and Evelyn shuddered when they heard these suggestions and began to catastrophize a bit by worrying that Erica would marry Jesse. However, as they reviewed the progress of their approach, they saw that direct methods just increased Erica's defensiveness by invalidating her position and tended to make Jesse look all the more appealing to her. By encouraging the relationship with Jesse, if there is a power or oppositional element ("I'll show you") to what Erica is doing, it will be undercut. She then would be freely deciding whether she wanted to see Jesse, rather than seeing him because her parents don't want her to. She could, therefore, evaluate the relationship on her own as she had done with all her previous boyfriends. By going with the flow, William and Evelyn are allowing the relationship to run its natural course, which in all likelihood will not be a long-term relationship. They are enabling the conditions through which Erica can step away from her extreme position of deep love for Jesse.

If Erica continues to love Jesse, then so be it. At least she is loving him on her own and not in response to pressure not to love him. In addition, even if the relationship continues, going with the flow prevents the ruining of an otherwise good parent–child relationship. Finally, if the relationship persists, the opportunity to get to know the young man better may result in some relief and can allow the parents to convey their values and have more overall influence.

William and Evelyn were able to implement going with the flow and were supportive of one another's restraint from falling back into the old patterns. They apologized to Erica and Jesse and included him in many family activities. They complimented him on whatever they could find that was positive: his car, holding down a job, helping his mother with the bills, and so on. Over time, they even found that he was a likeable kid, and William particularly respected Jesse's responsibility to his mother. Although they would have preferred Erica to be dating someone else, William and Evelyn felt informed about her whereabouts and relieved that they were all getting along well again.

Toward the end of Erica's senior year, she and Jesse decided to break up and just be friends again. They both agreed that they should date around since she was attending an out-of-town college in the fall.

Breaking Bad Habits

Larry and Karen had been happily married for five years when Larry decided he wanted to quit smoking. He convinced Karen to stop with him several times, but every time they stopped, she would ultimately begin smoking again. When she started smoking again after each unsuccessful attempt at quitting, he would resentfully start also, often blaming her for his inability to continue his efforts when she smoked around him. This cycle went on for about two years and was a source of a few arguments.

Finally, Larry announced that he was going to quit smoking regardless of Karen's continuing or not continuing to smoke. It was difficult with her smoking the same brand, but he was determined and ultimately successful. He was extremely pleased with himself and felt better both physically and emotionally. He thought that she would see how much better he felt and would follow suit and quit smoking. But she did not.

After becoming convinced that Karen would never quit on her own, Larry began an antismoking campaign with her. He regularly spoke about the benefits of stopping and about the health consequences of her continuing for both of them. He left brochures from smoke-ending programs around the house, as well as articles addressing the dangers of smoking. Every time he ran across another health implication of smoking or some disease in which smoking was implicated, he, ad nauseam, made sure that she was made aware of it.

At first, Karen was good-natured about Larry's concern, and she listened politely as he pleaded his case against smoking. Of course, she already knew about the health hazards of smoking; awareness was not the problem. She had not yet come to the realization herself that she was ready to quit. But as time wore on, Larry's persistent barrage began to get on her nerves. She shared her annoyance with him and requested that he back off his attempts to get her to stop smoking. He responded each time that he couldn't idly stand by and watch her kill herself, and him, without doing something about it. After all, he was only after her to quit because he loved her and was tired of living with the hazards of secondary smoke.

Karen's resentments only served to intensify Larry's resolve. He posted "no smoking" signs throughout the house. He banned her smoking in the car or around him at all. Every time she lit a cigarette, he would make sarcastic comments and leave the room. He seemed to do his best to make her feel miserable when she smoked, in hopes that she would quit. He refused to buy cigarettes for her when it was his turn to go to the store. Unfortunately, she was smoking even more than before.

Karen became defensive about her smoking and the first hint of Larry's saying something about it often led to an argument. She told him that she couldn't take any more pressure about smoking because her employer had just banned smoking at the office. Larry was delighted, but not for long. Karen followed through on her threat to leave if he said one more thing about smoking. Although she only left for one night, the fact that the situation escalated to that point scared him and he consulted with a therapist.

Hopefully, the nine-dot puzzle aspects of Larry's solution attempts are obvious to you at this point. His solutions of direct confrontation, persuasion, and education only made it more likely for Karen *not* to quit smoking. As he intensified his efforts, the smoking issue escalated into a power struggle, which ultimately precluded the possibility that Karen would address her smoking on her own.

The therapist suggested going with the flow. In Larry and Karen's case, it first required Larry to genuinely accept Karen's right to smoke as her own personal choice. The therapist suggested that Larry begin by apologizing to Karen for harassing her and give her the message both verbally and nonverbally that quitting was entirely up to her and that it was okay with him if she didn't. The therapist also suggested that Larry actually encourage Karen's smoking in every way possible. This would entail picking up a pack of cigarettes at the store for her when she didn't ask, or picking up two packs when she asked for one, bringing an ashtray or her cigarettes into the room when she left them in another room, asking for smoking sections at restaurants without waiting for her to ask, and so forth.

The goal, of course, was to alleviate the pressure and undercut the power struggle so that Karen could freely decide to quit smoking on her own. By accepting her decision to smoke and even by encouraging her smoking, the conditions are set for her to move away from her entrenched view of smoking. Aligning with the frame of reference of an individual permits that person to let go of the given issue as a symbol of his or her independence or autonomy.

Larry implemented the go-with-the-flow strategy. Nothing much happened for a while except that they were no longer arguing about Karen's smoking. Several weeks later, after he had purchased an extra pack for her, Karen thanked him but asked him not to purchase any more cigarettes for her because she was thinking about quitting. Larry resisted the temptation to become a cheerleader and instead agreed not to buy her cigarettes in a matter-of-fact way. A few weeks later, she enrolled in a smoke-enders class at a local hospital and successfully stopped smoking. By going with the flow, Larry stopped being an obstruction to change and permitted Karen to reach her own conclusions about quitting smoking.

Encouraging the Conditions for Change

Let us refresh your memory about Sharon and Jeff from Chapter 1 and show how Sharon successfully implemented going with the flow. Sharon had become increasingly aware of Jeff's propensity for giving instructions and pointing out imperfections in her methods of doing things. She explained to him that when they were first married she needed and appreciated the benefit of his knowledge and experience, but that now she sometimes felt he was treating her like a child and that she didn't like it.

Initially, Jeff agreed with Sharon and held his comments in abeyance, but fairly soon he began sharing his observations and making suggestions. When Sharon pointed this out to him, he became defensive and accused her of overreacting and not being able to accept constructive criticism. Sharon continued to make Jeff aware of his now "critical, paternalistic, and sexist nature." He responded by defensively backing off and withdrawing from conversation in general. When conversation did occur, he seemed more apt to criticize her, now about her "crazy," feminist ideas, as well as the way she did almost everything.

Sharon decided to try a different approach. She went "on strike" and discontinued doing anything that Jeff criticized. He decided to not only stop making comments and suggestions, but to also stop talking altogether.

Sharon couldn't take the tension any more so she decided to see a therapist. She invited Jeff's participation, but he angrily refused. After a thorough exploration of the problem and the identification of Sharon's goals as wanting to reduce the tension and receive less criticism and advice from Jeff, the therapist suggested going with the flow. Recall that all of Sharon's solution attempts were variations on the theme of "I will make my dissatisfaction apparent to him and he will respond with less criticism." Making her dissatisfaction apparent to Jeff largely involved direct confrontation, persuasion, and lectures in the form of pointing out to him the sexist nature of his actions. Of course, these solutions only served to make things worse and he responded defensively. By suggesting that Sharon go with the flow, the therapist was not implying that Jeff's behavior was not sexist, but rather that her attempts to help Jeff realize his sexist inclinations were ineffective. Going with the flow required Sharon to just *accept* Jeff's position that he was only trying to help her when he gave advice or criticized her approach to things. Sharon's task after accepting Jeff's point of view was to *encourage* or *promote* that point of view and the actions that flowed from it. Encouraging Jeff's position would entail (1) thanking Jeff for his input, recognizing the valid elements of his advice or criticism; and (2) genuinely asking for Jeff's advice in his areas of competence when it really might provide some helpful guidance.

If Jeff was feeling threatened by Sharon's independence and competence, going with the flow would enable him to re-evaluate his position and work on acceptance of the changes that she was making. Validating his competence in areas that were not strengths of hers might enable the context for him to criticize or give advice less in areas where she was equally or more competent than he.

Going with the flow made a lot of sense to Sharon. She shared with the therapist that perhaps she had been contributing to the problem by coming across as superwoman and as not wanting Jeff's help in any way. Her "systemic" insight was impressive.

Sharon responded to Jeff's advice and criticisms with grace and tried to see the validity of his comments, although she continued doing things the way she wanted to do them. More importantly, she began asking him for his input about what cars her company should buy for their sales force. Jeff was a car buff and was on top of the latest data on dependability and cost-effectiveness. She also requested his help in other areas in which he was knowledgeable. He was delighted, and the relationship improved significantly.

Jeff responded by giving less advice and offering input into fewer of Sharon's affairs. Surprisingly, he began asking her for her opinions about areas of her competence. He shared with her that perhaps he was frightened a bit about her recent job success and increased independence. He said that for a while it seemed that she was so self-sufficient that her relationship with him was for convenience only and not for any emotional needs. He said that he was worried that she would leave him. Finally, he agreed that he had been criticizing her too much and promised to keep an eye on himself. Her behavior enabled him to challenge his view or attributed meaning to the situation and permitted him to step away from his defensive position. He re-evaluated his behavior and was able to see her point of view about his advice giving and criticisms. By accepting his position and encouraging his advice in areas of his competence, Sharon set the conditions for Jeff to reach different conclusions and ultimately criticize her less.

Going with the flow can be very useful in a variety of situations in which there appears to be a stand-off involving radically different points of view. We hope that you may think of ways to apply this strategy. Please keep in mind that *acceptance* and *validation* of the other person's point of view is a crucial first step.

Chapter 13

Indirect Discouragement

The kind of situation appropriate for the strategy of indirect discouragement is one in which one person is doing something that has a direct negative impact on the other. Direct attempts to address the issue, such as assertiveness (with a peer) or discipline (with a child), have not been effective. The clear implication is that the person is deriving enough benefit from the behavior that its getting on the other's nerves is not sufficient reason for him or her to stop.

At times, the benefit to the person is not clear, and the behavior may even appear self-destructive. For example, the bright teenager who is doing poorly in school is hurting himself or herself and directly accomplishing nothing. Indirectly, the adolescent may be fitting in with a peer group that devalues good grades, or is finding a way to get his or her parents angry. This idea is referred to as "secondary gain" and is particularly relevant to many teenaged rebellious behaviors. The direct effects of many of these behaviors (school failure, drug abuse, fighting) are self-destructive but indirect effects seen as positive by the teenager (secondary gains) include expressing independence, fighting the system, and distancing from parents. In situations with teenagers deriving indirect benefits from negative behaviors, punishment and expressions of parental displeasure can boomerang, since getting parents upset can be seen as a plus.

Another factor to keep in mind when trying to influence another person's behavior is that it is tempting to try to influence the other person even when the effects of his or her behavior on you are minimal or absent. The urge to control or influence other people's behaviors in order to make one's own life more comfortable is a common one. In many cases, it is better to back off and cope with behavior that is mildly annoying or irritating. Indiscriminate attempts to change others is disrespectful to them and, ultimately, exhausting and time-consuming. We strongly suggest keeping your own impulses to control in check and utilizing our strategies only when the effects on you are negative *and* significant.

When the effect of one person's behavior on another is both negative and significant, and direct attempts to change the behavior fail, a spiral of escalating conflict and confrontation frequently results. The following examples illustrate this type of situation.

Jason is a sixteen-year-old who is irresponsible with and inconsiderate to his father, Howard. Jason's behavior not only inconveniences Howard, but it also causes Howard a great deal of emotional distress since he is afraid Jason will fail in school and do harm to himself as a result of his rebellious behavior. Neither compassion nor discipline has been effective, and it appears that Jason enjoys irritating Howard.

Paul has always done everything for his wife Leslie. The problem is he manages to sabotage any attempts she makes to assert her independence. When she confronted him about this, he seemed genuinely unaware he was doing it and got very defensive. Leslie got progressively more frustrated and angry as her attempts to assert herself had no positive impact on Paul's behavior.

Indirect discouragement involves finding ways to make it more difficult or less pleasant for the other person to do what bothers you without being direct or obvious. There are two aspects to the general strategy of indirect discouragement: constructive payback and creation of confusion.

Constructive payback occurs when one person surreptitiously attaches a negative consequence to the irritating behavior of another person. On the surface, it does look like a payback, or "You did that to me, so I'll do *this* to you." However, there are important differences. The main one is that constructive payback is used only after more direct, straightforward methods have been tried and have failed. Also, this strategy is to be done in an indirect and totally nonconfrontational way. It is best if the strategy is presented from a "one-down" position, that is, a position that looks like weakness instead of power.[64] By not obviously challenging the other person for power, one can avoid a lot of the conflict and rebelliousness that would likely accompany more direct methods.

Perhaps a brief example will help explain this further. Let's say a teenaged girl was supposed to do the dishes after dinner. Instead, she is on the phone with her boyfriend. Her mother, apparently absentmindedly, decides to run the vacuum. When the daughter complains, her mother says, "Gee, I'm sorry. I didn't realize you were on the phone. I thought you were in the kitchen. Don't worry, I'm almost done," yet she continues to vacuum for more than a few minutes.

This strategy was also used in Chapter 5, in the context of dealing with a domineering spouse. Giving a painfully detailed account of one's activities to a jealous partner, as outlined in Chapter 6, is another application of this strategy.

Constructive payback is based on sound behavioral principles. Punishment, like reward, can be effective even if it is not fully explained to or understood by the person receiving it. Parents are told that reward and punishment work better if they explain to their children why one or the other is being administered, for example: "You can stay up late because you got all your homework done," or "You can't watch television because you hit your sister."

However, reward and punishment work even without the explanation. (They work well with pets who most likely do not understand any verbal explanations.) This concept is particularly important with adolescents and adults, for whom not being told that they are being controlled may make any punishment worth enduring. In other words, if a teenager hears, "If you swear at me, you are grounded," he or she may swear as a way of saying, "You can't tell me what to do." In that case, the punishment is less important than feeling independent. Constructive payback makes the reason for the punishment less obvious and looks less like an attempt to control. It still works, but provokes less resistance.

There is another benefit to constructive payback beyond the ability to more effectively influence someone else's behavior. In the kinds of situations for which this strategy is being recommended, anger is usually present and growing. The other person's behavior is irritating, or worse, and it will not stop. Constructive payback allows a person to channel that anger into doing irritating things back to the other person, but in a planned way, designed to achieve a specific purpose. Still, it just feels good to do something back to someone who has been a constant source of irritation. This may sound childish, but it is realistic. It is all right, and even natural, to get a little secret enjoyment out of constructive payback, and it can prevent the build-up of anger and resentment.

A second type of indirect discouragement is the creation of confusion. Most people are quite predictable in the ways they act and react. Their predictability allows other people to anticipate and prepare responses for actions that are likely to occur. Unpredictability, and other methods that create confusion, produces an atmosphere in which change can occur. When people get confused, they become uncomfortable. Discomfort motivates people to find ways to change situations so as to reduce discomfort.

Roles, and the expectations they create, can make people predictable by limiting the ways in which they are "allowed" to behave: "A good parent is reasonable and consistent," "A good spouse is understanding and giving," "A good therapist is reserved and proper." These beliefs lead to limitations on the kinds of behavior a parent, spouse, or therapist can engage in. These limits reduce flexibility, and inflexibility reduces a person's ability to cope, especially with the unexpected. When two people are engaged in a conflict, the one who is willing to try anything to win often does. Sometimes a parent needs to act in nonparental ways to cope with a child who is rebellious and testing all limits. Being flexible involves doing what works as opposed to what is expected.[65]

When a person has been predictable, confusion is easily created by doing something very different from the predictable pattern. This strategy is particularly effective if a person who has been reasonable begins to do and say things that don't make sense. The authors have seen time and time again how teenagers who have been engaging in outrageous and senseless behaviors are stopped in their tracks when one parent (or both) "gets weird" on them.

Like constructive payback, creation of confusion can be fun for the perpetrator. We all like to let our hair down and be spontaneous. This strategy allows that to occur in the context of an effort to help a relationship. Probably one of the most significant effects of this strategy is that it interjects looseness and fun into situations that have become tense and desperate. In fact, the authors have noticed that many of their clients have reported feeling a lot better just by thinking about these strategies, without even having tried them.

These strategies can be applied to situations in a number of different kinds of relationships. Creation of confusion can be used in any relationship in which the participants interact enough to expect certain behaviors from each other: parent–child, spouse–spouse, friend–friend, colleague–colleague. Constructive payback is usually limited in its scope to situations in which the person using it has some control over things or situations important to the other: parent–child, spouse–spouse, employer–employee. The following examples have been selected to demonstrate more specifically how these strategies can be applied and the kinds of results they can produce.

Creating Confusion

Earlier, we introduced you to Howard and his sixteen-year-old son Jason. Howard and Jason's mother divorced when Jason was eight years old. Jason lived with his mother and his older sister after the divorce. Jason's mother did not work and lived on the alimony and child support paid by Howard. When the alimony stopped, she went on welfare. She harbored a great deal of anger toward Howard, whom she blamed for ruining her life, and she didn't hesitate to let Jason and his sister know her opinions. What she didn't tell them was that she had had numerous affairs when she was married to Howard, and that they divorced only when she refused to stop seeing her boyfriend.

Jason's sister got heavily involved with drugs, and her mother sent her to live with Howard. He got her into a treatment center, but it didn't help much. When she was released, she got back into drugs, seldom went to school, and got into trouble with the law. Howard spent a lot of time going to meetings with a family therapist, her probation officer, and her school counselor. Nothing seemed to help, and at age seventeen, she got pregnant, dropped out of school, and moved in with her boyfriend.

During this time, Jason continued to live with his mother, who lived in another state. She left him alone a lot and gave him very little structure or supervision. He frequently cut school and spent most of his time at home listening to music with his friends. Eventually, he decided he could live more comfortably with his father, and his mother agreed to let him go live with Howard.

Howard was delighted to have Jason with him. He disapproved of his ex-wife's life style and believed Jason was not getting the proper guidance from her. Also, he felt very guilty about his children since the divorce. That guilt was amplified tremendously when he was unable to help his daughter as he had hoped to. He resolved to succeed with Jason.

However, there were a number of factors he had not taken into account when he had made that resolution. First of all, Jason was not used to having any rules or supervision. In addition, he had expected to begin living the high life when he moved in with Howard, since his mother had told him for years how rich his father was (which was not true). Finally, Jason felt a lot of resentment toward Howard, since he had heard his mother bad-mouthing Howard for years.

Jason immediately began acting in an irresponsible and inconsiderate fashion. He missed a lot of school and seldom did his homework. He didn't do any chores around the house, or else did them very haphazardly. He played music very loudly and watched television at all hours.

Howard realized that Jason had lived a very unstructured life, and he had expected some adjustment problems. He tried to be very reasonable in setting limits with Jason and always explained at length his reasons for any rules he made. However, whenever he attempted to enforce any rules, Jason either ignored him or rejected angrily, calling Howard names and blaming him for all his and his mother's problems. Howard tried to listen to Jason and let him know he understood and empathized with his anger and frustration. Unfortunately, Jason seemed to have a virtually limitless supply of rage, and no matter how long and compassionately Howard listened, Jason was just as angry the next time Howard attempted to enforce any rules.

When Jason did not seem to be adjusting to his new environment, Howard decided to institute a plan of rewards and punishments. He tried to sit down with Jason and develop a plan jointly, but Jason was uncooperative. So Howard explained to Jason how he could earn allowance money and privileges (like driving the car) and told him what kinds of behavior (cutting school, swearing at Howard) would lead to grounding or phone restrictions.

Not only did this not work, but things also began to deteriorate. Jason did chores when he needed a little money, but more often he neglected them. He cut school and swore at his father, but was unperturbed by his punishments. When he was grounded, he made sure he did all he could to make Howard miserable. If Howard wasn't home, Jason would leave. One night, he waited until Howard was asleep, took the car, and got caught speeding at three o'clock in the morning, twenty miles from home. He and Howard regularly got into shouting matches, and Howard found himself neither able to reward Jason nor able to punish him effectively. The angrier Howard got, the more Jason appeared to enjoy it.

Howard entered therapy at a point when many people do: when he had tried everything that made sense to him and nothing had worked. Since Jason seemed to be resistant to direct attempts to influence him and seemed to seek out ways to provoke Howard, indirect discouragement was suggested. Howard and his therapist developed a strategy that relied heavily upon creating confusion, and Howard proved to be very adept at it.

One way Jason earned money was by washing the car. He hadn't done it for a few weeks, so Howard began washing it one Saturday. Jason came running outside and said, "I was going to do that later."

Howard replied, "You were? Great." But he kept on washing the car.

Jason repeated, "Dad, I was going to do that later."

Howard said, "Great," and kept on washing.

Occasionally, Howard reversed reward and punishment. He gave Jason a dollar for swearing at him, but later restricted his phone privileges for doing his homework. In the middle of a calm, superficial conversation, Howard would begin to yell: *"I think I'll read the paper now!"* As soon as he noticed an argument starting, he would laugh and say, "Jason, you really crack me up."

Trying to describe all the different methods Howard used to create confusion cannot do justice to how creative and downright weird he got. He also used a little constructive payback. For example, he would let the air out of one car tire when he knew Jason was in a hurry to get somewhere. But he mainly relied on confusion.

He did this so well that Jason became genuinely concerned about his father's mental health. He started swearing and yelling much less at Howard and seemed to be "walking on eggshells," when he used to do whatever he pleased. Howard overheard

Jason on the phone with his mother, saying, "I'm worried about Dad. I really think he's cracking up." Howard took advantage of this opportunity to act even stranger. One night Jason heard a strange, thumping sound in the laundry room. He went in to find a dictionary in the clothes dryer. Howard explained that he had spilled a little water on it.

Jason did become more cautious and considerably more respectful with Howard. He also somewhat toned down his antisocial activities. He still missed school occasionally and wasn't all that reliable about his responsibilities. For his part, Howard was relieved to be doing something that had some positive effect. In addition, he was thoroughly enjoying himself. His only complaint to his therapist was that he didn't really know what to say when Jason's guidance counselor asked him what he had done to improve things at home. He said he thought about it for a minute and answered, "I put the dictionary in the dryer."

Constructive Payback

When Paul came along, Leslie was looking for a knight on a white charger, and Paul was the perfect man for the job. Leslie had married her first husband, Jim, right after high school. They had three children and she was very happy. Jim treated her much better than her parents had, and he really seemed to love her. Then, after ten years of marriage, Leslie discovered Jim was having an affair. It hadn't been going on for long, but he freely admitted it when she confronted him and refused to give it up. Leslie tried to live with the situation, but couldn't. After six months, she filed for divorce. Against her attorney's advice, she went easy on Jim in the settlement, trusting that he would take care of her. He didn't. Leslie had to go to work for the first time in her life. She gave up the house and moved in with her parents. This situation was much less than ideal.

Then, along came Paul. He was a successful professional, five years her junior, and had never been married. Her having three children didn't bother him. Paul seemed too good to be true. He promised to take care of her and to help her raise her children. Leslie was a little leery, but she agreed to marry Paul.

He turned out to be all he had advertised. He was a very good provider, and Leslie found herself in a much larger house than she had with Jim. Paul didn't expect her to work and even suggested she get help with the housekeeping, an offer she declined. He had trouble getting along with her older son, but he was a good step-father to the children.

Things went well for Paul and Leslie until a few years after the youngest child had left the house. When her youngest was in college, Leslie had begun working part time for Paul, managing his office. Since he had had trouble with his employees in the past, he was happy to work with Leslie, who was very organized and detail-oriented. Still, he always checked her work and gave her suggestions and orders regarding the way things ought to be done.

Leslie began to notice a pattern with Paul, which she had not been aware of previously. She started to see him as a "control freak." Whenever they went out, he made all the arrangements, and he planned all the vacations. In spite of the fact that Leslie ran his office, he still balanced both the business and household check-books himself. He tended to dominate the conversation when they were out with friends, and he thought nothing of interrupting her when she was talking.

Paul hadn't changed, but Leslie was now viewing him through different eyes as a result of her own developmental changes, as well as of working with him at the office. Much of what had drawn her to him now irritated her. When they met, she wanted to be taken care of and to have someone else make the decisions. He was still good to her in most ways. She got whatever she wanted, and he went out of his way to compliment her and dote on her. She felt she was in a dilemma and was not without guilt. After all, she wanted to change things after all these years, and that wasn't fair.

She tried telling herself she was being silly or was going through a phase, but she got steadily more angry and resentful toward Paul. She tried doing little things to express her autonomy, but he squelched them—in nice ways. She would make plans for dinner, but he would always find an excuse to make a small change in them (a different restaurant, a different time). She tried asserting herself verbally in little ways. He listened and seemed to accept what she was saying, but his actions didn't change at all. Finally, one night, she blew her stack. She started screaming and yelling and told him she was sick of his treating her like a child and running her life. She told him he wanted to control people just like his mother had controlled him and that she was sick to death of it.

Paul was genuinely startled. He felt he had always taken good care of Leslie and thought she had appreciated it. He said that he was being no different than he had ever been, and that he was shocked and hurt by her outburst. He suggested that she might be suffering from "empty nest syndrome." Then he told her that he had to do things his way, and that if she loved him, she would accept that.

Leslie was confused and depressed when she first talked to her therapist. In some ways, she felt like a spoiled child. Paul had given her everything, and now she was complaining about how he was doing it. He loved her, was faithful to her, and never abused her physically or verbally. On the other hand, she didn't feel like a worthwhile person. The only job over which she had maintained control, raising her children, was essentially completed. It was time for her to establish herself in a different way, and she felt very stifled by Paul. She surprised herself with the extent of her resentment toward him.

In this situation, as in most situations like it, there wasn't a "bad guy." Paul was doing what he thought was best for Leslie. He did it the way he did everything else: by taking charge. She had appreciated that and accepted it once. However, she had come to a point in her life when she needed something else. She certainly did not want to end the relationship, but she was not willing to keep going along with it as it was. Direct attempts to address this with Paul had not gone well, so it was time to try something else.

A change strategy was developed for Leslie that utilized a combination of constructive payback from a one-down position with behavioral assertiveness. The constructive payback was very easy to set up, since Paul really did depend on her for a lot of things. He liked to plan and be in control, but for his plans to work, she had to perform as expected. She began to become forgetful and inefficient in response to his attempts to be in charge. She forgot to run errands for him, to take phone messages, or to have his laundry ready before business trips. She became a little less organized and effective at home and at the office. This quickly became very disconcerting to Paul. At times, he questioned her about why she had changed. She told him her depression (for which she had sought therapy) had made her "forgetful and scatter-brained." He couldn't argue with that.

At the same time Leslie became more behaviorally assertive. She pursued interests she had neglected (golf lessons, community college courses), spent more time with her friends, and planned trips on her own. This was somewhat upsetting to Paul since they had always done things together, or she had consulted with him and let him help with whatever she was doing. He was uncomfortable, but he didn't want to interfere with her therapy.

As Paul resisted Leslie's independence less, she became less forgetful and more efficient. Over time, he became considerably less involved in influencing her actions, and she was able to go back to her effective, organized self. He knew something had changed, but he wasn't sure how. Their new way of interacting was still difficult for him at times, but he and she got along well again, and he was satisfied.

The two examples just presented show how confusion (Howard and Jason) and constructive payback (Leslie and Paul) can be used in effective and nonconfrontational ways to help different kinds of relationships. They were not used to usurp power, but rather to restore, or create, the appropriate balance of power in the relationships (equality between Leslie and Paul, and some degree of parental authority for Howard with Jason). The outcomes in both situations were less tension and upset and more satisfactory, effective relationships. The final example in this chapter combines confusion and constructive payback in a relationship between two parents and their teenage son.

Combining Confusion with Payback

Scott, the eighteen-year-old son of Stan and Dena, dropped out of school and got a job .working as an elementary school janitor. His parents were almost relieved. He had been a constant source of frustration to them through both his failures in school and his insensitive and irresponsible behaviors. He left his clothes lying all over the house, came to meals if he felt like it, came and went according to his own whims, demanding meals at inconvenient times and either coming home late or not until the next morning.

Stan and Dena tried everything with Scott: reason, reward and punishment, threats. Nothing seemed to work. They were angry and felt used and abused. They saw him as completely self-absorbed and not at all concerned about their needs or feelings. Stan and Dena were ready to try just about anything. Since Scott had turned eighteen, they knew their influence on him was even more limited than it had been when he was a minor. Yet they were concerned with his future and, as he was still living in their house, wanted to use whatever leverage they had.

The therapist working with Stan and Dena took great pains to explain to them the kind of situation for which the confusion/constructive payback strategy was relevant. First of all, the situation would involve a teenager who had a problem attitude and who was acting in ways that were contrary to his own best interests. Secondly, the kid would have to be so wrapped up in himself that he would think that the impact of his behaviors on the people close to him was unimportant or totally irrelevant. Finally, the parents needed to be angry and frustrated to the extreme so that they would be truly motivated to act on the therapist's ideas.

A strategy of confusion creation and constructive payback was then outlined for Stan and Dena. The therapist acknowledged that his suggestions might sound weird,but that their purpose was to have a positive impact on Scott. Confusion induction was explained as a way to get him to put some effort into thinking about what was going on with his parents instead of being totally absorbed in himself. Constructive payback was presented as a way to discomfit him in response to his thoughtless and irresponsible behaviors.

Stan and Dena stayed with constructive payback for a few weeks and were delighted both with the effects on Scott and with their enjoyment in carrying it out. They targeted his irresponsibility about laundry and his inconsistent demands about meals. One night, they went out for dinner and "forgot" to tell Scott. Of course, they apologized profusely and prepared last-minute-demand meals, but the food was always over- or undercooked. And they always offered to cook something else, knowing he was in a hurry and didn't have time to wait.

Clothes he neglected to pick up were "overlooked" by Stan and Dena and never made it to the washing machine. Wearing dirty clothes bothered him, but not much. What did get to him was the dryer not "operating correctly" and that his clean clothes were always damp. Even Scott couldn't deal with that. He accused his parents of conspiring against him. They were shocked and mortified that he would even consider such a thing.

Stan and Dena decided to utilize confusion as a method for dealing with his staying out all night in defiance of curfew. In spite of the frequency of his curfew violations, he always promised to be home on time. His parents decided to use that promise to confuse him.

After a night during which he neither returned home nor called, he phoned his parents at 7:00 A.M. As soon as he said, "Hello," his mother hung up on him. This was repeated a couple of times. On his next call he pleaded, "Don't hang up, it's me, Scott!" Dena replied, "My son is upstairs asleep. I don't know who this is, but you're not funny." Then Stan got on the phone and said angrily, "Quit harassing my wife or I'll get the cops on you." In desperation, Scott had the friend he was with call. The friend swore Scott was with him, but Stan said, "David, we're really disappointed in you. We never thought you would take part in a tasteless prank like this."

When Scott finally got home, his parents ignored him as he came in and went to his room. He came downstairs and was greeted by Stan, "Well, Sleeping Beauty, you finally got up. Some of your friends were playing games with us on the phone. I'm surprised you didn't wake up as many times as the phone rang."

Scott said, "Dad, I wasn't here. I stayed out all night."

Stan laughed, "Oh, so you're in on it too. Very funny, young man."

Exasperated, Scott replied, "Either you're both trying to mess with my mind, or you've gone seriously weird."

Scott became noticeably more responsible. He actually began doing his own laundry. He tried very hard to stick to his curfew and was reasonably successful. Stan and Dena also noticed changes in themselves. Their desperation had changed to enjoyment. Before therapy, they had gotten to the point where they were starting to blame each other for Scott's problems. Now they felt as though they were acting as a team and that they were able to share in the creative process of handling Scott differently.

Chapter 14

Individual Applications
Help Yourself

In this chapter, we come full circle to the beginning of this book. Early on, we discussed how systems theory differed from traditional thinking about emotional problems. Systems theory looks at individuals as parts of larger systems and therefore has a great deal to say about addressing problems in relationships, families, and organizations. Traditional psychotherapy has focused on the individual as a separate entity, while systems theory sees the individual as part of a larger whole.

Nevertheless, the strategies derived from systems theory can also be useful for individuals dealing with problems that are not directly related to interactions with other people, such as worrying, procrastination, and overeating. Systems theory looks at *elements* of a system and how they interact with one another. In interpersonal situations, those elements are people. Within an individual there are many elements which interact with each other.

The human body is a system composed of many subsystems: the central nervous system, the circulatory system, and so forth. Elements of those systems—cells of various kinds, fluids—interact within and with other subsystems to allow the body to function as a whole. To understand physical health and illness, a knowledge of both the individual systems and their complex interactions is critical.

Human personality functioning is equally complex and is considerably less well defined than the physical sphere. Personality theorists agree that there are many elements and processes that comprise human thought, emotion, and behavior, but that there is tremendous difference of opinion as to what those elements and processes are and what they are called. Freudians talk about "ego," "defense mechanisms," and "fixation." Rogerians refer to "congruence," Gestaltists to "introjects," and cognitive theorists to "internal dialogue."

Perhaps knowing what all those elements are and what to call them is not as important as recognizing that they are components of the systems that are involved in thought, emotion, and behavior. Problems can be created by individuals in the same ways problems occur in other interpersonal systems, such as by repeating unsuccessful solution attempts or focusing on when the problem occurs rather than when it doesn't.

People who come to therapists are acutely aware that there are many different, and often conflicting, elements operating within them. Scarcely a week goes by in which one of the authors fails to hear from a client, "Doc, I think I must have a split personality," or "I feel like 'Sybil' sometimes."

Most of us are aware of different parts of ourselves which come into play at different times or which cause confusion for us in certain situations. For example, when starting a new job, one part of us can be excited and another scared. One part wants to stay in a relationship, and another wants to leave. One minute a person can be happy, and the next down in the dumps.

If these examples were indicators of "split personalities," this diagnosis would be seen more frequently than the common cold, since confusion, mixed feelings, and internal conflicts are endemic to the human condition. However, for some people, these conflicts are not effectively resolved or tolerated, and they become ongoing problems that create chronic emotional distress, cognitive confusion, or behavioral paralysis.

The problem areas we will address in this chapter can be emotional (anxiety, anger), behavioral (procrastination, overeating), or cognitive (obsessive worry). They differ from problems discussed in previous chapters in that they are not primarily related to interactions with other people. They do not occur in a vacuum, and people and situations can make them better or worse. However, they mainly involve a person in relation to him- or herself.

We will describe a variety of strategies, situations in which they can be helpful, and examples that demonstrate how the strategies can be implemented. They are similar in many ways to the interpersonal strategies outlined earlier in the book, but they have little in common with each other beyond their basis in the various schools of systemic thinking outlined in Chapter 7.

Inviting Problems

Individuals face many different problems in which trying to prevent them not only doesn't help, but also frequently makes them worse. A person giving a speech tries to look calm and confident, only to stutter, perspire, and shake. Someone prone to panic attacks tries so desperately to avoid panic that he or she brings it on and then escalates it. Few of us have not had the experience of trying to fall asleep, while succeeding in staying up most of the night. A number of sexual problems also fall into this category: the man who strives to achieve an erection, but remains impotent, or the woman who pulls out all the stops in her efforts to reach orgasm, only to become more and more frustrated.

A factor many of these situations share in common is that tension makes the problem worse. It is easy to see how tension can sabotage efforts to sleep or stay calm. In most cases trying produces tension, regardless of what specifically is tried. When we try, we concentrate, put forth effort, and often struggle to overcome obstacles. All these activities add to tension, which in turn produces the very problems we seek to avoid.

People manage to come up with very clever ways to prevent these problems. Woody Allen lampooned this in *Play It Again Sam.* His character credits his ability to postpone orgasm to his thinking about baseball during sex, and his partner replies that she now understands why he kept yelling "slide." For most men, distraction, no matter how clever, is not sufficient to prevent premature ejaculation, and attempts to distract often make it worse.

Rather than trying something truly different to help with these problems, people usually do variations on one theme. What their coping efforts have in common are attempts to *prevent* the problem. A more effective solution to this type of difficulty can be to try to bring on or invite the problem.[66] Since many of these problems occur involuntarily, it is difficult to know what to do to cause them. Consequently, "trying" is interrupted, as it is not clear what to try. As effort is reduced, so is tension, and the problem is less likely to occur. If a person *is* able to bring on the problem, he or she has the opportunity to observe the problem and what makes it better and worse, since all effort is not being poured into trying to prevent it.

One of the authors (J. R.) worked for a time as a consultant to an impotence clinic. A physician there told him of a patient who was so frustrated by his inability to achieve erections that he got a penile implant. The implant, which had to be put in surgically, mechanically made his penis rigid and allowed him to have intercourse whenever he pleased. When he came in to see his doctor for a post-surgery check-up, he was ecstatic. The doctor asked him how the implant was working (it operated by pushing a "button" under the skin which pumped fluid into the implant). The patient said that he didn't know, since he hadn't used it. He now got erections with no problem! Just knowing that the implant was there allowed him to relax and stop trying, and as a result, he got erections naturally.

The ways this strategy can be implemented are usually pretty straightforward. A person afraid of looking nervous during a speech needs to try to perspire, stutter, and make his or her hands shake. The insomniac should try his or her level best to stay awake. In some situations, the way to approach this strategy is not so obvious. The following example shows how to use this strategy and the kind of results that can be produced.

Mike, twenty-eight years old and single, had had emotional problems since he was a teenager. He had been hospitalized three separate times for what most people would call "nervous break-downs." During those times, he heard voices that weren't there, isolated himself from people, and had paranoid thoughts. He was put on medication and received individual and group counseling at a public mental health clinic. By the time he was twenty-eight he had been "stabilized" for four years, that is, he no longer heard voices or thought people were plotting against him, and he had not had to return to the hospital during that time period.

Mike was living with his mother and had a job as a janitor at his church. He came across as a bright and pleasant young man, but he was painfully shy. He had always kept to himself, but since his first hospitalization, he found it even harder to socialize than before. If he was in a one-on-one situation with a person with whom he felt comfortable and whom he had known for some time, he could carry on an intelligent and witty conversation. He had a self-effacing sense of humor and was able to see the irony in many run-of-the-mill events.

However, when Mike was with a person he did not know well or in a group, he couldn't think of anything to say. His emotional problems had made him extremely sensitive to appearing different. So he tried very hard to look and sound "normal" and to fit in. He censored every idea before he verbalized it to make sure it didn't sound weird. As a result, he got so wrapped up in thought that he lost track of the flow of conversation and really felt at a loss. As he became aware of his perpetual silence in these situations, he tried harder to come up with things to say. He read the paper every day to remain conversant with current events and rehearsed small talk as he drove places.

Mike's counselor suggested to him that whenever he found himself in one of the social situations he couldn't handle, he would follow one rule: "I am not allowed to talk unless I am asked a direct question." In other words, he was being asked to invite the problem, silence, that he had strived so hard to avoid. Mike was reluctant, at first, to try this and was skeptical about how it could help. Nevertheless, he agreed to give it a try. He would report back to his therapist on what he had observed about himself and the situation.

To his surprise, Mike discovered that it quickly became difficult for him to remain silent. Evidently, he had been speaking up all along, just not as much as he thought he should. He noticed other interesting things as well. When he stopped thinking about what to say, he followed the conversation better, and ideas spontaneously came to him. Some people had said things that he had been thinking. Also, some people said things that sounded "off the wall" to him, but nobody had seemed to mind or notice.

The overall effect on Mike was that he felt more confident and less pressured. He found himself breaking his "rule" and speaking up. When he began to feel tongue-tied, he just reminded himself that he could always try to be silent.

Trying to prevent something that happens involuntarily and made worse by tension can be a counterproductive strategy. Shifting gears by looking to bring on the problem can reduce the tension and pressure and allow the problem not to occur, or to produce the problem under circumstances under which it can be observed and analyzed instead of futilely battled.

Permission Not to Change

This strategy is very similar to the one just described. In both cases, the focus is taken off trying to rid oneself of a problem. The difference is that in the strategy of "permission not to change" there is no attempt to produce the problem, it is accepted or allowed to exist.

Once a problem is identified as a problem, a person tends to go about trying to remove it. The wisdom of doing so is seldom questioned. After all, who wants a problem? When efforts to resolve the problem are effective, it is not given a second thought. However, when the problem persists other things can happen. As we pointed out in the last section, sometimes trying to solve a problem makes it worse. Other times, failed solutions just lead to frustration and futility.

By calling a situation a problem, a person categorizes that situation as uniformly negative and can lose sight of benefits he or she may derive from that situation. For instance, a person who has been hurt in love can find he or she has a problem with intimacy. Defining that as a problem overlooks the positive aspects of that situation. Not being able to get close prevents one from becoming too vulnerable and getting hurt again before adequate healing has had a chance to take place.

Getting rid of a problem can be a risky proposition. Systems-oriented therapists often warn their clients who find themselves stymied in their efforts to change to beware of the "dangers of improvement."[67] Change is always stressful, and in their zeal to get out of unpleasant situations, people can easily overlook the possibilities that the present situation isn't all that bad and that change could result in worse discomfort. The message of this particular strategy is that there are at least two ways to solve a problem: alter the situation or accept it. We live in an action-oriented society, and accepting things is not always seen in a positive light. It is often construed as giving up or running away.

A young man entered therapy primarily because he was concerned about his inability to meet women. It turned out that the only place he tried was in crowded singles bars. He didn't drink, and he found the noise disconcerting to the point where he felt "spaced out" in those settings. He wanted to learn how to function more effectively in the "bar scene." Instead, he learned to accept that he wasn't cut out for that kind of life-style and stopped putting himself in those situations. When he began doing other things, he met a woman in a church group, and within a year they were engaged.

This strategy bears a number of similarities to the interpersonal strategies outlined in Chapters 10 and 12. By giving himself or herself permission not to change, a person changes the meaning of the problem situation and uses creative interpretation to create a more helpful reality. In the previous example, the young man changed his interpretation of himself from a failure with women to someone who didn't fit in the world of singles bars. It is also easy to see how allowing oneself not to change is a form of going with the flow, as in the strategies in Chapter 12.

Of all the individual strategies described in this chapter, permission not to change might be the most widely applicable. It can be used with virtually any problem. We are suggesting, however, that it be considered particularly for situations in which change has been tried and found difficult to achieve.

An interesting application of this strategy is to the problem of procrastination. This is a problem that is notoriously difficult to deal with. One of the authors was on a call-in radio show with a colleague, and a gentleman called in asking for ideas on how to deal with procrastination. Jokingly, it was suggested he call back the next day. He was more than happy to oblige. That is what makes procrastination so hard to handle, since people put off dealing with the problem the way they put off everything else.

In order to understand procrastination, it is necessary to get back to the idea of dualistic elements of personality. Fritz Perls, the father of Gestalt therapy, referred to the two opposite parts of the personality as "top dog" and "underdog."[68] The top dog, the part that is in charge and has most of the power, says to the procrastinator, "Do this." The underdog, the part that has relatively less power, is strong enough to sabotage and prevent the top dog from getting things done.

People generally attempt to handle procrastination by siding with the top dog and trying to find creative ways to get things done more quickly. The "permission not to" strategy suggests instead saying that it is all right to continue not to do things. In a sense, this could be construed as listening to the underdog. When we discussed communication theory, we looked at how words and behavior often conflict. The procrastinator is saying to himself or herself, "I want to get things done," but his or her behavior says the opposite. This strategy allows a person to listen to behavior instead of staying bogged down in thinking, or self-talk.

Dan began therapy when he was released from the hospital following a suicide attempt. He was nineteen-years-old and had graduated from high school the previous year. Since high school, Dan had held a few part-time jobs, but he still couldn't decide what he really wanted to do. His reasons for trying to kill himself were complex, but his self-destructive behavior had a lot to do with the pressure he was putting on himself to find a career. He lived at home, and his parents were being very patient and were putting no pressure on him to make a decision.

After Dan had been in therapy for a few weeks, his mood had improved and he started feeling more like his old self. Unfortunately, that also meant he began putting pressure on himself to begin looking for a job. He had been neglecting his friends since he got out of the hospital and told himself it was time to socialize more. However, Dan was ashamed of what he had done and was not eager to face his friends. Nor was finding a job any less intimidating than it had been.

As a result, Dan kept putting things off. He looked through the want ads, but never got around to calling any of the numbers. His friends called asking him to do things with them, but he made up excuses. He lied to his parents and his therapist about his lack of follow-through on employment possibilities because he was embarrassed. He really did want to get a job, and he missed spending time with his friends.

When Dan's therapist learned about Dan's procrastination regarding a job search, he immediately suggested that Dan allow himself not to look for a job or see his friends. After all, he had almost died, and then spent three weeks in a hospital. He needed to let himself heal.

At first, Dan had a hard time believing it was really all right to do that. Granted, it was what he was already doing, but the idea that it was permissible to keep putting things off was hard to get used to. As he got more comfortable with his relative lack of activity, Dan was able to see more clearly what had been going on in his life. He had been so worried about not letting his parents down that he had not spent much time thinking about what *he* wanted to do with his life. He realized that neither his parents nor his friends were disappointed in or disgusted with him, but he had been so afraid that that was the case that he became immobilized. He eased into socializing when he felt ready, and when he resumed his job search, he felt the stakes were not so high and was much less nervous.

Procrastination is certainly not the only kind of problem for which this strategy is useful. Maria had taught high school English ever since her youngest child had started school. When she retired, she vowed to finally take it easy. She wanted to read, play bridge, do gardening, and spend more time with her husband. He owned his own business, but had many employees he trusted to run the business, so he could make his own hours.

Very soon after her retirement, however, Maria found herself doing volunteer tutoring, playing in three bridge groups (and organizing many of their functions), serving as a curriculum consultant to the school district in which she had worked, and redecorating the house. She spent relatively little time with her husband, who felt let down, and she felt bad about her inability to follow through on her own plans to relax and live a peaceful, slow-paced life. She was busier than she had been when she was working.

In therapy, she sought help to slow down, not overschedule herself, and just do nothing sometimes. But she just couldn't follow through on any of the plans she and her therapist came up with to help her reach her goals. When she tried to slow down, it felt strange and uncomfortable to her, as new behavior patterns often do.

After viewing her problem different ways, her therapist suggested she consider allowing herself to stay the way she was. She came in for her next session and said, "I better stop kidding myself. This is how I am. I'm only happy when I'm busy and I've always been that way. It's time to stop pretending all that will change just because I've retired. It's time to stop making promises to my husband and myself that I can't keep."

Sure enough, when her therapist followed up with her six months later, she was as busy as ever and happy about it. This is the way "permission not to" strategies often work out. People try hard to change into someone whom they think they should be, only to find things work out better when they allow themselves to remain who they are.

Putting on the Brakes

When people are in emotional pain, they want to do what they can to remove it as soon as possible. This desire creates a sense of urgency, which can create new problems and worsen existing ones.[69] It increases pressure and produces stress. Not that stress is all bad. In the absence of stress, people often find themselves unmotivated. However, people experiencing problems are already facing uncomfortable levels of stress, and amplifying that stress usually reduces coping abilities.

Also, in the face of pressure to do something quickly, a person can act before he or she knows the best direction in which to go. And since the person is in a hurry, many steps are rapidly taken, and it becomes difficult to change back when the actions don't help. Even in the event that the actions do help, quick change is stressful, regardless of whether it is positive or negative; and this stress can produce new problems. Finally, changes that are made overnight tend to be less permanent. Gradual adjustment to new ways of thinking and behaving isn't given a chance to work and, thus, it becomes easy to revert to the old ways.

In spite of all the reasons to slow down when under pressure, people give themselves rationales for rushing the pace of change: "Life is short," "I've felt this way long enough," "I can't stand this another minute." It is easy to overlook reasons for hitting the brakes instead of the accelerator pedal. Slowing down allows a person to relax and reduce the stress that could well be contributing to the problem. Living with the emotional pain rather than frantically trying to get rid of it gives a person a chance to learn to handle the pain and not blow it out of proportion. Urgency narrows a person's focus on immediate ways to resolve the problem. Backing off fights tunnel vision, helps a person broaden his or her focus to consider a variety of alternative paths (some of which may take a little longer to work), and places the problem in a more realistic perspective.

Putting on the brakes is not so much a specific strategy as it is an attitude or a style. As such, it applies to virtually all situations. It can be particularly useful for a person whose general coping style involves rushing, striving, and perfectionism. Slowing down and acting more deliberately can keep those tendencies in check. Problems that involve a significant anxiety or stress-related component also respond well to this approach.

Pacing is a more general form of putting on the brakes. Where a person driven to resolve a problem quickly can benefit from applying brakes to his change attempts, pacing oneself is a process that can be applied to most activities. Regardless of how smart or resourceful a person is, he or she can only effectively do one thing at a time. Yet, there are few people who don't find themselves regularly doing one thing while thinking about doing something else. This is like functioning in the present while at the same time running to catch up with the future.

This looking ahead creates anxiety and reduces one's ability to do the task at hand well. A slogan in a popular self-help program goes something like this: "Get your head where your feet are." Staying focused in the present by doing and thinking about one thing at a time and approaching that one task at a comfortable pace is a key component of any program geared toward managing stress. In fact, many of our clients find that focusing on pacing themselves is, by itself, enough to significantly reduce stress. Rushing and trying too hard gives the behavioral message, "This is a big deal." Slowing down and acting more deliberately places matters in a better perspective.

Terri was thirty-one years old when she decided that her life wasn't going the way it should. She was unmarried and working as a clerk in a department store. Early in her first therapy session she said, "I need to meet a compatible guy soon because I don't have much time left to have kids. I also have to find a new career or go back to school and get some more training. At my age, I should be a lot further ahead in a lot of areas than I am."

Since Terri knew so clearly what she wanted, her therapist wondered why she felt she needed counseling. Terri explained that she had been trying to reach her goals, but that she was getting more and more anxious. She would make plans to attend a singles group or talk to a college guidance counselor, but she would get so nervous that she had to back out at the last minute. On a few occasions she was able to get herself into social situations around single men, but by the time she arrived she was so anxious and self-conscious that she couldn't carry on a conversation with a friend, much less a stranger.

Her anxiety had gotten so bad that she had begun having trouble driving too far away from her apartment, even if she was just going shopping or visiting a friend. The less she found herself able to do, the more pressure she felt. "After all," she said, "I'm already thirty-one years old, and what have I done?"

The irony in this situation was that Terri was not unhappy with her job or with living alone. She had friends and interests that she pursued. But for her, thirty-one was a magical age. It symbolized being over the hill, or at least out of her youth. The goals of settling down and pursuing a new career became demands. They changed from "I want to do these things" to "I have to do them *now.*"

By changing her goals to demands and drastically shortening the time she gave herself to meet these demands, Terri created more stress than she could handle. She produced a problem by pressuring herself to reach her goals more quickly and responded to the problem's worsening with more pressure. She was nervous about changing careers and had had some experiences with men who had hurt her. Pushing herself to deal with this tapped into a lot of fear, and she also became obsessed about this night and day. She lost all objectivity.

Her therapist urged her to apply the brakes a little and slow down the pace with which she pursued her goals. At first, as in most situations like this, slowing down felt like standing still. As she gradually got used to a much slower pace, her anxiety began to subside. She made plans, but took them one step at a time. If a situation didn't feel right to her, she let herself pass it up.

She discovered that there was a man with whom she worked who had been sending her signals that he was interested, but she had been so intent on going to singles functions that she had not paid attention. They began to date and got along well. She did have to remind herself constantly not to begin planning the wedding after each date. She signed up for a business course at a local junior college to see how she liked it.

Terri's goals were reasonable ones, and the crisis she went through at age thirty-one was painful, but not unusual. Putting on the brakes allowed her to access her own resources to deal with her crisis and work toward her goals without rushing and pressuring herself.

Setting Time Aside

Some types of problems can be addressed effectively using an approach involving complete cessation of the problematic behavior. For example, an alcoholic can totally abstain from drinking as a major part of a recovery program. Other types of problems, such as overeating, have to be managed or controlled, since the behavior creating the problem cannot be stopped altogether.

People who suffer from excessive worry, obsession, or painful feelings (anger, resentment, grief, sadness) would prefer to solve the problem by having the uncomfortable experience cease. However, few people are able to totally eradicate unpleasant experiences. Instead, they find themselves having to manage or control their problems in other ways. The strategy of "setting time aside" offers ideas on how to manage difficulties, such as those mentioned above, which (1) occur just about every day, (2) are excessive and intrusive, and (3) have not responded to attempts to stop them completely.

Generally, what this strategy involves is putting aside fifteen to thirty minutes per day, preferably in the early evening, to devote exclusively to worry, obsession, experiencing grief, feeling anger, or doing whatever it is that is being defined as a problem. Of course, the problem will occur at many other times during the day. At those times, attempts should be made to recognize the onset of the problem as quickly as possible and to postpone it until the specific time allotted to it later that day. One should not expect these attempts to always be successful, but they often will be.

Becky was carrying around a lot of resentment, even though she tried very hard to deny that she did. She felt that she had been treated unfairly by her parents, her husband, her ex-husband, and two of her children. Every day, thoughts would pop into her head that reminded her of the things these people had done to her that she saw as unkind or unfair. She tried to push these thoughts out of her mind, but they lingered and always returned. Becky was, by nature, a pleasant and accepting person, so these intrusive, angry thoughts galled her. She sought professional help when she noticed her resentment spilling over onto other people (friends, store clerks) and manifesting itself in a short fuse and sarcastic humor.

Her therapist assigned her the task of channeling her resentment into a specified time period each day, during which she was to contemplate all the wrongs done to her by her parents, husbands, and children. She was not to distract herself away from her anger, but rather to allow herself to feed it. The first thing she noticed was that she was bothered by the anger and resentment much less often outside of her "resentment time." Next, Becky decided that two or three times a week was sufficient for her to focus on her resentments. Gradually, she also found herself forgiving some of the people and draining the reservoir of anger she had allowed to build up over the years.

There are a number of possible explanations for why setting time aside works. One is that the behavior trying to be eliminated serves a useful purpose for the person. Some people believe that worry prepares them for future crises, and others believe that it can help prevent them. Also, obsession can be a way of not letting go of a person, even if that person is no longer around. It is true that these reasons are not logical, but important parts of our minds do not operate on logic. Setting time aside can reduce time spent on uncomfortable activities without eliminating them and their potential benefits altogether.

This strategy also circumvents "black-or-white" thinking, which is common to many emotional problems. It is easy to think of things as being present or absent. If there are two conflicting parts to a person—one that wants the behavior eliminated and one that prefers to hang onto it—this strategy offers a compromise.

Within a period of six months, Danny suffered the loss of both his father and his younger sister. Over a year later, he still found himself thinking of them every day. He tried to put the thought out of his mind, since he thought that by this time he should have finished grieving. Still, so many things reminded him of his father and sister that he often thought about them and cried. When he set aside grieving time daily, as his therapist suggested, he sometimes spent as little as ten minutes and at other times over an hour. Gradually, he discovered he needed less time and could skip days at a time. Also, things that used to churn up sad memories no longer had that effect on him.

So, by grieving only at home and at a certain time, Danny reduced the number of situations that reminded him of his grief. This suggests another explanation for how setting time aside works. When people grieve, obsess, or worry all day long in many different places, a wide variety of stimuli (cues) come to be associated with the troublesome thoughts and can subsequently trigger them. Limiting the times and places at which such thinking occurs reduces the number of things the mind associates with the thoughts and, therefore, how frequently the thoughts occur.

Thomas Borkovec, a "worry" researcher, suggests that this explanation is part of the reason that "worry time" helps decrease the amount of time chronic worriers spend worrying.[70] His research showed that setting aside a thirty-minute "worry time" at the same time and place every day reduced worry significantly. This strategy did not work for everyone and did not eliminate worry altogether, but it was effective.

Dolores had always been an involved mother, but she was somewhat relieved when her three children grew up and moved out of the house because she thought she could stop worrying about what they were doing. Much to her chagrin, she found that the less contact she had with her adult children, the more she worried about them. She worried about their doing drugs, contracting AIDS, going out with the wrong people. There was little she did not worry about.

She was happy to comply with her therapist's request that she do a half an hour of concentrated worry about her children daily, because she felt she "needed" to worry but hated how it had taken over her life. Dolores became very proficient at postponing her worry until her daily worry time. During that period, she gave air time to all her many concerns about her children. The relative lack of worry she experienced during the rest of the day freed her up to spend more time with her friends and pursue neglected hobbies. She apologized to her therapist when she sheepishly admitted she had cut her worry time back to every other day, since other things had become more important to her. However, when her therapist contacted her three months after they had ended therapy, she was still using worry time two or three times a week. She had tried stopping altogether a couple of times, but the worry always came back.

Setting time aside for worry or other uncomfortable habits is a useful strategy for decreasing their frequency and intensity. It seldom eliminates them altogether, nor is it intended to. One factor to keep in mind when using this strategy is that it is important to follow through with the scheduled time. Some people will postpone this time until a later time that never occurs. Trying to trick yourself into not worrying at all doesn't work. If you make a deal with yourself to set the time aside, keep it.

Dare to Be Average

There are times when, by striving to do his or her very best, a person ends up doing something poorly, at the last minute or not at all. Elliott played jazz saxophone. He had been told since the time he was very young that he had a special musical talent. He nurtured that talent by taking music lessons, playing in a variety of bands with different musical styles, and studying music in college. Jazz had always been his main musical interest, and during and after college he got a reputation around his home town (a fairly large Midwestern city) as one of the best players in the area.

As a result of his growing reputation, Elliott began getting opportunities to play with national artists who came through town on national tours, or to play jazz festivals. Elliott had always been somewhat of a perfectionist. He practiced long and hard and held himself to high standards. Some musicians disliked playing with him because he could be very critical of people who played below his standards. When he played with acts with national reputations, he found himself in situations in which the quality of his fellow musicians' performances was a cut above his own.

Elliott realized that if he wanted to get anywhere with his music, he had to improve. He worked even harder and put more pressure on himself to perform at his best every night. Then he started pushing himself too hard. He began to cancel gigs at the last minute, because he didn't feel he was ready. On a couple of occasions, he got so frustrated with himself that he walked off the stage in the middle of a set. He drank to calm his nerves before he played, and his performance deteriorated.

Elliott's therapist worked with him to get him to strive each night to give an "average" performance. Practicing extensively was out of the question, since it could lead to perfection. Mistakes would have to be made and he would need to blend in, not stand out. It was difficult to sell this concept to Elliott since perfectionism had always been a part of him and since recently he had become even more dedicated to reaching his full potential. His therapist presented this idea as a brief experiment designed to gather data. Fortunately, Elliott was miserable enough to give it a try.

The types of problems amenable to this strategy are ones in which there is strong pressure to do well, or great fear of doing poorly. Performance anxiety (leading to poor performance or inability to perform), procrastination, perfectionism, and the inability to meet deadlines can all be responsive to the "dare-to-be-average" strategy.

The strategy itself is quite simple. It involves attempting to perform in an average fashion instead of very well, the best one can, or perfectly. Ordinarily, conceptualizing this strategy as a brief and reversible experiment will be necessary, since people in pressured situations inflate the importance of their performance and catastrophize the consequences of doing poorly.

Allowing oneself to be average is helpful for a number of reasons. It removes pressure and allows one to go with the flow. Attention shifts from doing well to just doing. Just telling oneself to relax and stop trying too hard usually doesn't work. Attempting to be average can work, because there is no way to be average. People think they know how to do very well (try harder, make no mistakes, be perfect), but how can someone be average? Making too few mistakes misses the objective of being average because performance will be too good. Similarly, making too many mistakes will also miss the goal by making the performance below average. Basically, getting someone to focus on being average leads to confusion. This makes it easier to stop striving and just let things happen.

Different kinds of beneficial outcomes are possible with the dare-to-be-average strategy. One possibility is that performance will improve. Watzlawick and colleagues describe a situation in which a student dashes off a "mediocre" paper and winds up getting a B-plus, while receiving a C-minus for a "good" paper he labors over.[71]

Another possible outcome is an "average" performance that the person may discover is not so terrible. Of course, one man's "average" can be another's "excellent." When Elliott allowed himself to play "average" saxophone, he felt a lot more relaxed, enjoyed playing, and became much easier for his colleagues to work with. It was hard for him to believe the feedback he got from his fans—that it was the best they had ever heard him play. He believed he had gotten comfortable being average, while others thought his performance had improved. Regardless, he was able to play again and enjoy it, and he no longer saw himself as having a problem.

A third positive outcome of being average is the ability to get the job done. Mark prided himself on giving "110 percent" to every task he undertook. Unfortunately, this became exhausting. He was a carpenter by trade and quite a perfectionist. He gave the same care to every little job around his house that he gave to the most important task at work. Mark was also into martial arts. He enjoyed the discipline, but had to be the best at that, too. Gradually, he began sitting around watching television instead of taking care of his house or practicing martial arts. He became immobilized by his perfectionism, and it wasn't until he allowed himself to do a few things (not all) in an average way that he was able to get himself active again.

Shifting the Focus

An idea which runs through this book is that of variations on a theme, in which a person thinks he or she is trying a variety of different potential solutions to a problem, whereas they are really just slightly different varieties of the same basic approach. The individual problems addressed in this section have in common that attention stays focused where it is unhelpful (the theme) while the person attempts in different ways to feel better (variations). For example, a woman who has trouble achieving orgasm can focus her attention on orgasm and try a wide variety of different methods to achieve it. What she seldom thinks of trying is redirecting her attention away from striving for orgasm, a technique that is usually an important component of treatment for a number of sexual problems.

The strategy of shifting the focus also applies to persistent unpleasant emotions, worry, and physical pain. In many cases, there is an ongoing interaction between thought and emotion that causes the problem to escalate. An anxious person might think, "I feel a little queasy today. What if I go shopping and get sick in the store in front of everybody?" That thought creates some anxiety, which in turn motivates the person to think more about the potential problem, which hasn't even occurred yet. The next thought might be, "I had better just stay home. But if I keep doing that, I'll never get anything done, my husband will think I'm going crazy, and my whole life will fall apart." More anxiety ensues and the negative cycle continues: negative thought → anxiety → more negative thoughts → greater anxiety, and so on. It is easier to think anxiety-provoking thoughts when you are anxious and to get anxious while thinking anxiety-provoking thoughts. The same concept holds true for depression, anger, and other unpleasant emotions.

Thinking is instrumental in creating and maintaining the unpleasant feeling. Yet, the tendency is to *keep thinking* about how to resolve the problem. The focus remains *internal* (in one's own mind) and *future-* or *past-oriented*. People seldom, if ever, think about the present when feeling bad. They think about the future—what they have to do, what might happen—or the past—mistakes they made, how much better it used to be, something unfair someone else did. The strategy of shifting focus will involve moving one's attention to *external* reality and to the *present*.

To better understand this concept, take time out to try a brief experiment. For a few minutes, close your eyes and think about all the things you have to do in the next week and when you will get them all done. At the end of that time, notice how you feel, then open your eyes and describe in detail to yourself everything you see, hear, feel (sense of touch, not emotion), or smell at that moment. After a couple of minutes, note how you feel emotionally.

Most people notice a couple of things about the time they have their eyes closed and are thinking. They tend to be unaware of what's going on around them (they are in their own little worlds), and they feel uncomfortable emotionally. Conversely, when they are describing what their senses are picking up, they are very aware of their surroundings and feel more relaxed and calm. Shifting the focus is based on this kind of experience.

The process of shifting the focus involves three steps. The first is to recognize the problem (anxiety, anger, worry). The second step is interrupting the problem by slow, timed breathing, relaxing one's muscles, or just getting up and moving around a little. This step may seem inconsequential, but it is very important since it is difficult to shift one's attention to something new until the old focus is first interrupted.

In the final step, attention is focused outside of oneself and into the present. There are many ways to do this, but a couple are simple and widely applicable. One is sensory focus. One describes what one's senses (sight, smell, hearing, touch, and even taste) are picking up at the present moment. A second method for accomplishing this shift is *activity focus,* in which one describes to oneself in detail everything he or she does moment by moment: "I am picking up a plate, scraping it, running it under hot water, putting it in the dish drainer," and so forth. Both methods achieve a shift of focus from inside one's head to one's immediate surroundings, and from thinking of the past or future to thinking of the present.

Georgia lived alone and prided herself on being independent and responsible. She also liked to make sure things were done "just so." This worked well for her in some ways—she was very dependable and her home always looked great—but it also created some problems. She constantly thought about all the things she had to do and couldn't relax. She had a lot of trouble falling asleep because her mind was racing, and she developed stress-related stomach problems.

As an important part of her therapy, Georgia learned to shift her focus away from the things she had to do in the future back to the present. She used both sensory and activity focus. When she used activity focus, she was instructed to pay attention to pacing herself and to intersperse messages of "slow down, it's not that important" among her descriptions to herself of what she was doing. When Georgia had improved enough to stop therapy, she identified this strategy as being the most helpful aspect of her treatment.

When she first started shifting focus, she found herself having to repeat the recognize–interrupt–focus pattern three, four, or even five times in a given situation, since her mind easily wandered back to thinking about the future. This is not at all uncommon, since old habits die hard. As she became more skilled at this strategy, however, she usually had to shift only once to break out of her old pattern in any given situation. This is not to say that her problem went away. She will probably always have to use her shifting-of-focus skill to keep herself calm and centered.

The shifting-of-focus strategy works for a number of reasons. By bringing one back to the present, it refocuses attention in a place where one can deal with reality and have an immediate impact on one's surroundings, which is impossible in the future or past. It also breaks the chain of negative thought $\rightarrow$ unpleasant emotion $\rightarrow$ more negative thought. Finally, it helps one to go with the flow (see Chapter 12) better by making one more attuned to his or her environment.

The process of redirecting attention also works with problems related to physical pain and sexual functioning. In the case of a pain problem, attention paid to the pain worsens the situation by increasing tension (as the person "tries" not to hurt and gets upset by the pain) and by making the pain the center of attention, causing it to stand out even more. Shifting the focus away from pain, as part of an overall pain management program, is effective to the extent that it distracts attention from the pain, thereby placing it in a different perspective.

With sexual problems, attention to them can worsen the situation by increasing tension and by creating an atmosphere in which a person tries to force something that must come naturally. Going with the flow and letting things happen by themselves instead of making them happen is of primary importance in sexual functioning. Among the sexual difficulties sensitive to overattention are premature ejaculation and impotence for men and difficulty in achieving orgasm for women.

A third type of focus shift can be utilized in trying to deal with problems related to sexual function. This is called *sensate focus*, and it was developed by Masters and Johnson during their extensive, groundbreaking research on human sexual functioning.[72] This technique encourages shifting attention from orgasm or erection onto the sensual pleasures experienced during touching and caressing. It combines sensory and activity focus and applies them to sexual situations.

When Cal started seeing Betsy, he had not had much dating experience and had much less sexual experience. They got along very well and before too long they were sexually involved. Cal began having problems getting and sustaining erections. He was worried about how he would stack up sexually against other men Betsy had been involved with. He wondered what she really thought about him sexually, even though she had often told him she found him exciting. When he started to have problems with impotence, he became even more self-conscious and put more pressure on himself to perform.

Cal and Betsy were instructed by their therapist to engage in sensate focus as part of therapy. They were told to take turns being the giver and receiver of pleasure during sexual contact. They were to focus only on what they were feeling (touch, sound, smell) moment to moment. Intercourse was forbidden, as a way of preventing both of them from looking ahead instead of staying in the present. At first they followed their instructions well, but soon after, they began having spontaneous sex as Cal's difficulty with erections disappeared.

Regardless of the specific problem addressed, shifting the focus involves redirecting attention outside of one's head to the present. Early awareness of the onset of the problem is helpful, since the longer it has gone on, the more difficult it is to halt. Also, finding a way to interrupt the old pattern prior to focusing one's attention elsewhere should not be overlooked as a key intermediate step.

Self-Discouragement

Certain habitual behaviors such as overeating, smoking, and not exercising are notoriously difficult to change. People start out with a lot of motivation and the best intentions, only to quickly get off track and fall back into their old habits. The strategy of self-discouragement can prove helpful in the implementation of habit and life-style changes.

When a person sets out to change a habit, but fails (or at least finds it very difficult), mixed feelings are usually present. Part of the person decides change is needed, but another part resists. People obviously derive some benefits from their habits, or those habits would never have started or persisted. Many habits earmarked for change feel good and reinforce themselves. Food tastes good, smoking relaxes some people and gives them something to do with their hands, and laziness has its own unique appeal. In addition, aspects of a person's environment can trigger old habits. A cup of coffee can signal the need for a cigarette. A break at work might serve as a cue to visit the candy machine. A soft, reclining chair can beckon its owner to take a nap. People like to think they have free will to make decisions. The reality, however, is that many factors, including physical and emotional needs, and aspects of the surroundings exert some control over people's behavior.

People attempting to change habits try a number of approaches, such as making schedules, quitting habits on a certain date "cold turkey," or joining groups set up to assist people who are trying to quit smoking or lose weight. Many of these approaches are helpful for some people. None is universally effective. Many people simply try to exert will power. But few people seem to succeed using this strategy alone, since it often involves facing temptation and trying to stare it down (starting a diet with cheesecake in the refrigerator).

In self-discouragement, as in the indirect discouragement outlined in Chapter 13, a person uses less than direct methods to discourage behavior he or she would like to see decrease or disappear. Simple goal-setting and self-reinforcement for goal attainment are also effective, but they are often not sufficient when the person is ambivalent about change. Ambivalence involves giving oneself two conflicting messages at the same time: "I want to change/I don't." Self-reward strengthens the side that desires change. Self-discouragement interferes with the side that is resistant.

Simply put, through alterations in one's environment and change strategies, self-discouragement makes it easier to change and harder to stay the same. For instance, a person who has vowed to start exercising, but who has been relatively inactive, may make grandiose plans to begin going to a health club three or four times a week. If he or she fails to follow through, maybe the plan was too difficult to implement. It means packing work-out clothes, driving to the club, changing, working out, showering, dressing, and driving back home, not to mention deciding which club to join and paying for a membership. On the other hand, brisk walking probably just entails changing one's shoes and stepping outside. In other words, find a way to make it easy when trying to encourage yourself to do something.

Many people who try to stop smoking, on the other hand, have been helped by using techniques to make smoking harder and less pleasant. Those include buying one pack at a time, keeping a record of how much is smoked by marking a card prior to lighting up, only smoking outdoors, changing brands after each pack is finished, or sitting in nonsmoking sections in restaurants.

Self-discouragement can also be applied to overeating. Dana had been struggling with her weight since she was a teenager. She belonged to a nationally franchised weight-loss program, but still found herself cheating. With the help of her therapist, she introduced elements into her eating routine that made it much less convenient to overeat. She was allowed to eat only in one room in her house and was not permitted to do anything else while eating, like watch television or read. She was to chew each bit of food a minimum of ten times. Food that could be eaten without preparation (potato chips, cookies, snack crackers, etc.) were not brought into the house. Dana, who was right-handed, was told to eat only with her left hand.

These represent only a few of the eating rules Dana imposed to discourage herself from overeating. A sound, balanced diet and the support of her weight-loss group were also significant contributors to her successful weight loss. Six months later, she had kept the weight off, but she was cautioned to keep tabs on herself and to reinstitute aspects of her program should her old habits begin to return.

Self-discouragement, applied to any behavior change project, is basically self-control, which ought not to be confused with will power. Will power refers to attempts to change just by deciding to and by making oneself stop unwanted behaviors or start more desirable ones without making any concessions to wants, needs, or environmental obstacles. Self-control involves looking at the systems involved in maintaining old behaviors and supporting new ones, and making whatever changes are necessary to ease transitions, strengthen new behaviors, and discourage old habits.

Chapter 15

Criticisms of Our Ideas—Or, Why You Won't Try Them

Now that we've described in detail some new ways of handling familiar problems, let's take a look at how they relate to the ideas expressed in the first chapters of the book. In Chapter 2, we talked about systems theory and especially about circular causality and wholeness. As you will recall, circular causality refers to the idea that people in a relationship don't influence each other in a straight-line, A-causes-B way. This means that statements such as "I fool around *because* she's cold to me" or "I drink *because* he nags so much" cannot be true.

Rather, people's influences on each other in relationships are cyclical: I respond to you, and you respond to my response, and so forth. Choosing the point at which the causal chain begins is pointless and arbitrary. The positive upshot of this idea is that the circle of causality can be broken at any point and that a new pattern will result. That is, when your actions are noticeably different, and consistently different, the other person's reactions will change, which in turn can allow your reactions to his or her reactions to change as well, thus starting a positive cycle.

All the strategies for handling the problems that we discussed are firmly based in the circular causality principle. You will notice that in few of our examples were both members of the couple working toward change in the relationship. Thus, our assumption was that a demonstrable change in one person could lead to positive changes in his or her partner.

This is quite a different conceptualization of how change takes place in a relationship and what must occur to prompt that change. Many people still believe that both members of the relationship must be involved for change to be effective and lasting. We don't think this is always the case. The practical advantage of our viewpoint is that *one* motivated member of a relationship can positively change the quality of the relationship without the active participation of the other partner.

This idea is also consistent with the concept of wholeness, which holds that the relationship is more than the sum of its parts, or the sum of its two individuals. It also states that the system tends to behave as a whole. Therefore, when one part changes the way it functions, the other part must alter its responses, and the system as a whole changes. In other words, when one partner begins to behave differently, the relationship adjusts to accommodate that change. One person can't change without, in some way, changing the relationship.

Again, our examples assume that one person's change will affect the other person and the relationship. We certainly do not mean to imply that we can predict specifically what the other partner's response will be, or what exactly the ultimate effect on the relationship will be. Each system has its unique aspects and will respond differently. However, we do believe our strategies will allow change to begin in situations that had been characterized by stagnation or negative ripple effects.

Communication has also been emphasized in Chapters 2 and 3. We discussed honest communication, the relationship aspects of communication, and what communication consists of besides words. Our strategies obviously don't place a premium on totally open and honest communication. We'll talk about this in more detail shortly, when we discuss criticisms of our ideas.

The relationship aspects of communication refer to the influence of what we do and say. An example from Chapter 2 was how the words "my back itches" can mean "scratch my back" at the relationship level. The strategies we presented were primarily geared toward changing the implicit demands of relationship communication. If a person feels pressured for more sex, more communication, or more honesty, he or she may well respond in the opposite way. None of us likes to feel coerced or controlled. When we do feel that way, we will at times not cooperate just to show we can't be controlled. Unfortunately, in some of these instances, we fail to do what is best for us, or our relationship, in the long run.

Many of the new solutions we suggested operate very explicitly on the relationship level of communication. We discuss ways to get more sex by *not* asking for it and to get more communication by becoming *less* available for it. These strategies allow the other person to do what we desire and what the relationship may need without offending the person with relentless pressure and demands for compliance with our desires.

It was also pointed out in Chapter 2 that communication is more than words. Gestures, behavior, and lack of behavior all strongly communicate. Most of the strategies we have suggested involve behavior change as well as alterations in what is said. A behavioral change implicit in many of the strategies involves focusing less on the problem and doing more for oneself. This kind of activity communicates very clearly that you hold yourself, and not just the relationship and the other person, to be important. Once that is behaviorally communicated, you can begin to be seen by yourself and your spouse as important.

The way people create meaning in relationships was also discussed in Chapter 2. All of the strategies presented in this book in some way represented attempts to create meaning changes, as well as behavioral ones. People attach meaning to social interaction in an ongoing fashion. When you change your behavior in a relationship, you allow your partner to not only change the behavioral response, but also to reevaluate the meaning he or she is attributing to the problem and the relationship itself. Helping to create a different context by changing your own behavior permits your partner to arrive at more helpful meanings on his or her own.

In Chapter 3, we described five myths about people and relationships that get in the way of effective change: (1) what people say is very important and has a big impact on what they do; (2) people can, and should, understand and explain their own and others' motives; (3) in close relationships, being completely open and honest is critical if the relationship is to work; (4) a good relationship is one in which both people give unselfishly; and (5) in any situation, there is only one reality or truth. Should you choose to hang onto these myths, you won't implement our suggestions, since they directly contradict those myths. Our strategies downplay what people say, emphasize what people do, and sometimes encourage them to be inconsistent in word and deed. We explicitly tell people not to explain themselves in many instances. We discourage openness and total honesty in selected circumstances. We instruct people to be more selfish in the service of the relationship. We advocate searching for alternative, more helpful realities.

It is not that we believe those myths to be ignoble or immoral. On the contrary, they are ideals, and ideals tend not to exist in the real world. If you act based on what life should be like instead of how it is, you will often find yourself stymied and frustrated. The bottom line is that solving problems in ways consistent with those myths can, in many cases, lead to repetitively ineffective solutions. Our assumptions may not always sound as noble as the myths, but we believe they are more realistic, in certain situations, and can lead to more effective attempts to change.

Since our ideas advocate behaviors that don't make sense, given traditional societal assumptions, and are not always direct and assertive, not everyone will like them or agree with them. We would like to conclude by responding to some criticisms we anticipate you may have of our point of view.

Criticism #1: "What you are suggesting is blatantly manipulative. You are encouraging people to be sneaky and dishonest, instead of open and straightforward."

Let us respond to this criticism by saying that this is, to some extent, true. We readily agree that we advocate conscious, planned attempts to influence other people without their knowledge or active participation. However, please note that we are not advocating them generally. Rather, we have suggested ways in which you could influence the context of relationship problems that enable your partner to make changes on his or her own. We see this as manipulating or influencing the *situation* to permit the other person to independently change, not as manipulating others against their will. We think it can be helpful in a few fairly specific relationship patterns we described in this book. In these cases, either unplanned manipulation was already occurring (as with the domineering spouse who had seized the lion's share of the power in the relationship), or honest, open attempts to deal with the problem had already failed (as with the person who directly requests more sex, has his or her spouse agree, and then gets the same frequency or less).

Being honest is not entirely what it seems. We don't believe people always know all they feel, or what motivates their behavior. For example, I can "honestly" say to my partner that I want to make changes in our relationship, but I may be unaware of conflicting needs and desires that exist in my own mind and unconsciously may find ways to sabotage attempts to change. Now my partner can honestly say that my behavior is communicating that I don't want to change. So, honesty is not as clear-cut as we would like to think.

We have also repeatedly discussed the relationship level of communication—how each communication has an impact or influence on another person. Therefore, to reiterate what we contend in Chapter 2, each of us tries, consciously or subconsciously, to influence people with whom we communicate. These attempts are every bit as manipulative as anything we have suggested, and they occur constantly. Those attempts are usually unplanned and subconscious, and we tend to be insensitive to their consequences. In other words, we keep doing them the same way even if they don't work too well. So, the kinds of strategies we are suggesting happen all the time. All we suggest is that they be done *on purpose,* effectively, and in the best interests of the relationship.

If you still see what we suggest as sneaky and dishonest, it is certainly your prerogative not to try our ideas. Please keep in mind that we are only suggesting indirect strategies for situations in which more direct, open strategies have not worked. At times it may boil down to a choice between being sneaky and effective or open and honest and frustrated. We are *not* saying our way is right. We just want you to know you have a choice. There are many different ways to approach relationship problems.

Criticism #2: "These ideas can be used for selfish purposes, since your partner isn't directly involved in the decision to change."

There is absolutely no question that this criticism is true. The checks and balances that are present when both members of a couple work to change a relationship are absent when only one partner attempts to effect the change. However, this criticism is directed at people in general, as much as it is directed at us. People are already manipulative. If a manipulative person reads this book, it will just provide him or her with more weapons in his or her arsenal.

We hope more people will be sincerely interested in improving their relationships and will use the techniques judiciously, in the ways suggested. One way to check out your own motives, in many cases, is to see if your partner has expressed a willingness to change, but hasn't been able to. In this instance, you are working toward a common goal.

Also, keep in mind two perspectives on the idea of selfishness previously presented in this book. One is the idea that a certain amount of selfishness is important. If you give too much, you become resentful, and the other person doesn't know what you want and, therefore, can't give it to you. The other perspective is that there exist few, if any, truly unselfish acts. When we perform altruistic acts for other people, we selfishly enjoy the feeling of being good or righteous people.

Basically, we are saying that the idea of selfishness has gotten a bad rap. Instead, selfishness should be seen as a matter of degree. If you are totally unselfish, you don't learn to take care of yourself, and you either become overly dependent on the charity of others, or, in the worst case scenario, you die (how can you eat and be *totally* unselfish when other people are starving?). On the other hand, if you are too selfish, you can't coexist with other people. We believe there is a point between the two extremes that represents a healthy degree of selfishness.

Criticism #3: "Your solutions address only superficial, surface issues, so the changes won't be permanent, or other problems will crop up."

Yes, we do deal only with surface issues. We described in detail our lack of belief in the necessity of finding out "why." Nor do we believe that in order for change to be effective or lasting, the solution has to address all the deep, underlying causes.

A systems viewpoint focuses on current interactions within a relationship. Changes in one person set the stage for changes in the other, and a positive ripple effect can occur. Knowing "why" something happens says nothing directly about "how" to change it.

As far as the issue of permanence of change goes, of course changes aren't permanent. People change and their situations change. Belief in permanence, predictability, and consistency in the context of a human relationship is folly. The best we can hope for are ways to effectively deal with changes that threaten the relationship, not a solution that takes care of all problems forever. You don't master life; you cope with the things with which it confronts you. Hopefully, our ideas can give you more tools to facilitate your coping.

Criticism #4: "Every situation is unique. You are trying to give general solutions to varied individualized problems."

This is a trap into which all self-help books fall, to a greater or lesser extent. In order to make our ideas understandable, and to help people relate to them, we have to generalize and simplify. By doing so, we gain the ability to apply our ideas to a broader audience, but lose the richness and detail of the individual situation.

Our purpose is not to give anyone a "cookbook" describing

the precise steps to follow to resolve all relationship difficulties. We want to provide fresh, different ideas for you to think about and apply to your life situations flexibly. We want to encourage you to challenge some of your assumptions and to entertain new perspectives in old situations. Please don't confuse what we are doing with psychotherapy or relationship counseling. If your problems are severe, please get help.*

If your problems are annoying and longstanding, but not immediately dangerous or relationship-threatening, use what we have written as food for thought. We are giving you ideas, not prescriptions, and your ability to understand them and decide if and how they might help your situation will be the critical variable in your attempts to change your relationships.

Somehow, in our society, we got the crazy idea that love is demonstrated by words ("I love you") and isolated actions (buying gifts, sending cards). We believe that working hard and creatively to make a relationship last and stay mutually satisfying is clearly a more powerful statement of caring and respect. We hope you can use our suggestions to help in that process.

---

*For a referral for marriage and family therapy, call the American Association for Marriage and Family therapy at (202) 452–0109.

Notes

1. Paul Watzlawick, John Weakland and Richard Fisch. *Change: Principles of Problem Formation and Problem Resolution* (New York: Norton, 1974). 24–27.
2. Ludwig von Bertalaffy. *General System Theory* (New York: Braziller, 1973).
3. Walter Buckley, ed., *Modern Systems Research for the Behavioral Scientist* (Chicago: Aldine, 1968).
4. Steve de Shazer, *Keys to Solutions in Brief Therapy* (New York: Norton, 1985), 33.
5. Paul Watzlawick, Janet Beavin and Don Jackson, *Pragmatics of Human Communication: A Study of Interaction Patterns, Pathologies, and Paradoxes* (New York: Norton, 1967), 48.
6. Watzlawick, *Pragmatics*, 83.
7. Watzlawick, *Pragmatics*, 51.
8. Watzlawick, *Pragmatics*, 51.
9. Kurt Vonnegut, *Slapstick* (New York: Dell, 1976), 108.
10. Paul Watzlawick, ed., *The Invented Reality* (New York: Norton, 1984), 14–15.
11. Walter Buckley, *Sociology and Modern Systems Theory* (Englewood Cliffs, NJ: Prentice-Hall, 1967), 54.
12. William Morris, ed., *The American Heritage Dictionary of the English Language* (Boston, Houghton Mifflin, 1976), 869.
13. Watzlawick, *Pragmatics*, 212.
14. Gregory Bateson, Don Jackson, Jay Haley and John Weakland, "Toward a Theory of Schizophrenia," *Behavior Science* 1(1956): 251–264.
15. Watzlawick, *Change*, 56.
16. Watzlawick, *Change*, 85.
17. Watzlawick, *Change*, 99.
18. Steve de Shazer, *Keys to Solutions*, 122.

19. Richard Fisch, John Weakland and Lynn Segal. *The Tactics of Change: Doing Therapy Briefly* (San Francisco: Jossey-Bass, 1982), 155–166.
20. Don Jackson and William Lederer. *The Mirages of Marriage* (New York: Norton, 1968), 292–293.
21. Fisch, *Tactics of Change*, 205.
22. Watzlawick, *Change*, 142–146.
23. Watzlawick, *Change*, 142–146.
24. de Shazer, *Keys to Solutions*.
25. Barry Duncan, Bernadine Parks and Greg Rusk, "Eclectic Strategic Practice: A Process Constructive Perspective," *Journal of Marital and Family Therapy*, 16 (1990): 165–178.
26. Bateson, "Theory of Schizophrenia," 251–264.
27. Jay Haley, *Uncommon Therapy* (New York: Norton, 1986), 28.
28. Cloe Madanes, *Strategic Family Therapy* (San Francisco: Jossey-Bass, 1982).
29. Watzlawick, *Change*, 31–37.
30. de Shazer, *Keys to Solutions*.
31. Duncan, "Eclectic Strategic Practice," 165–178.
32. Erik Erikson, *Identity, Youth and Crisis* (Toronto: Norton, 1986).
33. Roger Gould, *Transformations: Growth and Change in Adult Life* (New York: Simon & Schuster, 1978).
34. Daniel Levinson, *The Seasons of a Man's Life* (New York: Ballantine Books, 1978).
35. George Vaillant, *Adaption to Life* (New York: Ballantine Books, 1977).
36. Debra Merrifield Carothers, Stephen McConnell, Barry Duncan and Eileen Buban, "Nuclear War Fears Across the Life Cycle," (Unpublished manuscript, 1990) 17–18.
37. Duvall, *Marriage and Family Development*, 5th ed. (Philadelphia: Lippincott, 1977).
38. Barbara Carter and Monica McGoldrich, *The Changing Family Life Cycle* 2nd ed., (New York: Gardner, 1988).
39. Betty Friedan, "How to Get the Women's Movement Moving Again," *New York Times Magazine* (November 3, 1985).
40. Fisch, *Tactics of Change*, 205.
41. Watzlawick, *Change*, 104.
42. Watzlawick, *Change*, 92–109.
43. Watzlawick, *Change*, 92–109.
44. Fisch, *Tactics of Change*, 162–166.
45. Watzlawick, *Change*, 92–109.
46. Watzlawick, *Change*, 92–109.
47. Watzlawick, *Change*, 92–109.
48. Fisch, *Tactics of Change*, 159–162.
49. de Shazer, *Keys to Solutions*, 34.
50. Steve de Shazer and Alex Molnar, "Four Useful Interventions in Brief Family Therapy," *Journal of Marital and Family Therapy*, 10, (1984): 297–304.
51. de Shazer, "Four Useful Interventions," 297–304.

52. Watzlawick, *The Invented Reality*, 95.
53. Robert Rosenthal, *Pygmalion in the Classroom* (New York: Holt, Rinehart and Winston, 1968).
54. Watzlawick, *Change*, 146–149.
55. de Shazer, *Keys to Solutions*, 137.
56. de Shazer, *Keys to Solutions*, 132.
57. Watzlawick, *Change*, 148.
58. de Shazer, *Keys to Solutions*, 137.
59. Watzlawick, *Change*, 148–149.
60. de Shazer, *Keys to Solutions*, 137.
61. Matteo Selvini, ed., *The Work of Mara Selvini Palazzoli* (Northvale, NJ: Jason Aronson, 1988), 305–310.
62. Watzlawick, *Change*, 114.
63. Duncan, "Eclectic Strategic Practice," 165–178.
64. Fisch, *Tactics of Change*, 205.
65. Mark King, Larry Novik and Charles Citrenbaum, *Irresistible Communication: Creative Skills for the Health Professional* (Philadelphia: Saunders, 1982), 9–11.
66. Watzlawick, *Change*, 124–127.
67. Fisch, *Tactics of Change*, 162–166.
68. Fritz Perls, *Gestalt Therapy Verbatum* (New York: Bantam, 1969), 18–20.
69. Fisch, *Tactics of Change*, 159–162.
70. Thomas Borkovec, "What's the Use of Worrying?" *Psychology Today* (December, 1985), 59–64.
71. Watzlawick, *Change*, 149–151.
72. William Masters, Virginia Johnson and Robert Kolodny, *Masters and Johnson on Sex and Human Loving* (Boston: Little, Brown and Co., 1985), 488–492.

Index